CHICKEN SOUP
FOR THE
MOTHER AND
DAUGHTER SOUL

Stories to Warm the Heart and Inspire the Spirit

Jack Canfield
Mark Victor Hansen
Dorothy Firman
Julie Firman
Frances Firman Salorio

Health Communications, Inc.
Deerfield Beach, Florida

www.hci-online.com
www.chickensoup.com

We would like to acknowledge the following publishers and individuals for permission to reprint the following material. (Note: The stories that were penned anonymously, that are public domain, or that were written by Jack Canfield, Mark Victor Hansen, Dorothy Firman, Julie Firman or Frances Firman Salorio are not included in this listing.)

A Mother is Born and I Love My Body . . . Now. Reprinted by permission of Regina Phillips. ©2000 Regina Phillips.

Light. Reprinted by permission of Jacquelyn Mitchard. ©1996 Jacquelyn Mitchard.

Spring of '59. Reprinted by permission of Jean Kinsey. ©1999 Jean Kinsey.

Confessions. Reprinted by permission of Linda Sultan. ©1997 Linda Sultan. Excerpted from *Family Life and Other Strife.* ©1996 Linda Sultan. Published by Worcester Publications.

The Reunion. Reprinted by permission of Kathy N. Jublou. ©1999 Kathy N. Jublou.

(continued on page 355)

Library of Congress Cataloging-in-Publication Data

Chicken soup for the mother and daughter soul : stories to honor mothers and daughters / [compiled by] Jack Canfield . . . [et al.].
    p.   cm.
    ISBN 0-7573-0088-X (tp)
    1. Mothers and daughters. 2. Conduct of life. I. Canfield, Jack, 1944–

HQ755.85 .C474 2003
306.874'3—dc21

2002032921

© 2002 Jack Canfield and Mark Victor Hansen
ISBN 0-7573-0088-X (trade paper)

Publisher: Health Communications, Inc.
          3201 S.W. 15th Street
          Deerfield Beach, FL 33442-8190

Cover design by Andrea Perrine Brower
Inside formatting by Dawn Von Strolley Grove

What People Are Saying About
Chicken Soup for the Mother and Daughter Soul . . .

"Dorothy and Julie Firman have been teaching a mother-daughter workshop at Omega Institute for twenty years. That means that more than 1,000 mothers and daughters have had their relationships uplifted and healed by this dynamic and talented duo. Now they bring their understanding to a book of touching stories that awaken the strong feelings between mothers and daughters. A beautiful reminder for anyone who has a mother or a daughter (or both!) to communicate love, support and gratitude."

Elizabeth Lesser
cofounder, Omega Institute and author, *The Seeker's Guide:*
Making Your Life a Spiritual Adventure

"This wonderful collection of experiences in the lives of real mothers and daughters is heartwarming and provocative. It inspired me to examine all of my close relationships and to reflect on where my life is going."

Alice Hopper Epstein, Ph.D.
author, *Mind, Fantasy and Healing: One Woman's*
Journey from Conflict and Illness to Wholeness and Health

"Scratch the surface of any mother and you will find a profound story of birth, death, survival and rebirth. As a daughter of immigrants, I know this, as a mother of daughters, I know this, and as the founder of an organization dedicated to speaking the truth in motherhood, I also know this. When we see a mother pushing a stroller, a mother trying to reason with her teenager, or a daughter helping her own mother up a curb, *Chicken Soup for the Mother and Daughter Soul* reminds us to honor each of these unique mothers and daughters and their unique stories. Thank you for reminding us to notice."

Annette Cycon
editor, *MotherWoman! Journal* and author
of the forthcoming, *Mother Woman!*
The Truth About Motherhood in the 21st Century

"Like a therapeutic massage, this book is full of short, easy-to-read pieces that give you a welcome break."

Ellen Story
Massachusetts State Representative

"This book presents the deep wisdom, grace and heart of the stories of women—mothers and daughters. It is a recipe for soulfulness, for finding authentic values amidst daily life—this book is a treasure for all to explore."

Stephan Rechtschaffen, M.D.
CEO and Cofounder, Omega Institute and
author, *Time Shifting*

"You don't have to be a mother or daughter to love *Chicken Soup for the Mother and Daughter Soul*. I'm a father and son, and the book brought tears to my eyes. It is filled with love, joy and healing."

Michael Leach
editor, *I Like Being Married* and *I Like Being American*

"As a psychotherapist and parent educator, I am moved by the many stories of healing, love and timeless wisdom that are shared by mothers and daughters in this book. Stories like this help to heal the soul and inspire the best within each of us."

Ilene Val-Essen
author, *Bring Out the Best in Your Child and Yourself*

"In this exceptionally poignant book, the authors weave deeply touching and personal stories attesting to the timelessness of this emotionally complex relationship. A must-read for all mothers and daughters!"

Robert Friedman
author, *The Healing Power of the Drum*

"The mother-daughter stories that the Firmans have gathered reach for the deep bond of love that underlies this most complex relationship. In a time that is fraught with stories of despair and confusion, this collection offers a message of hope for us all."

Jeanne Lightfoot and Bill Ryan
authors, *In the Woods, at the Water: Healing Journeys into Nature*

"All too often, my male clients believe that they can only experience real emotions in response to a marquee event or highly dramatic moment. These engaging stories can teach men that opening ourselves to the simple and poignant moments may be what most stirs our hearts and reminds us of the treasures in our intimate connections with others."

Kevin Quirk
author, *Not Now, Honey, I'm Watching the Game*

"The difficult task of 'species bonding' faces all of us in a world filled with alienation and disconnection. These beautifully crafted stories about mothers and daughters both remind and inspire us fathers and men to refocus our attention away from what separates us, to what matters the most—each other. This is a must-read for fathers, too."

John B. Franklin, Ph.D.
author, *FatherBirth: A Close Encounter of a Fourth Kind*

"*Chicken Soup for the Mother and Daughter Soul* is a book that I highly recommend. The stories range from tales of pain and recovery to stories of laughter and friendship. The book moves one from tears of sadness to smiles of happy recognition and reconciliation. I could see my life with my own daughter in many of the stories.

Shirley Rich Krohn
casting agent

"Although I had a problematic relationship with my mother, *Chicken Soup for the Mother and Daughter Soul* took me to those poignant moments before and after her death when I saw the gifts she had passed on to me, the wonderful qualities that had been so hidden by her wounding. Moreover, I found myself affirming all those who have mothered me in my life: my grandmother, my mother's best friend, a neighbor, and even my husband's mother, and I recognized all those who have been my daughters as well.

Ann Gila
coauthor, *Psychosynthesis: A Psychology of the Spirit*

"The authors have put together an intriguing, easy-to-read series of vignettes that will keep you reading until you reach the back cover, and make you wish there were more. "

Dick Teresi
author, *Lost Discoveries* and coauthor, *The God Particle*

"Since Demeter and Persephone, the mother-daughter bond has held eternal fascination. The stories in *Chicken Soup for the Mother and Daughter Soul*—funny, mysterious, tragic, searingly real, whimsical—really do speak powerfully to the soul."

Judith Hooper
author, *Of Moths and Men* and *The Three-Pound Universe*

"As surely as the telling of stories must have begun not with the first hunter but with the first mother, this collection of the stories of mothers and daughters reaches to something deep inside that is very ancient. Though written by mothers and daughters, the reflections reach to our common humanity and the web that weaves us all together, which is, at its heart, maternal."

The Rt. Rev. Stacy F. Sauls
Bishop of Lexington

"These stories are so heartfelt and wise, you are propelled from one to the next. Once you pick this book up, you will find it very hard to put down."

Janine Roberts
coauthor, *Rituals for Our Times*

"Miracles occur within every story of *Chicken Soup for the Mother and Daughter Soul*: the miracles of birth and resulting transformation for the mothers; ordinary acts of love seen with new eyes as memories emerge; daughters coming into their own with the encouragement and blessing of their mothers; mothers deepening through the gift of their daughters' love, attention and, sometimes, pestering. This beautiful collection is a gift of hope and transformation that spills over into the reader's own life. Even for those of us whose mother-daughter relationships were less than perfect, we are healed in the reading."

Becky Jones
Chaplain, Cooley Dickinson Hospital

"For those of us who are interested in familial relationships—and who isn't—this grand array of autobiogaphical vignettes will illuminate the compelling world of mothers and daughters, with its commonalities and its uniqueness: a world of which we are all a part."

Aylette Jenness
author, *Families: A Celebration of Diversity, Commitment and Love*

"I am a father. I have two daughters. When the first was in her mother's womb, I had two dreams in which I was asked, 'Do you want a girl or a boy?' Both times I said, 'A girl.' I have been continually blessed by this visitation and doubly blessed by the presence in my life of our second daughter. And now, by the arrival of the stories in this book that invite quivering in the chest and wetness in the eyes, carrying within their fold an overwhelming sense of gratitude for my dear wife and daughters. This book is a celebration of all life bearers—past, present and future."

Saki Santorelli
author, *Heal Thy Self: Lessons on Mindfulness in Medicine*

GLASBERGEN

"My teacher says little girls can grow up to be anything they choose! Why did you choose to be an old lady?"

Dorothy, Frances and Julie dedicate this book to
Linsay Firman, our niece, our granddaughter,
Tom and Katherine's daughter, cousin to
our children, our friend. You bring out
the mother in all of us, and we know you
will heal and continue to be a source
of joy and creativity to everyone you touch.

Jack and Mark dedicate this book to their mothers,
Ellen Angelis and Una Peterson,
and their daughters Riley, Elisabeth and Melanie.

Contents

2. A DAUGHTER'S LOVE

3. MEMORIES

4. CHALLENGES

5. LESSONS

6. LIKE MOTHER, LIKE DAUGHTER

7. LOSS AND HEALING

8. TIMELESS WISDOM

Acknowledgments

The path to *Chicken Soup for the Mother and Daughter Soul* has been made all the more beautiful by the many "companions" who have been there with us along the way.

Our heartfelt gratitude to:

Our families, who have been chicken soup for our souls! Inga, Travis, Riley, Christopher, Oran and Kyle for all their love and support. Patty, Elisabeth and Melanie Hansen, for once again sharing and lovingly supporting us in creating yet another book.

Computer guru, husband, son-in-law, brother-in-law and friend, Ted Slawski, without whom this book could never have been done. Jody Slade, Sarah Slawski, Tom Slawski and Kendy Slade; Cynthia Salorio, John Salorio and David Court; Tom, Lore, Linsay, Ashley and Tim Firman, our children and grandchildren, and the true meaning of our lives. Win Firman, husband and father, who started this all more than sixty years ago by falling in love and who has kept it all together by being the paterfamilias in grand style. Sarah Slade, granddaughter, great-granddaughter, great-niece and our future. Katherine Firman, who continues every day, in the face of adversity, to show us what mothers really are. The women who have been mothers to us, Sarah Fisher, long gone and still missed, Julie, coauthor and mother, and Catherine Slawski, mother-in-law and good friend. And to each other, Julie, Frances and Didi, for believing we could do this together!

Our publisher Peter Vegso, for his vision and commitment to bringing *Chicken Soup for the Soul* to the world.

Patty Aubery, for being there on every step of the journey, with love, laughter and endless creativity.

Heather McNamara and D'ette Corona, for producing our final manuscript with magnificent ease, finesse and care. Thanks for making the final stages of production such a breeze!

Leslie Riskin, for her care and loving determination to secure our permissions and get everything just right.

Nancy Autio and her wonderful assistant Barbara LaMonoco, for nourishing us with truly wonderful stories and cartoons.

Dana Drobny and Kathy Brennan-Thompson, for listening and being there throughout with humor and grace.

Maria Nickless, for her enthusiastic marketing and public relations support and a brilliant sense of direction.

Patty Hansen, for her thorough and competent handling of the legal and licensing aspects of the *Chicken Soup for the Soul* books. You are magnificent at the challenge!

Laurie Hartman, for being a precious guardian of the Chicken Soup brand.

Veronica Romero, Teresa Esparza, Robin Yerian, Vince Wong, Kristen Allred, Stephanie Thatcher, Jody Emme, Trudy Marschall, Michelle Adams, Carly Baird, Dee Dee Romanello, Shanna Vieyra, Lisa Williams, Gina Romanello, Brittany Shaw, Dena Jacobson, Tanya Jones, Mary McKay and David Coleman, who support Jack's and Mark's businesses with skill and love.

Christine Belleris, Allison Janse, Ronelle Fleming, Lisa Drucker and Susan Tobias, our editors at Health Communications, Inc., for their devotion to excellence.

Terry Burke, Tom Sand, Lori Golden, Kelly Johnson Maragni, Randee Feldman, Patricia McConnell, Kim Weiss, Paola Fernandez-Rana and Kathy Grant, the marketing, sales, administration and PR departments at Health Communications, Inc., for doing such an incredible job supporting our books.

Tom Sand, Claude Choquette and Luc Jutras, who manage year after year to get our books translated into thirty-six languages around the world.

The art department at Health Communications, Inc., for their talent, creativity and unrelenting patience in producing book covers and inside designs that capture the essence of Chicken Soup: Larissa Hise Henoch, Lawna Patterson Oldfield, Andrea Perrine Brower, Lisa Camp, Anthony Clausi and Dawn Von Strolley Grove.

All the *Chicken Soup for the Soul* coauthors, who make it so much of a joy to be part of this *Chicken Soup* family: Raymond Aaron, Matthew E. Adams, Patty and Jeff Aubery, Nancy Mitchell Autio, Marty Becker, John Boal, Cynthia Brian, Cindy Buck, Ron Camacho, Barbara Russell Chesser, Dan Clark, Tim Clauss, Barbara De Angelis, Don Dible, Mark and Chrissy Donnelly, Irene Dunlap, Rabbi Dov Peretz Elkins, Bud Gardner, Patty Hansen, Jennifer Read Hawthorne, Kimberly Kirberger, Carol Kline, Tom and Laura Lagana, Tommy Lasorda, Janet Matthews, Hanoch and Meladee McCarty, Heather McNamara, Katy McNamara, Paul J. Meyer, Arline Oberst, Marion Owen, Maida Rogerson, Martin Rutte, Amy Seeger, Marci Shimoff, Sidney Slagter, Barry Spilchuk, Pat Stone, Carol Sturgulewski, Jim Tunney, LeAnn Thieman and Diana von Welanetz Wentworth.

Our outstanding panel of readers who helped us make the final selections and made invaluable suggestions on how to improve the book: Gloria Ayvazian, Debra Best, Marilyn Bodwell, Kathy Broderick, Eleni Chase, Kobie

Cook, Pat Coscia, David Court, Marilyn Dahl, Fred Angelis, Clare Goodwin, Jillian and Robin Diamond, Pat Drobny, Tanya Everett, Konnie Fox, Jean Gran, Ann Grose, Kathleen Holwell, Judy Gans, Rebecca Law, Dottie Lathrop, Barbara LoMonaco, Kristi Palacito, Pamela Powell, Arthur and Rose Quentin, Marc Rubin, Barbara Snoek, Nancy Sperry, Anne Stein, Nancy Toney, Alayne Vlachos, Jae Way and Charlotte Willenborg.

And, most of all, everyone who submitted their heartfelt stories, poems, quotes and cartoons for possible inclusion in this book. Each and every woman and man who shared with us recognized how beautiful the mother and daughter relationship can be. While we were not able to use everything you sent in, we know that each word came from a magical place flourishing within your soul. May your love continue to heal the world. May all human beings know peace.

Because of the size of this project, we may have left out the names of some people who contributed along the way. If so, we are sorry, but please know that we really do appreciate you very much.

We are truly grateful and love you all!

Introduction

Every woman is a daughter and every woman had a mother. The bond of the mother and daughter relationship is so profound, so deep and long-lasting, that women often miss their mothers fifty years after they are gone. Once birthed, a mother/daughter relationship is perhaps immortal. It is in honor of that eternal relationship that we offer this book, not only to every woman who is a daughter or a mother of daughters, but to every person who knows and loves a woman, because her heart will be touched by the stories of love, courage, loss, reunion, sacrifice, redemption and everyday caring that make up this book.

Being a mother is more than a role or an outcome of biology. Mothers are not just those women who give birth to the daughters they raise. Perhaps *mother* is more expressive as a verb than as a noun. To be truly mothered teaches us how to love, how to think, how to grow into our own potential, into our womanhood. At its best, being mothered teaches us to be whole. To mother is to give of oneself in service of another, to truly see and honor another and to care for her. Thankfully, in a world that brings hardship as well as joy, mothers show up in all sorts of wonderful and magical ways. You'll read stories about sisters, adoptive mothers, grandmothers and even a cat, each one mothering a daughter in such a way that both become the better for it.

And daughters, what about them? You will read again and again how daughters come into their mothers' lives as a gift from heaven. Daughters allow their mothers to see themselves through a new life, to see how they are carried in their daughters and how their daughters are unique and absolutely new. Daughters allow (sometimes push) their mothers into seeing a larger world, the new world that their daughters inhabit. Daughters offer their mothers an opportunity to become whole, just as mothers offer the same to their daughters.

In celebration of love and wholeness, we invite you to join us in the never-ending story of mothers and daughters.

Share with Us

We would love to hear your reactions to the stories in this book. Please let us know what your favorite stories were and how they affected you.

We also invite you to send us stories you would like to see published in future editions of *Chicken Soup for the Soul.* Please send submissions to:

Chicken Soup for the Soul
P.O. Box 30880
Santa Barbara, CA 93130
fax: 805-563-2945

You can also access e-mail or find a current list of planned books at the *Chicken Soup for the Soul* site at *www.chickensoup.com.*

We hope you enjoy reading this book as much as we enjoyed compiling, editing and writing it.

1

A MOTHER'S LOVE

Mother's love grows by giving.

Charles Lamb

A Mother Is Born

*Faith and doubt are both needed, not as antag-
onists, but working side by side to take us
around the unknown curve.*

Lillian Smith

My first child, a daughter, was born on July 27, 2000, and
I found I was completely unprepared. I thought I was
ready for her birth. I had read my books and articles on
childbirth and baby care; I had bought everything on my
shopping checklist. The nursery was ready for use, and
my husband and I were anxiously awaiting her arrival. I
was prepared for wakeful nights, endless diapers, sore
nipples, crying (both hers and mine), and the feeling that
I can't get anything done. I was prepared for sitz baths
and hemorrhoids.

What I wasn't prepared for was the way the entire
world looked different to me the minute she was born. I
wasn't prepared for the fact that the sheer weight of my
love for her would reduce me to tears on a daily basis. I
didn't know that I wouldn't be able to get through my first
lullaby to her because I wouldn't be able to sing through

my tears. I didn't know that the world would suddenly become unbelievably beautiful and yet infinitely scarier. I didn't know that it would seem like a new place had been created inside of me, just to hold this incredible love.

I had no idea what it would feel like when the nurse wheeled my daughter in to me saying, "She's looking for you," and the way the image of her deep-blue eyes looking right at me would be seared in my heart forever. I didn't know that I could love someone so much it literally hurts, that a trip to Wal-Mart would make me feel like a protective mother bear guarding her cub, or that my first trip to the grocery store without her would break my heart.

I didn't know that she would forever change the way my husband and I look at each other, or that the process of giving birth to her and breast-feeding her would give me a whole new respect for my body. No one told me that I would no longer be able to watch the evening news because every story about child abuse would make me think of my daughter's face.

Why didn't anyone warn me about these things? I am overwhelmed by it all. Will I ever be able to leave her and think of anything but her, or see a crust in her eye or spot on her skin that doesn't make me nervous? Will I ever be able to show her and express to her just how deep and all-encompassing my love for her is? Will I ever be able to be the mother I so desperately want her to have?

I have heard it said, and I now know that it is true, that when a woman gives birth to her first child, there are two births. The first is the birth of the child. The second is the birth of the mother. Perhaps that is the birth that is impossible to prepare for.

Regina Phillips

Light

Reach high, for stars lie hidden in your soul.
Dream deep, for every dream precedes the goal.

Pamela Vaull Starr

It was only two weeks before Christmas, but fear, not cold, made my hands shake as I stood in the darkness of the hotel parking lot, trying to unlock my rental car. The Texas predawn air was balmy, and if I'd bothered to ask them, my relatives and friends would have assured me that I was about to set out on an errand as balmy as the weather. I was heading out to navigate my way alone, through a city of unfamiliar streets, to drive a nine-months-pregnant woman I'd met only the previous night to the hospital to deliver . . . my child.

A widow for one year, a mother of four—three sons under twelve and a stepdaughter just starting college—a freelance writer with a hole in her kitchen floor the size of Lake Michigan, and a hole in her heart the size of an ocean, I had decided that what I needed to do was not to fix my linoleum or get a steady job—but to become a single mother to a baby daughter. This choice I'd made against all reason. It was a choice so controversial even among people who truly loved me that it had prompted more than one serious breach of friendship. After all, I was hardly fossilized, just enough past the age of forty to feel it in my knees. I could and would love and raise another child, a daughter.

But alone?

With my husband, who'd died of colon cancer at forty-four the previous year, I had joshed longingly about another child, but I struggled with infertility. Adoption, our only possible route to parenthood, was both risky and expensive. My dreams of another child should have faded in the cold light of reality. But though many of the illusions of youth had indeed died with Dan, the idea that one day I'd sit myself down and write a big, fat bestselling novel and my fantasy of a baby daughter had not. I was determined. Since I knew for certain that over-forty moms (particularly those with big fannies and big families) were not exactly the dream dates of the millennium, I was reasonably sure I wouldn't marry again.

I wondered why it was so dark. I searched the frontage roads for a bank clock, and to my horror, realized it was only two o'clock in the morning, instead of six. In my confusion, I'd set the alarm wrong! So I spent the next few hours in an all-night diner, slugging down cups of coffee, regarding my reflection in the window and wondering who I was.

How had all this happened?

I'd found out about the adoption agency from a friend. We'd met at a holiday craft fair, and delighted as I was to see my pal, it was the occupant of her shoulder backpack I couldn't take my eyes off. He had a thick shock of dark hair and fine chiseled features of a baby Byron. His name was Jack, and my pal and her hubby had adopted him through an agency in San Antonio. I thought the agency would laugh so hard when I called that they'd never get to the point of sending me the application.

But the agency director had no problem with single parents, even widows with big holes in their floors. A few months later, I was filling out voluminous applications. And a few months after that, in the middle of Thanksgiving dinner, I got a phone call. There was a nineteen-year-old birth mother who, against all reason, seemed to think I had the right stuff. Until just a week before, she'd been "matched" with the perfect couple, but they'd left her in the lurch when an ultrasound exam proved that the baby she was carrying was not the boy they dreamed of, but a girl.

That had been my only qualification. I wanted a girl. I figured luck would favor a little girl with three older brothers to protect her. The birth mother, whose name was Luz, thought the same thing.

I pulled the car up close to the stairs of the second-floor apartment where Luz, pretty and shy and grindingly poor, but already a good and proud mother to two unplanned babies, was watching for me through a crack in the window blinds. Luz had chosen me over dozens of other two-parent families. She'd even asked me to coach her labor. She believed in me.

Luz waved to me. She'd be down in a moment. The nanny the agency had sent to mind Luz's children had just arrived. I had five more minutes alone with my doubts.

This was the first really huge decision I'd ever made entirely on my own in my adult life. It made refinancing my house look like a game of beach volleyball and starting my own business seem like getting a perm.

Now, as I watched Luz open her apartment door and negotiate the slick pavement like a tightrope walker carrying a bowling ball, I let my smile show more confidence than I felt. For the moment, the lifetime commitment wasn't all I was worried about. There was the immediate future to contend with. For though I'd given birth myself, I'd never seen a baby born.

In the hospital, as Luz was hooked up to lines and monitors that would attend the induction of labor, I noticed shafts of watery winter light sliding through the blinds. It had been a cloudy morning, but the sun would shine today, after all. I took it as a sign. I was ready to accept any tiding of comfort and joy.

The medicine began to drip into the tubes, and quickly, contractions commenced. Luz breathed and blew; I counted. The hours crawled past. I looked up at the clock. I called my son and my friend at the hotel, and the director at the adoption agency. No, no one new was in the world yet. The contractions became more commanding, their clench gathering speed like a runaway sled. I phoned my older sons and daughter, and a sweetly intuitive nurse placed the receiver against the fetal heart monitor so that my nine-year-old son, Dan, a thousand miles due north in Wisconsin, could hear his baby sister's beating heart. The light was changing. The sun was bright at the west window; it was late afternoon and time for Luz, soothed by pain medication, to rest before pushing. I sat beside her as she moaned and slept, my cheek resting on her extended hand.

We were two single mothers—one probably too old for this and one certainly too young. It was December 8, in Catholic tradition the Feast of the Immaculate Conception, and outside in the hall an Army choir was singing ancient songs about another single mother and the baby in the barn.

Soon it was time for Luz to push, and she gathered herself, silent and stoic, her clenched face like the image on an Aztec coin. Twice, she told me, "I can't go on." Twice, I told her she had no choice—neither of us did. I put my arms around her and we held on to one another, and in the light of that one bedside lamp, its cone the shape of a golden trumpet, in the whole universe, there were only the two of us.

And then, suddenly, slippery, just one minute after the doctor came rushing into the room, there were three—the third a baby woman who would grow up to understand all this and someday to endure it.

Together, Luz and I marveled over her tiny, flossy dark head. Our daughter for this moment. My daughter ever after. "Let Mom hold the baby," the doctor said gently. And Luz slowly raised one hand and pointed to me.

So I stood up alone and held her for the first time. And there she was, fairest of the fair she was, seven pounds and fifteen ounces of earth angel and nobody's baby but mine. I named her Francie Nolen, for a little girl in an old book, *A Tree Grows in Brooklyn*, a little girl who came up strong and sure in circumstances that might have daunted a lesser spirit.

Francie might not have the inestimable benefit of a father. Her mother would have a crinkly smile and creaky knees, not bounce and sparkle. But there was some wisdom and not a little patience behind that crinkly smile. Francie would have siblings to champion her, as well as the support and comfort of all those doubters back home who'd be converted as soon as they laid eyes on her. Let them say I already had my hands full—weren't these big hands? I would not let any of my children down, nor let them feel that raising them had strained me past my limits.

As I looked down at Francie, I could feel those limits stretch and grow. I made a promise to her and the gallant girl who had given her life and given her up. My little girl would have laughs. She would have stories, good pasta twice a week, a house full of comforting noise. And most importantly, she would never, ever go to sleep except in the knowledge that she was loved beyond . . . beyond reason.

That December night was five years ago. And indeed, Francie has grown up unique in many ways, but most especially in her boldness. She has the stride of a tiny prizefighter and the will of a lion cub.

Six months after her birth, my first novel, *The Deep End of the Ocean,* was published, and suddenly, we got not only a new floor where there had once been a hole, but a new chance at life. And as for the hole in our hearts, Francie's personality helped shrink it to bearable proportions, and one day, along came a brave young man who wanted not only me, squeaky knees and all, but all my brood, for his very own.

My husband and I were married just weeks after my second novel was published. It was called *The Most Wanted,* and it was in part about a young teenager who gave birth to a baby girl in terrible circumstances, but who, because of the intervention of an older woman who longed for a child, got a second chance. It was my attempt, in fiction, to correct what I could not correct in life for the birth mother of my little girl. I dedicated that book to my daughters, and also to Luz, whose name, in Spanish, means "light."

Jacquelyn Mitchard

"Mommy used to go to Club Med and to the Bahamas
and once to Cannes . . . but you know, this is nice, too!"

Reprinted by permission of Stephanie Piro.

Spring of '59

Since you get more joy out of giving joy to others, you should put a good deal of thought into the happiness that you are able to give.

Eleanor Roosevelt

Mama didn't know how to drive a car or write beautiful words. She didn't have money to take me shopping. But she could copy the latest fashions from looking at the Sears, Roebuck & Company catalog and sew me a dress when I needed it. Mama didn't have a convection oven. Her wood-burning stove sufficed. She baked cakes from scratch that Martha Stewart would envy today.

I remember the morning Mama came into my room and sat on my bed. She was quiet for a moment and seemed embarrassed. Then she looked me straight in the eyes and asked the question, "How would you like to have a new baby in the house?"

I knew there was no possibility of that, because I was seventeen, my sister twelve, and the two boys nine and eight. You couldn't start having babies after eight years! "Mama, don't be foolish." I didn't hesitate to tell her we had more kids than we had money as it was.

A shadow crawled across her face. "I'm three months pregnant." She walked out of my room and closed the door. I was sorry I'd hurt her feelings, but being the thoughtless teenager I was, I didn't apologize.

Mama tried hard to take care of the house and kids, but she had a difficult pregnancy that forced her to stay in bed much of the time. I hoped by helping out with the kids and the meals I might make amends for the things I'd said about the baby, although she never mentioned them.

I worried about Mama sometimes, but my head was filled with something more exciting. Soon it would be spring, and I would graduate from Franklin-Simpson High. Our class began working and earning money for our senior-class trip four years earlier. Starting in our freshman year we held bake sales, car washes and play productions. Finally, we did it: We earned enough money to charter two Greyhound buses to take the entire graduating class to Florida for a week! My parents were poor. I'd never been off the farm, let alone three states away—and be able to see the ocean! This trip was the epitome of a dream come true.

Mama, who had only finished the fourth grade, was almost as ecstatic as I was. She was happy about my Florida trip and had sewn some pretty clothes for me even after she had gotten sick. I had blue, red, pink and yellow skirts and blouses to match. I even had a petticoat made of a rainbow of colorful ruffles. But my graduation would be her dream fulfilled.

By early spring, Mama's face looked gray and unwell. Even I could see something was wrong. And her eyes didn't laugh anymore. Mama's eyes always laughed. Four days before I was to leave, the doctor admitted her into the hospital. I knew this was serious. In those days, farmers didn't have insurance and very little money to pay doctors. People didn't go to hospitals unless there was a chance they might die.

Dad worried about Mama. He couldn't afford to pay anyone to come in and help. We managed the best we knew how. Someone had to take care of the younger children and the farm; milk cows couldn't wait. I volunteered to stay with Mama nights while Dad managed the home and kids. I spent the nights sleeping in a chair beside Mama's bed, praying for God to spare her life, then walking across town to school in the mornings, riding the bus home, helping Dad with the kids, and later, going back to Mama's side for the night. I was so tired I ached all over.

I watched the calendar as the days passed. I didn't think Mama realized what day it was until she took my hand in hers and asked if I had my luggage packed. She said, "I want you to see Florida. Then you can tell me all about it, so I can feel like a part of me went to see the ocean." Mama longed to see the places that we read about in my geography books, but she could never afford to travel.

"I'm not going, Mama," I muffled a sob.

"Oh, but yes you are." She was very adamant, but I was my mother's daughter and just as stubborn. Mama finally gave in and said I could stay, then added, "But miracles do happen. One never knows. There's still one day and a night left."

"It's all right, Mama, I don't mind. Really. I want to be here with you." I stuffed my face into a pillow that night so she wouldn't hear me cry.

A surprise awaited us at the hospital the next evening. When Daddy and I arrived, Mama was packed and waiting for us. "Remember that miracle I spoke of. I've been dismissed," she announced. "Doctor said I could go home." The three of us hugged each other and cried happy tears. I was happy for Mama, but, truthfully, my first thought was, *Now I can go to Florida.*

I boarded the Greyhound at 6:30 the following morning. Mama looked at me so pleased and proud, her soft gray eyes were hazed with tears. Several years later, I learned she had walked out of the hospital without her doctor's permission. She returned afterward, but not until she saw me off on my dream vacation.

The baby didn't arrive while I was gone. My little brother, Alan, waited until a week before graduation to make his appearance. I was in the room with Mama that Sunday morning when she went into labor, a very appropriate day, Mother's Day, May 9, 1959.

The hospital was busy but quiet. There were no monitors in the rooms or intercoms at the nurses' stations. Only one nurse worked the maternity hall of the small community hospital, and no physician was on duty. By the time they called Mama's doctor from across town, the nurse and I had delivered Alan. The cord, wrapped around his neck, made him all black and blue and purple. I thought my little brother was dead and Mama was dying. I've never been so scared in my life. Her face was covered with beads of sweat, her face white as the cotton sheets and her eyes looked like glazed windowpanes.

Doctor Beasley walked into the door and Mama immediately demanded, "Get her out of here, she's only seventeen!" She lay in a crimson pool, yet she was concerned about me.

"No use of that now, she's seen the worst of it." He patted my head and grinned. "Mama and baby are both fine. The cord had him constricted for a short while. Caused a little discoloration, that's all." He pulled my brother up by his feet and laid him on her breast while he cut the cord. I'll never forget the look that Mama gave that baby. In one swift, precious second, her eyes told him he was worth all the suffering she'd endured.

The doctor ordered complete bed rest before he released Mama from the hospital. I hugged her and told her I understood why she wouldn't be at my graduation ceremony. Her eyes brimmed with tears as she squeezed my hand and told me how proud she was. That evening, when Daddy and I were ready for the drive into town, Mama, donned in a blue Sears, Roebuck copy, joined us. Daddy gave her a questioning look. "And just what do you think you're doing?"

"I'm going to see my daughter walk across that platform," she stated so matter-of-factly that neither of us had the nerve to refute her.

Twenty-five years later, I sat by Mama's bedside again. This time she was the one preparing for a phenomenal voyage. The angels lifted her from her cancer-ridden body and carried her to her heavenly home, her dreams fulfilled.

Jean Kinscy

Confessions

When I was just a little girl
My mother once confessed,
Of all us kids (and there were five)
My mother liked me best.

I never told my brother
Though he always was a pest.
Of all us kids (and there were five)
My mother liked me best.

I never told my sisters
Cause they might become distressed.
Of all us kids (and there were five)
My mother liked me best.

All five of us are almost grown.
I mentioned it in jest.
Of all us kids (and there were five)
My mother liked me best.

The smiles across their faces
Told the story I had guessed.
She had, of course, to each of us
Identically confessed.

Linda Sultan

The Reunion

Gratitude is not only the greatest of virtues, but the parent of all the others.

Cicero

My kids knew something was up the minute I took a phone call during dinner and failed to return for three hours. After twenty-five years of wondering and praying, that long-awaited call finally came. To be frank, I can barely even remember what we said. How do you fit twenty-five years of unanswered questions into one conversation? Having learned that she lived less than twenty-five minutes from my home, we made immediate plans to reunite, the sooner the better. I emerged from the phone call with a very heady feeling and a date to meet her the next evening.

My husband knew about Nicole from our first date. I had a very well-developed sense of what I wanted in a life-mate. I knew I would spend the rest of my life with him and felt the need to share with him the story of Nicole. I told him with the hope that she would eventually rejoin my life. I wanted him to know that she would also be joining his.

I had gotten pregnant at the age of sixteen, after having been the victim of what is now called date rape. Nicole's biological father was nineteen at the time, and I broke up with him immediately after he forced himself on me. My family fortuitously moved shortly thereafter. Having had sporadic menstrual cycles, I wasn't concerned with the missed periods. I must have attributed the baby's kicking to gas. Being a healthy teenager, I carried her entirely inside, never showing until a month and a half before her birth, and then only slightly.

It was Christmas Eve, after an argument with my mom, when she looked at me in a very serious manner and asked if I was pregnant. I was indignant and vehemently denied the possibility. It did give me plenty of food for thought, and a week later, I asked her to take me to the doctor. I'll never forget her face as she was putting on her mascara, and I casually asked the question. She had forgotten about the Christmas Eve argument. It was one of the hardest things I've ever had to do, mustering up enough courage to stop the denial and face the facts.

Upon learning that I was indeed pregnant and due within thirty to forty-five days, my parents rallied around me and assured me that they would support whatever decision I made. They also made certain that I understood the ramifications of each of my potential choices. It wasn't a hard decision to make, since I really had no bond yet with the baby. I chose to place the baby for adoption.

In those days, if the baby was to be placed for adoption, the mother was not allowed to see the child after delivery. Neither was any other family member, but the hospital staff didn't know my mom. She managed to sneak into the nursery every day of my stay and get as many looks at Nicole as she could steal. As we were leaving the hospital, my mom casually reminded my dad that this would be his last opportunity to take a look at Nicole. He had not joined my mom on any of her stealthy trips to the nursery. The social worker was scheduled to pick Nicole up from the nursery that day. Dad unlocked the doors of the car, got us all settled, was about to drive off, then said, "Wait, I'll be right back." We waited, and on his return he simply said, "Kathy, she's beautiful."

I believe it was the hand of God ensuring I never had the opportunity to emotionally bond with the baby growing inside of me. When Nicole was two weeks old, we met at the Social Services office, where I was to spend time with her in a contrived living room setting. This meeting was to ensure that I still wanted to give her up for adoption. They brought her to me and left me there, alone with her, for fifteen minutes. That was a long fifteen minutes. I was a very young woman and terribly frightened I might drop her. I do remember thinking she was the most beautiful thing I'd ever seen, but I knew I couldn't keep her.

We finalized the paperwork, the adoption process was initiated, and as far as we knew, she went to a family in Richmond, Virginia. I returned to school, finished out the year, and we moved at the end of the year. I went on to graduate from college and gained a commission as a naval officer. It was there that I met my husband. We married three months after meeting each other, nineteen years ago.

We went on to have two children of our own, and thanks to the Naval Reserves, I am now a retired reserve commander. Throughout the years, not a single day went by that I didn't think about Nicole, and pray that she had a good, happy and healthy life. On her eighteenth birthday, I put a letter in her adoption file which detailed how to contact me in the event she ever came looking. My husband and parents were very supportive of this.

When Nicole decided to search for me, my letter made it very easy. The long-awaited phone call had finally come, and my husband shared with me the excitement of the prospect of finally meeting my daughter. The day of the reunion, we sat our boys down and explained the situation. They were wonderfully supportive about it, and asked some frank questions, which we answered very honestly. Excited at the prospect of actually having a sister, they wished me well, gave me big kisses and sent me on my way to my reunion.

Nicole and I met outside the church after my bell choir rehearsal. I will never forget watching her climb out of her Mazda RX7 and just keep going up, up, up. She was tall, she was blond and she was gorgeous. We very slowly hugged each other with the gentleness afforded only the most precious, fragile treasures in your life. The rest of the evening was spent in a cozy booth at a restaurant down the street. The waitress was observant enough to realize that something very special was going on, and she prudently left us alone to try to catch up on a lifetime.

That night, Nicole told me that if she were to be limited to saying only one thing, she would thank me from the bottom of her heart. "Thank you for having me, for giving me up, and for welcoming me back into your life so warmly and openly." We sat there and compared our hands, feet, the same laugh, the same way we hold our mouths, all the answers to Nicole's questions of "Where did I get that?" This continues to be a resounding thread through our lives, "Oh, that would explain where I got *that.*"

After twenty-five years, I felt as though a tremendous weight had been lifted, and I remember feeling as though there was simply nothing that could beat the joy I felt at finally knowing she was safe, healthy and had grown up with a very loving family. We went on to spend time together each week. She got to know her new brothers, and she very bravely accompanied me to many outings with our friends, getting to know all the people who are special in my life, as I met all those who were special in hers.

My husband took particular pleasure in our reunion since Nicole is almost a mirror image of what I looked like at her age. He loves to go out with us, feeling as though he has the best of both worlds, me at my current age, and me at the age we got married. Even now, more than two years after the reunion, he marvels at the fact that we have the same mouth, smile and laugh.

I don't know if I can ever adequately express the gratitude I owe to her parents for having given her such a wonderful upbringing. They are two very special people, and I am deeply indebted to them. They welcomed me and my family into their lives with the same open arms that welcomed Nicole. The card her mom gave me for Mother's Day that year said it all: "I truly believe children are gifts from God, on loan, for us to raise to become independent and assets to society. Ever since we adopted Nicole, you have been in my thoughts—each February 17, but especially on every Mother's Day. So, Happy Mother's Day, not only have you found a daughter, but a best friend." And to her, I also say thank you.

Kathy N. Jublou

The Needle

*Remember happiness doesn't depend upon who
you are or what you have; it depends solely on
what you think.*

Dale Carnegie

"Honey, will you see what you can do about these arm
covers that keep slipping off?" asked my husband for the
second or third time. I had watched him struggle to keep
the too-skimpy but necessary protective covers carefully
in place and end up with one or the other on the floor.

The house was empty when I decided to tackle the task.
I had a vision in my mind of an unusual and special needle
that I had seen somewhere among my sewing things. So I
began a rather haphazard search through various sewing
boxes and my sewing machine, and then I went to the old
Martha Washington walnut sewing cabinet that had been
my mother's. I sat down beside it and began to go through
the drawers. Why had I saved so many crochet hooks? I
rarely crocheted more than one or two loops. Oh, look,
there is the box of old lace and the old beaded bag that
mother's aunt sometimes carried to keep her change at

hand. Before long an hour had passed, and I had certainly not begun to fix the chairs. I gave up that idea for the present and continued to savor the memories that flooded over me as I sorted through the chest. Then there it was: the needle that had floated into my memory bank and given me the idea that I could fix the chairs. It was rather thick in the middle but had a good-sized eye, and it was curved in a rather sharp and useful arc.

Mother died over thirty-five years ago, and I remember so clearly asking for that needle as we three children chose the things of hers that were meaningful to us. I also asked for her painting supplies and to this day I use her brushes and sometimes almost feel that she is there beside me as I paint with the short stubby brush that makes such wonderful clouds.

But the needle was a mystery to me. Why had I wanted the needle and kept it for so many years, through at least five moves to different towns and homes? Now even in my retirement years, I still kept the needle. I have never used it. In fact, I'm not sure I even know how it is used.

Nevertheless, as ignorant as I felt, I took the needle and threaded it and went to the chair and sat down to study the situation. Then I felt tears on my cheeks, and I knew why I had kept the needle. I think I was about fifteen, and I was having a party. I complained over and over again to Mother how ugly our couch was with the torn places on the arms and the shabby pillows. "What will my friends think of us?" I whined.

Mother hugged me and told me not to worry, that my friends would have a good time because they cared about me and that she would make the room very pretty. I went up to my room to do my homework, and when I came down a couple of hours later to kiss Mother good night, there she was sitting on the floor with the needle going in and out, sewing a piece of matching fabric over the worn places in the couch. The needle just went into the flat overstuffed surface, and she pulled the curve around and out over and over again. Now I knew why I had kept that needle for so many years and why I knew that I could fix those chairs. No lesson from a book, no homily, no class could have taught me more powerfully how to make someone you love feel comfortable with what was available as well as my mother's love in fixing the couch for me.

I fixed the chairs, and I carefully put the needle away and hoped that some day one of my daughters would find a way to use it.

Julie Firman

The Education Ring

Arrange whatever pieces come your way.

Virginia Woolf

It is a hot July afternoon, typical of most Alabama summers. The air hangs heavy in rural Morgan County as storm clouds gather in the west. I pull up to the entrance of the Somerville Community Cemetery. I feel sad, yet somehow elated at the sight of this old place. I feel right at home, having spent many "Decoration Days" here as a child. Decoration Day always followed a frantic week of cleaning off graves, cutting grass and repairing any damaged tombstones. Every grave (some dating back to the early 1700s) received new flowers.

My family's graves are near the front or "new" part of the cemetery. The "old" part is deeply shaded with giant pines and fragrant cedar trees. It always seemed dark, musty and more than a little mysterious. On my left is a section for loyal coon dogs, and a small, fenced section on my right holds the remains of black members of the community. Some of these stones date back to pre-Civil War days.

In my hand, I am holding an envelope addressed simply "To Mama." I start at the oldest of my family's plots, those marked Campbell and Smith. There's my grandfather who was adopted and grew up to become a cowboy in Oklahoma at the turn of the century. My grandmother, who made clothes for my Barbie doll, lies beside him. I move slowly by the graves of aunts, uncles and cousins to stand at the foot of Mama's grave.

The memories are bittersweet. This is the end of a long journey for me, a journey that spans nineteen years. Mama died at age forty-seven, just ten months before her first grandchild was born. It's finally time to say good-bye. I open the envelope and read its contents one more time. Something buried deep in the corner of my heart brims over and rolls down my face as I read.

"Mama, I remember when we gave you 'the ring.' Daddy, Diane and I woke you up on your birthday by piling on your bed, giggling and filled with excitement. I was clutching the tiny white box in my hand. When you opened it, the contents were large and sparkling to my five-year-old eyes. Daddy had whispered beforehand that it was a whole carat and cost five hundred dollars. I could not imagine that vast amount of money, or even what a carat was. I just knew that you squealed with delight, eyes out-sparkling the diamond, and you kissed Daddy for a long time. I didn't know until many years later that Daddy had sold his gold Hamilton pocket watch for money to buy the ring.

"Happy and sad years followed in quick succession. I fell in love with the Beatles, and watched Alan Shepard take the first space ride. I watched in horror and fascination when John Kennedy was killed in Dallas. High school proms came and went, and I graduated one warm May evening in 1965. You gave me a beautiful silver watch for graduation. It no longer works, but I look at it often. I'm sure my graduation meant a lot to you and Daddy, since you married in your senior year, and he went off to World War II without either of you graduating.

"You were already ill that summer of '65, and any extra money went for medical bills. College seemed an impossible dream, but you found a way, Mama. I had no idea what I wanted to be, but I already knew I was in love with history. To me, it was an endless adventure in which I could always play the main part.

"The only time I remember seeing you cry, Mama, was the day you and Daddy left me at college the first time. I was only seventeen.

"The next four years were full of new experiences. I loved every minute of school. I cried when a bomb killed four little girls in a Birmingham church, when Robert Kennedy was murdered, and when Martin Luther King Jr., died on a Memphis balcony. But I cried the hardest for Fred Smith. He sat next to me in physical science class. One semester he didn't return after summer vacation. He had been killed in Vietnam. He was just twenty years old.

"Through all this, it never occurred to me each semester to worry about the money my student loan didn't cover. Somehow you always had it, even when you and Daddy filed for bankruptcy because of the overwhelming medical bills. You made it through two life-or-death operations during those four years. I know that you wanted desperately to see me walk across that college stage as the first on either side of the family to receive a college degree.

"Only later did I learn where the extra money came from. Each semester, 'the ring' disappeared only to reappear weeks later. It spent more time in Wiley's Pawn Shop in those four years than it did on your finger. You gave up your most prized possession to guarantee me one of the greatest gifts a parent can give a child—a good education.

"Your sacrifice paid off, Mama. I will begin my twenty-second year as a high school history teacher next term. I still can't sleep the night before the first day of school, just like a child on Christmas Eve. Every year my students and I build and destroy great civilizations, fight wars, paint the Sistine Chapel with Michelangelo, build a flying machine with DaVinci, cry over the bombing of Hiroshima and contemplate the horrors of the Holocaust. They keep me young with their fifteen- and sixteen-year-old excitement about life. My body says I'm forty-four, but my mind says I'm still twenty-two and teaching my very first class. Some of my students have become doctors, lawyers, teachers, social workers, engineers, policemen and ministers. I am now teaching some of their children.

"Mama, your grandson, Joshua, will be starting college this fall at my alma mater. I imagine it will be the first time he will see me cry. Thanks for the ring, Mama. It may come in handy again."

I fold the letter and put it into the envelope. I gently lean it against the stone under the words "Arleta Smith Maxwell, 1925–1972." As I turn to leave, a gentle, cleansing rain begins to fall.

Brenda Jordan

Selfless Support

A mother is a person who, seeing there are only four pieces of pie for five people, promptly announces she never did care for pie.

Tenneva Jordan

I was born on the twenty fifth of February, which just so happened to be my mother's birthday, too. It was as though this single piece of timing foretold the future depth of our relationship. Through my childhood, adolescence and adulthood, our bond grew stronger. Every year, as we celebrated our birthdays, we became more attuned, closer to each other in understanding, knowledge and spirit. We shared dreams, troubles, hobbies, shopping trips, in-depth discussions, everything. Through it all, Mum and I worked as a team.

Our long talks covered many things, including my future and the natural progression of our friendship when I married. Never did either of us consider the possibility that anything might happen to change the foundation of our relationship.

As I grew up and stretched my wings, I was drawn by an

overwhelming desire to visit Australia. There was no reason for it; I didn't know what was there or really where the country even was. But it was something I couldn't ignore.

As I stood in the airport with my plane ticket and a year's holiday visa in my hand, Mum and I struggled to say goodbye. We had never been apart for so long. Both of us knew the break would not be easy, yet we both knew it had to be faced. Some of the last words Mum said to me were, "Don't fall in love and marry an Aussie." It was a brave attempt at humor, but it was a sentence I would never forget. One year later, when I returned home and tried to settle back into my old way of life her words came back to haunt me. I hadn't fallen in love with an Australian. But I had fallen in love with an Englishman living in Australia, which meant the same thing when a month later he proposed.

In the short time leading up to my wedding and emigration, Mum and I spent many hours together, each of us trying to make the most of our time together in England. Through it all Mum never once mentioned how she really felt about my moving twelve thousand miles away or the loss of our regular chats or the loss of her dream of spending time with any children I might have. She never spoke of her disappointment at not being able to afford the expensive plane ticket so that she could be at the wedding. She chose instead to tell me only of her delight in the happiness I had found, how proud she was and how much she would miss me when I left. Yet, beneath all her excited words I could see the heartbreak. How could I not?

Eighteen months after my first plane flight we stood again, at a loss for words, at the airport. As I walked alone through the doors that led toward my future, my heart ached for all that I was leaving behind. It was only the flow of people around me that kept me heading toward the plane. But as I sat there in my window seat, the enormity of my decision hit me. Holding back the tears caused by the physical pain I felt, I willed away the nagging knowledge that I didn't know when I would see my mum again. Desperately, and unsuccessfully, I tried to block out all except that within days I would again be with my fiancé.

It was the height of summer when I arrived in Australia. As I unpacked my wedding dress and gifts from England I couldn't help but think about how different my wedding would be from the one I had thought about for so many years. My Australian cousin would be giving me away but there would be no other members of my family there. In fact, most of the guests were friends of my fiancé—people I had never met. In my heart, I knew it was the right decision, but as every day moved closer to the wedding the distance away from my mother weighed heavier.

Days before the wedding my cousin phoned to say that he needed to discuss with me his duties regarding the marriage service. Pulling into his driveway I was filled with a dread. What if he couldn't make the wedding after all? Would I be married with none of my family there? Panic gripped me as I knocked on his door. Eventually, the door opened, and I stood there dazed by the sight. For there she stood, my mother.

It turned out that as she had seen me walk through the airport doors, she, too, had felt the shearing wrench. And in the five days since then she had moved heaven and Earth to make sure she would not miss my wedding.

At eight o'clock in the morning, a few days later, my wedding took place. It was twelve thousand miles away from where we had expected it to be. It was in a picturesque park instead of the traditional church. There was no long flowing gown or organ music. But it didn't matter, because my mum, loving, selfless and supportive, was there to give me away to the man I loved.

Elizabeth Bezant

The Princess Dress

There are souls in this world which have the gift of finding joy everywhere and of leaving it behind them when they go.

Frederick Faber

The phone rang on a Saturday night. It was Kelly.

"Mom, where were you?" she said. "I tried to call you from a store because I want you to help me make up my mind. Oh, Mom, I found the most beautiful dress for my formal! I feel like a princess in it, but it's really expensive. What do you think I should do? Should I buy it?"

I didn't have a moment's hesitation. "Yes," I told her. "Buy the dress." But in those few short minutes on the phone I didn't have the time or the words to explain why I thought she should have the "princess" dress she'd found. There are so many reasons I would give my daughter. . . .

For growing up without many clothes or vacations, because there was never enough money, and not complaining about either one—that would be one reason.

For studying so hard and doing every extra-credit

assignment she could get her hands on, so she could go to college.

For all those times she passed the soccer ball, when she knew she could have easily run and scored but valued being a team player more than being a star.

For that fierce determination when she was slammed in the nose during a game, and despite blood running down her face, kept yelling, "I'm fine, Coach! I'm not bleeding anymore. Put me in, Coach!"

For giving up varsity soccer at college because she had to work and couldn't (wouldn't!) let her grades suffer.

For giving up her spring break one year to build houses for the poor in Tijuana and coming home scraped and bruised and sick and exclaiming, "Mom, that was the most wonderful thing I've ever done in my life!"

For deciding that even though she was supporting herself she could still find the money to sponsor a child in El Salvador who has less.

For deciding that faith is the most important thing of all.

For telling me when I wished I could give her more, "Mom, I think of you as my angel," and reminding me just how priceless love is.

Oh yes, I do think that daughter of mine should have that dress. And she's right that no one will notice that her shoes don't match (since there's no extra money to buy new shoes). I know that people will only see the shining joy in those big brown eyes of hers, and that radiant smile that could light a midnight sky. But Kelly was wrong about one thing. I don't think that she'll look like a princess in that dress of hers: To me, my darling daughter is a queen.

Anne Goodrich

The Birth of Daughters

Life is what we make it, always has been, always will be.

Grandma Moses

I am finally and victoriously pregnant after seven years of marriage. I am also absurdly worried about what my mother will think. I've recently gone back to school for a master's degree. My husband is not quite finished with a Ph.D. program. I feel like we're being a little reckless, like we have no business even thinking about a child, let alone strategically planning the optimal conditions to make one.

So I nervously rehearse the "big news." My worst fear is a raised eyebrow asking, "And just how do you think you're going to raise this child on a student's income?" Asking, in fact, the very question that I'm nervously asking myself, *What are you? Crazy?!*

I end up telling my parents by inviting them to Thanksgiving dinner even though it's only Easter. "Well, it's a little far ahead to make plans . . .," my dad says. I tell him I already know what I'll be doing—getting ready to deliver his first grandkid. He looks surprised, but definitely not elated.

My stomach starts to sink.

I think I wince as I look to my mother for her response. It's my turn to be surprised. She rockets off the couch, doing a little victory dance, exclaiming, "I knew it! I knew you were pregnant! I'll be right back!"

And she runs off upstairs. She returns with a little gift bag. "Here!" she says, thrusting it at me, "Presents for the baby! I just knew you were pregnant! I was wondering when you'd tell us. I've had this stuff for over a month."

I've only known for a month myself.

I admit to my mom that I was expecting a lecture from her regarding our financial situation. I can tell that the thought has never even crossed her mind. I hear the words, "Oh, don't worry about the money. Everything will work out just fine."

Now I find out we are not expecting a baby. We're expecting *two*. It took a while to sink in. This time, my mother, a twin herself, is the first person I called. From that moment on, she's my constant pregnancy companion.

Looking back, I'm embarrassed by my ignorance, but I guess I thought maybe she'd pat me on the head, tell me to eat saltines when I felt like barfing, and send me some flowers in the hospital.

Instead she acts like she's just won the lottery. She tells everyone who will listen that she's going to be a grand-mother of twins. She buys me maternity clothes. She "picks up" things for the babies. ("Hi, honey, I just bought a couple of wardrobes for your embryos.") She sends me cards.

She calls me regularly.

I go into labor early and unexpectedly. Mom sounds nervous but thrilled.

I wish she could be with us, but we're hundreds of miles apart.

About six hours later, the nurse tells me I have a visitor in the waiting room. In walks Mom. I actually think that fatigue and pain are making me see things.

"How did you get here?" I ask incredulously. I know shecan't possibly have driven—there hasn't been enough time. "I flew, and then I took a taxi."

She tells me matter-of-factly, as if this is the kind of thing she does on a daily basis. She, like me, hates to fly, probably even more than she hates to drive. "Did you think I'd miss this for the world?" she asks me.

"All I know is I really wanted you to be here."

"I know that, honey, that's why I came."

When she sees her tiny, squalling granddaughters for the first time, she makes it as far as my husband. She hugs him and starts to cry. It's as if she'll never stop. And I know her tears are tears of deep relief. I know they are tears of intense joy and intense love. I know they are the tears that a mother cries for a child. I know it because I can taste it in the salt of my own tears.

I offer her up two tiny bodies and feel the ties that connect us bind tightly as she takes her granddaughters into her arms for the first time.

"There are some things you'll never understand until you have kids. You'll see," she has always told me. And sitting there in that hospital bed, totally exhausted and emotionally raw, seeing my mother holding my two impossibly light brand-new daughters, I think I do see. I see that becoming a mother has not only given me the gift of loving a child with an intensity that I never knew existed, but also the gift of my own mother—and the sudden realization that I am, and have been all my life, loved the same way.

May the circle be unbroken.

Karen C. Driscoll

Moving in with Mom

Each day provides its own gifts.

Martial

Five weeks before my daughter was due, I went into pre-term labor and was sentenced to bed rest. I could get up only for weekly doctor's appointments, twice-weekly non-stress tests and bathroom privileges.

While giving me my instructions, my doctor said that I shouldn't be alone; I needed someone to get me to the hospital at the first twinge of a contraction. My husband, Jack, had been saving his vacation days for after the baby was born, and we both hated the thought of using them up. We also found out that it would be impractical for me to return home since our bedroom is on the second floor—and going up and down stairs was on my list of forbidden activities.

As Jack and I were exhausting our possibilities, my mother (who hadn't left my hospital room) piped up: "Why don't you stay with me?" she asked in her here's-what-we're-going-to-do voice. Jack thought that was the perfect solution; my mother could be with me all day, she lives a block from the hospital, and she has a first-floor guest room. I was more doubtful. Like most daughters, I have had my share of conflicts with my mother, and I didn't know if I could handle weeks of constant togetherness. Eventually, though, I realized it was the best option and moved back "home."

I spent my days sulking—acting more like a surly teenager than a gracious houseguest. When Jack came after work, and my mother visited friends or ran the errands she couldn't do during the day, I cried. I wanted to go home. I wanted to be away from my mother. Most of all, I just wanted everything to be normal again. I snapped at my mother incessantly.

"Do you have to tell everyone about my medical problems?" I yelled when I overheard her phone conversations. "Can't I have any privacy around here?" I whined when she checked to make sure I hadn't fallen during my two-minute showers. My mother, who had never hesitated to tell me to "knock it off" when necessary, apologized.

Thanksgiving came a few days later. I wasn't feeling very thankful, but I was craving my mother's mashed potato casserole. The night before Thanksgiving, my mother went to the grocery store and bought everything I wanted.

The next day, I lay on the couch and watched my mother prepare a gourmet meal for three—even straining the gravy because the slightest lump would make me gag. I could see how difficult the day was for her; my father had died six months earlier, and this was our first "family" holiday without him. When dinner was ready, my mother sat and looked down at her plate for a long time. "Aren't you going to eat?" Jack finally asked her.

"In a minute," my mother said, tears glistening in her eyes. "I was just thinking about how thankful I am to have a grandchild coming. I never would have gotten through the past few months without this baby to look forward to. And I know you're going to love being parents as much as Daddy and I always did."

I realized then just how lucky I was: While my husband was working all day, then pulling all-nighters assembling the crib, setting up the swing and changing table, and getting everything ready for the baby, I had my mother to take care of me.

For the next ten days, I let my mother fuss over me—and I let myself enjoy her company. She told me stories about her pregnancy and my childhood. We read baby books and magazines together. We laughed at trashy talk shows and cried over sappy movies. We ate all my favorite foods. I got to know my mother as more than just my mother.

I can't say everything was perfect, though. I had to take an "anti-contraction" pill every six hours, including one at 2:00 A.M., and my mother had a tendency to wake me at 2:15—after I had already turned off my alarm clock, taken the pill and drifted back to sleep. She was convinced that if I raised my arms, I would strangle the baby (despite repeated assurances from my doctor that this would not happen), so she panicked whenever I reached for something. And she said things like, "Maybe after you have the baby, you'll shave your legs again."

I didn't mind. In fact, I thought it was kind of funny. And I was grateful. I knew my husband and I would have managed on our own if we had to. But having my mother around just made things easier.

When my mother took me to the hospital for my third non-stress test, the nurse said, "Come on in, Grandmom. Don't you want to hear the baby's heartbeat?" As the sound of my baby's heart filled the room, I heard another sound—the sound of my mother's sobs.

"Is the baby's heart okay?" she asked. "Is everything all

right?" When the nurse said everything sounded great, I could see my mother beaming through her tears, and I was so glad she was there. My father had died of a heart attack, and I realized what a gift it was for my mother to hear her first grandchild's strong, healthy heartbeat. She squeezed my hand as we listened. Then she turned to the nurse and said, "And you're sure Carol is okay?"

"Yes, Carol is just fine," the nurse smiled. "You're taking good care of her."

"Well, she's my baby," my mother said and kissed my cheek.

At that moment I saw that, while I was putting my life on hold to do what was best for my baby, my mother was putting her life on hold to do what was best for her baby, too. And as I held my mother's hand, I knew that I would follow her example. Whenever my daughter needs me— no matter how old she is or how cranky she is—I'll be there, just like my mother taught me.

Carol Sjostrom Miller

Why, don't be silly . . . raising my daughter
hasn't cramped my style a bit!

The Rocker

There is as much greatness of mind in acknowledging a good turn, as in doing it.

Seneca

I stumbled with exhaustion, searching for the ringing telephone. Colicky three-month-old Max slept only two hours at a time, and my husband was away traveling again. My fatigued body ached. I found the phone under a receiving blanket and answered it.

My mother asked, "Is Max sleeping any better?"

"A little."

"You're not getting any sleep, are you?" She sounded worried.

My gritty eyes burned. "Not much."

"That must be so hard."

My throat closed. "Oh Mom, I'm exhausted! I can hardly think."

"I'm coming up."

Outside my window a December blizzard moaned through the darkness. My mother would have to navigate icy canyon roads to reach my house. I said, "It's snowing hard here. Don't come. I'll be okay."

"I'm on my way." She hung up. Tears of exhaustion and relief blurred my vision. My mother has always been my rock.

The usual thirty-minute drive took her an hour. My mother arrived looking rosy-cheeked from the cold, snow frosting her reddish-brown hair. She took baby Max from my arms and ordered me to bed. I said, "But Max needs to eat in the night."

She shook her head. "I know how to warm up formula. Go to bed!" Her determined look told me not to argue.

My soft pillow beckoned to me, along with my cozy down comforter. I headed upstairs feeling relieved, but lying in bed I couldn't sleep. Guilt overwhelmed me. I should be able to take care of my baby. At least I could have offered to help. My mother wouldn't have let me, I realized. I heard her coo to Max as she climbed the stairs. Soon the rocking chair in baby Max's room creaked, back and forth, back and forth.

Suddenly I remembered my mother rocking me when I had the chicken pox. I was too big for rocking, but blisters invaded my throat, my ears, even the back of my eyelids. As we rocked my mother sang, "Rock-a-bye my big-big girl." The monotonous chant comforted me. I slept. When I woke in the night my mother offered sips of water and laid cold washrags across my burning forehead. I slept fitfully, but in the morning the blisters had crusted, and I felt better.

Now I could hear my mother chanting to Max, "Rock-a-bye my ba-by boy." Her monotone relaxed me, just as it had when I was a child. I slid toward sleep, knowing my baby was in capable hands. In the morning, I'd hug my mother, thank her, and tell her how her love had rocked both Max and me to sleep.

Kendeyl Johansen

Always a Mother

Is there anything more precious, more steadfast, more constant or enduring than a mother's love?

To watch her worry and fret as she waited for news of how her little girl came through brain surgery was almost more than I could bear. Through her tears she recounted stories of her little girl and voiced her longing to be right there with her. As she continually checked her watch, counting down the time that the doctor said surgery should take, I tried to think of comforting things to say. My words did not seem appropriate, for she was in a place I had never been. How could I understand her vigil, the agony that waiting was causing her?

Finally, the telephone rang. Marie had come through surgery fine and would recover with time. The look of relief flooded her face as her body visibly released its grip on her nerves. At last, this eighty-six-year-old mother could relax, knowing her seventy-year-old "little girl" was going to be fine.

Elizabeth Sharp Vinson

2

A DAUGHTER'S LOVE

My mother wanted me to be her wings, to fly as she never quite had the courage to do. I love her for that. I love the fact that she wanted to give birth to her wings.

Erica Jong

Abigail's Dove

To love another person is to see the face of God.

Victor Hugo

It had been the worst snowstorm in ten years, and I'd been caught in it. After hearing earlier that it was supposed to snow later in the night, I had volunteered at our church to take groceries and medical prescriptions to elderly members in need. Since my husband was away on business, I called my mother and she immediately came over to my house to watch my three-year-old daughter, Abigail.

"Can't someone else help those people?" she had asked me, concerned for my safety. "I have a bad feeling about this, and it looks like it might snow at any minute."

I glanced out the window and had to admit that the sky looked threatening. I began to feel uncertain.

"Mama will be okay," my daughter smiled, taking her grandmother's hand. "She likes helping people. Besides, I'll be praying for her!"

My heart swelled at her words. We had such a close relationship that sometimes when I breathed, it was as though Abigail exhaled. I decided then that I had to act on what I'd been instilling in my daughter: that sometimes we just have to step out in faith and believe that God will keep us safe. Kissing my mother and daughter good-bye, I set out to make my rounds. On my last stop, the snow began to fall.

"You shouldn't have come here," Bill Watkins, a ninety-two-year-old member of our congregation, scolded. He coughed, trying to get out of bed, but the effort proved too taxing. Giving up, he settled back onto the pillows. "I told the pastor that I didn't expect anyone to come to the boonies for me."

"Nonsense," I grinned, positioning snacks and drinks by his bed. Beneath his gruff exterior, Bill was sweet as candy. His heart medication had to be taken every day, and living on a modest income without any surviving family members, he needed as much help as possible.

"Well, look what your stubbornness brought you," he said, pointing to the snow-covered road outside the window. His fingers clasped my hand. "Stay here, Karen. I want you safe."

I kissed the top of his head but decided to brave the road conditions. It would be worse later, I reasoned.

"I'll be okay," I told him, remembering my sweet daughter's words before I left. Thoughts of Abigail made me more determined to get home. I missed her already.

I got into my Volkswagen and gradually tried making it down the steep hill. Remembering old instructions about driving in the snow, I kept the compact car in second gear. The wind increased, creating waves of blinding white. As I squinted through the windshield, holding my breath, I screamed and jerked the wheel, narrowly missing the deer that stood frozen by my headlights.

The Volkswagen hit the embankment, plummeted off the side of the road, and skidded to the bottom of a ravine below. When the rolling motion finally stopped, I opened my eyes and realized that I had been unconscious for some time. Night had arrived—and with it the forecasted accumulation of snow. Panicking, I tried opening the door, but it wouldn't budge against the resisting snow. Sliding over to the passenger's door, I realized that the door had been jammed shut by a tree. I turned the key to start the engine, but the battery was dead. My hopes of rolling down the power windows to crawl out vanished. Without heat and adequate clothing, I curled up on the back seat and waited for help.

The frigid air enveloped me. Shivering, I chastised myself for not preparing for a circumstance like this. My toes and fingers were already numb. An eternity seemed to pass, and as I listened to the wind and snow hitting against the car, I prayed for my family, who would be sick with worry by now. Abigail would probably be drawing pictures for me when I arrived home. Since she'd been old enough to hold a crayon, she'd drawn pictures to brighten the days of her loved ones.

To calm my growing concern about my safety, I closed my eyes and concentrated on pleasant thoughts. Drifting into sleep, I saw Abigail. Abigail in the warm sunlight, laughing as she held out a beautiful white dove to me. The dove's graceful, serene presence and the love shining in my daughter's eyes filled me with peace.

The night grew colder, and as I floated in and out of consciousness, I fixed my mind on the image of Abigail and her dove. Together, they kept me company throughout the night. Hours later, as the first rays of daybreak appeared, I heard tapping on my window. Relieved to see an emergency rescue team, my stiff lips tried to smile as they hoisted me onto a stretcher and into an ambulance. At the hospital, I was treated for mild frostbite and a head wound before being told I'd have to stay overnight for observation. Anxious to see my family, I propped myself up on the bed pillows and waited impatiently.

Before long, the door opened and my mother burst into the room. "We were so worried about you!" she cried, rushing over to hug me. "I knew you were in trouble! Mothers sense these kinds of things." Her maternal instincts surfaced as she appraised the food tray nearby. "Your tea is cold! I'll be right back."

Seizing the opportunity to have me all to herself, Abigail climbed onto the bed and buried her face in my neck. I scooped her closer. "I've missed you so much," I murmured softly, brushing a silky strand of hair from her face. "And what have you been doing while I've been away?"

"Oh, I forgot!" she exclaimed, jumping out of my arms to grab a large tube of construction paper nearby. "I drew this for you last night when we didn't know where you were. I thought you might've been scared, and I wanted you to feel better."

As if it were a treasure map, I unrolled it and oohed and aahed over the images. "Well, that's our car," I said, pointing to the red square. "And that's me," I laughed, touching my fingertips to a stick person with long hair. "But what am I holding?"

Abigail's eyes brightened as she pushed her fingertip to the small object on the paper. "That's God's spirit," she said excitedly. "I drew it as a dove like I saw in Sunday school." She pressed her soft lips against my cheek and added, "I didn't want you to be alone, Mama, and so I gave you the best friend I could think of."

"Oh, darling," I exclaimed, recalling the white dove that had given me comfort in the darkest of nights. "Your dove *was* with me." Taking her hand, I marveled at the heavenly bond between mothers and daughters.

"And what are you two looking at?" my mother interrupted, placing a steaming cup of tea on the nightstand. She started to move away, but I grabbed her hand and brought it between Abigail's and mine. It was a remarkable feeling, this incredible connection of three generations.

"We're looking at the love that flows between us," I whispered, kissing the top of my daughter's head as I met my mother's understanding eyes. Returning my gaze to Abigail's picture, I studied the beautiful bird that had, on such a dismal night, connected my daughter's heart with mine.

Years later, that extraordinary event in our mother-daughter relationship became known as the "miracle." The miracle of Abigail's dove.

Karen Majoris-Garrison

The Mother of Mother's Day

Who ran to help me when I fell,
And would some pretty story tell,
Or kiss the place to make it well?
. . . my mother.

Jane Taylor

While she might not have been the first person to suggest a day devoted to mothers, it is clear that the efforts of Anna M. Jarvis are directly responsible for today's celebration. Jarvis was born in Webster, Virginia, in 1864. After college and a brief teaching career, she moved to Philadelphia with her blind sister and well-to-do mother, Anna Reese Jarvis, to whom she was devoted.

When Jarvis was forty-one, her mother died, and she became the guardian of her sister and a considerable estate. During the period of mourning, she came up with the idea for Mother's Day. On the second anniversary of her mother's death (the second Sunday of May 1908), Jarvis announced to her friends that she wanted to establish a Mother's Day.

Ironically, the U.S. Senate actually voted against

Mother's Day in 1908. According to research, some senators noted that, "We might as well have a Father's Day or a Grandfather's Day or a Mother-in-Law's Day." But the following year, Jarvis began the tradition of a Mother's Day church service and persuaded the city fathers in Philadelphia to hold a city-wide Mother's Day observance. By 1912, West Virginia made Mother's Day a state holiday, with Oklahoma, Washington, Pennsylvania and other states following suit. In 1914, the senate changed its mind, and in May 1914, President Woodrow Wilson signed a joint congressional resolution, calling mothers, "The greatest source of the country's strength and inspiration."

Anna M. Jarvis died in 1948, penniless and sightless in Philadelphia, having devoted the last part of her life and most of her fortune to promoting Mother's Day. Her legacy is her gift to the mother she loved so well.

Hallmark

In Your Eyes

In your eyes, Mom,
I have always been the prettiest,
The smartest, the funniest
The one with the potential
To do anything

In your eyes,
My failures are but
Practice for success
My weaknesses
But strengths in the making
My mistakes
But an opportunity to learn

In your eyes,
I am the strongest
And the softest.
I am the shoulder
The world can cry on
And the rock
It can lean on

In your eyes,
I am the most creative
And artistic
My every stick figure
The Mona Lisa
My every clay figure
David

In your eyes,
I am the most loved and loving
Everyone's best friend
The perfect daughter
The perfect mother
The perfect wife
A beautiful person to know

And when I see myself
Reflected in your eyes
I see someone
Ten times the person I'll ever be—
I see you.

Melissa Peek

A Bus Trip for Mom on Mother's Day

I don't want to be a passenger in my own life.

Diane Ackerman

One early May, I had to attend a convention in New Orleans. It was just what my eighty-six-year-old mom wanted to hear.

"Why can't I go, too? I'd love to see New Orleans again!"

I had misgivings about Mom traveling, especially since an old hip injury was acting up. But she was so enthusiastic I figured a nice, quick plane trip would be just fine. That was not what Mom had in mind, however.

"Remember when you were a kid and we traveled all over on the bus? Wasn't that fun?" Mom asked with a grin.

Memories of harrowing hours in bus stations and rushed sandwiches in roadside diners made words other than "fun" leap to my mind. But then Mom brought out the big guns: "It is almost Mother's Day. That can be your gift to me. A bus ride to New Orleans."

So much for my protests.

So off we went, leaving San Diego one chilly morning and heading east. Mom quickly made friends with the

Hispanic men going home to the Imperial Valley after working all week in San Diego. Before I could hoist her bag up and down from the overhead rack, two darker-skinned young men were beating me to it. And Mom was raving over the sights of the mountains and the desert.

"Look at all the vegetables growing," she cried, "even more than when we went through the Imperial Valley before."

The giant sahuatob of Arizona delighted her, and Texas was everything she dreamed it would be: the wildflowers, the hills, the bubbling little rivers and the goats grazing in the brushy fields. Mom had raised goats when I was small. Most of the bus passengers in Texas were African-American, and Mom reminisced with them about the time our family first moved to California in the late 1940s. I could always tell which row of the bus Mom was in when I would return with snacks. She was where the laughter was.

The chili in the San Antonio bus station was so good that Mom insisted on congratulating the girl dishing it up. From then on long after we got home, Mom wanted chili, though it never tasted quite as good as it had in San Antonio.

By the time we reached New Orleans, I was worried that Mom was getting tired. I kept remembering the dim view friends took of an eighty-six-year-old lady spending so long on a bus.

"We'll get a hotel room in New Orleans and rest for a couple of days before heading home," I told Mom.

"No," she laughed, "I want to get back on the bus and see everything from the other direction!"

And so after a day of watching Mississippi river boats, being serenaded by jazzmen and strolling through the French Quarter, we were heading west.

Mom remembered all the landmarks and looked

forward to the lights over Sierra Blanca and the goats again.

Seeing Mom enjoy herself turned out to be the highlight of the trip. My convention appearance sank into insignificance.

When we got back to San Diego, Mom regaled everyone with our adventures. She had friends and family in stitches over the snafu of "losing" our bus in Phoenix. Somehow we got off without boarding passes and then couldn't find our bus. I told someone that all we remembered was that our driver was about fifty with glasses. When we relayed that description to an annoyed agent, he growled that, "All the drivers are about fifty with glasses."

Our family had taken many trips by bus, train and finally our family car with Mom at the wheel pulling a travel trailer. But this was the first trip for just Mom and me. It frightened me when I realized how close I had come to not going on a trip with my mom, an experience that proved to be one of our sweetest memories.

Mom remained with us for another seven years and almost to the last she mentioned the trip to New Orleans at least once a day. Her eyes would light up, and she'd say, "Do you remember all those goats?" and "I still can't believe we had to ride the escalator up to see the Mississippi River!"

Three years ago, Mom left us for the shores of a better world, but I still savor the memory of the best Mother's Day gift I ever gave her, and what a gift it was to me. I had feared eighty-six was too old for such an adventure, but it turned out to be just right. Mom was usually the oldest passenger on the bus, and always the one having the most fun.

Anne Schraff

Arm in Arm

What a pleasure life would be to live if every-body would try to do only half of what he expects others to do.

William J. H. Boetcker

When I have not thought about my mother in a little while, and someone or something brings her to my mind, I see her first as she looked when I was ten. She is walking down our street, wearing a checked coat, grasping a grocery bag or two. I stand in the living room window and watch, and when she is close enough for me to see her face, I bolt from the house and run to meet her. She smiles in greeting, and my heart swells. I may take a bag from her, or she may refuse my help. In either case, I tuck my hand in the crook of her elbow, and we walk the rest of the way together.

The image holds me fast because it represents the essence of our relationship: two together, overcoming all odds and obstacles life could present for a woman abandoned by her husband and raising her only child alone.

There are in my memory a handful of images that shine as bright.

Our house sits on a curve, so whenever I began the half-mile trek from the corner, I could already see the light in the window. Beyond that light, I knew, she would be working in the kitchen, or in later years, waiting in her big armchair for the sound of my step on the front porch.

Always there was that exchange of smiles, that instant of delight shared with this woman who has been my parent, my dear friend, my companion in life.

I remember her sturdy frame bent over a shovel or a rake in the yard. Her lot was not to tend fragile blossoms or burgeoning vegetables. She was the one who mowed and pruned and raked and hauled big bags of brightly colored leaves to the curbside. I watched her one summer take down six eight-foot-tall pine trees with a meat saw because it was small enough for her to handle.

In the early days, I held the leaf bags open for her to fill. Then we worked side by side. Much later, the task became mine, then was passed to a hired man. But she always liked to "survey her estate," as she said wryly, clipping a branch here, picking up a stray paper there, allowing me to slip a palm under her forearm for balance. Then she could do even that no longer.

And so the years passed for us: Christmases with trees that became smaller each year, then disappeared, leaving two angels in red velvet the task of heralding the season; birthdays with cakes that also dwindled in size, countered by cards whose sentiments grew more expansive and more bittersweet.

We once imagined that I would have a life quite apart from hers, a life filled with triumphs she could share. There were a few. If there were as many heartbreaks, it did not matter much; they were shared by her as well. We had thought that she would visit me in another house, another town, another world. We did not plan that I should grow middle-aged down the hall from her. But that is how it turned out, and I have no regrets. She gave me laughter and wisdom and boundless love.

She grew old, and often in the early morning, well before dawn, I would wake and peek in on her to be sure she was breathing, completing the circle of concern begun by her when I was born.

Sometimes we would sit together in the late evening, reading or watching a movie, and I would look up to see her engrossed in the story, or dozing quietly, and I would think, *This is enough.*

Now she has had to leave our home, and it has become for me only a house. I go where she is and sit beside her there. I look at her frail hand clasping mine as she sleeps, and I can say, finally, "This is not enough. Not for her."

"Two hearts that beat as one," she used to joke about us. "Cut one, the other will bleed." Yes, but in the end, one must go on without the other.

I like to think there is an afterlife, though I lack certainty and the comfort that would bring. Still, I think, so much love, so much energy must go somewhere. I like the stories people tell of passing through tunnels into white light and meeting loved ones on "the other side."

Life being what it is, I cannot even be sure my mother will go first. Perhaps, I will precede her, felled by the burden of anticipated loss.

Whatever happens, I hope the stories are true: that we will meet again. If we do, I know we will smile in greeting, just as we did a lifetime ago when I was small and she was young and hope was invincible. Our hearts will swell then, and we will walk the rest of the way together.

Pam Robbins

The World's Worst Mother

*F*lowers grow out of dark moments.

Corita Kent

After mothering me for thirty years, my mom stood in the kitchen of my home and announced these words, "I was the world's worst mother, and I am so sorry." She then proceeded to apologize for all the things that she did wrong in raising me. I realized that she was filled with guilt about the strict rules of her child-raising years, causing me to miss many school dances. She was mortified that she and my father were too poor to afford my high school ring. She was ashamed of herself for punishments that lasted for weeks. She was sad that she tried to choose my friends. My mother went on and on about her mistakes and regrets as tears of pain streamed down her face.

Right at that moment my mom looked so beautiful. I wondered why my entire family, including me, took her for granted. How do you tell your mother all that she is to you? I wanted to tell her that the punishments and strict rules of my childhood have a small spot in my memory in comparison to my recollections of the nights she let me stay up late and bake cookies with her. I kept silent instead of telling her how much it meant that she scraped together the money for my wedding shoes and matching purse. I couldn't swallow the lump in my throat so I could explain all of the millions of ways she makes me feel so special. I should have told my mother, on that day, that of all the people in my life, no one has ever loved me in the unconditional way that she does.

Four years have gone by since the day I didn't tell my mother that her mistakes were tiny molehills, and her love and understanding were big beautiful mountains in my life. But I'm telling her now. Thank you, Mom, and thank you, God, for the world's worst mother.

Polly Anne Wise

"I can't believe you threw me a
sweet sixteen party and served *sugar-free* cake."

My Original Role

When I stopped seeing my mother with the eyes of a child, I saw the woman who helped me give birth to myself.

Nancy Friday

"Don't stay out too late," my mother says, handing me her car keys.

"Do you want to wait up for me?" I ask her.

She shrugs. "I won't be able to sleep anyway."

When I left home to come visit my mother, I was a mature woman. But once I enter my mother's house, I revert to my earliest, most practiced role, that of daughter.

Every mother knows so much more than her daughter. Every mother sees the beauty, the secret hollows and lost potential of her daughter. The mother saves these insights like precious unread love letters. She prays that somehow, someday her daughter will ask her just how much she knows. I, too, am a mother. I know the exact words that could change my daughters into happier women. And like my own mother, I wait helplessly for them to open their ears to me.

I return to my mother's house before midnight. Though my old friends were yearning to go to another jazz club, I felt my mother waiting for me. She opens the door before I even knock.

"I have something to show you," she says. I follow her into the breakfast room.

"Look at this," she says, pointing to a photo of a beautiful woman sitting coquettishly under a tree. Her lipstick is a taunting red, her hair a provocative black. "This was taken when I was in nurse's training," my mother says. I see her secret smile, her joy in how beautiful she was.

I sit down and study the picture, knowing that she had already lost her mother and her first husband, that deep sorrow stretched underneath her beauty. Then my mother spreads more pictures. Me at age five, playing jacks on the front porch. Me and my daughters sitting in a mimosa tree.

"No one can hurt you as much as your own daughter can," my mother says as she hands me another photo, one of my wedding. "I knew you were making a big mistake," she says, jabbing her finger at my ex-husband's picture.

Before when my mother made remarks like this, I resented it. But this visit, I listen. I allow the words to soak in. I hear their translation: "I love you. I think of you all the time. You are so important to me." Has she been speaking in a foreign language all these years, so I never noticed the real meaning of her words?

I call home to check on my fifteen-year-old daughter.

"Hi, how are you?" I say.

"Fine," she answers.

"How was your day?"

"Okay."

I know when she is done talking to me, she will call her friends and they will laugh and chat for hours. I feel like a thirsty woman, wanting too many drops of water.

"Want some coffee, dear?" my mother asks, when I get off the phone.

I take the coffee, made the way she likes it, too strong. We sit together on the sofa, and she asks me if I eat properly.

I want to answer, "Yes," in a voice crisp and clipped as my daughter's.

I take a deep breath before I answer. "Yes," I say, "I eat properly."

"Do you get enough rest?" she asks.

My friends and I talk about money, work, relationships, children. No one else asks me these basic questions: Am I surviving? No one dares get so deep, so primal.

In the beginning, the mother is the everything, the arms and the heart and breath of her daughter. The mother is the leader, the model. She takes a step, and her daughter follows. But gradually, the child pushes away from her mother. Like a swimmer, kicking off from the side of the pool, the child moves herself into deeper water.

I know that moment, standing alone at the edge of the pool, watching my daughter swim faster and farther. It is a moment of "hallelujah" success and heartbreaking loneliness. To be a good mother means to lose your child to the world.

My mother's child has returned. I am old enough to allow her to renew our original bond, my original role in life. I am old enough that I truly treasure having a mother.

Deborah Shouse

A Secret for Mom

*If one is lucky, a single fantasy can transform a
million realities.*

Maya Angelou

As I contemplate the arrival of the holidays, I think
about all the warm and wonderful Christmases as a child,
and I feel a smile cross my face. They were truly a time to
remember. As I grew older, the Christmas memories
become less vivid and more of a sad and depressing time
for me . . . until last year. It was then that I believe I learned
how to recapture that childhood wonder and joy I felt as a
child.

Every year I flounder, never knowing what to buy my
mother for Christmas. Another robe and slippers, per-
fume, sweaters? All nice gifts, but they just don't say I love
you like they should. I wanted something different, something she would love for the rest of her life. Something
that would put that beautiful smile back on her face and
the quickness in her step. She lives alone, and much as I
may want to spend time with her, I can only manage an
occasional visit with the schedule I keep. So I made the

decision to become her Secret Santa. Little did I know that this would be just what the doctor ordered.

I went out and bought all sorts of small gifts and then headed to the more expensive areas of the mall. I picked up little nothings, things that I knew only my mother would love. I took them home and wrapped each one differently. Then I went to my computer and made a card for each one. It went according to the song "The Twelve Days of Christmas." Then I began my adventure. The first day was so exciting, I dropped it off and put it in the screen door. Then I hurried home and called her, pretending to inquire about her health. She was bubbling over. Someone had left a gift for her and signed it "Secret Santa."

The next day, the same scenario played out. After four or five days, I went to her house, and my heart just broke. She had laid out all the gifts on her kitchen table and was showing them to everyone at the apartment complex. Wrappings and all were spread out and each one had the note attached. She never stopped talking about this secret admirer the entire duration of my visit. Her eyes sparkled, and her voice was lilting. She was in seventh heaven. Every day, she would call me with news of the new gift she found when she woke up. Then she decided to try to catch the person responsible and slept on the couch with the door cracked open. So I left it later that day, and she worried that the gifts weren't coming anymore. She had me just as excited as she was. On the last day, the note told her to be dressed on that Saturday, and she was to go to Applebee's for dinner. There she would meet her Secret Santa. She went wild. The note also told her to ask her daughter Susan to bring her (that's me). It said she would know her Secret Santa by the red ribbon she would be wearing. So I picked her up and off we went.

When we arrived the hostess seated us at a table, and my mom looked around. She lost the smile and asked when she was going to meet her Secret Santa. I slowly took off my coat, and there was the red ribbon. She began to cry and fuss over how much I spent and how did I do this. She was happier than I have ever seen her.

When it was all said and done, I thought about how good I felt, and just as quickly, I remembered something very important. When I was a child, it was my mother who taught me that it is better to give than to receive. Reality slapped me hard. All these years when I had been sad during the holidays was most likely because I was looking at the "getting" instead of the "giving." I was humbled by this realization, and now I am certain, Mom does know best. . . .

Susan Spence

And You Always Will

I opened the dish-towel drawer for about the sixth time, hoping the towels had somehow magically appeared. But of course, the brand-new towels still weren't there. "What did Mom do with them?" I wondered aloud. I knew they had to be around somewhere because I'd given them to her for Christmas only a few months ago. Not that the towels were so terribly important. It's just that when you're expecting guests, you'd kind of like everything to look nice. Okay, so maybe I wasn't going to find the dish towels. But then again, the guests wouldn't arrive until tomorrow. Plenty of time to worry about dish towels later. On second thought, maybe I ought to forget about the towels altogether.

My father's niece and her husband didn't seem like the kind of people who'd leave in a huff because their host hadn't put out new dish towels. What next? Perhaps I'd better see if I could lay my hands on Mom's best table-cloth. A tablecloth was always one of the things my mother insisted upon when we had company. I went to the drawer where Mom kept her tablecloths, and sure enough, there it was. But when I pulled out the hand-embroidered tablecloth and shook it open, I gasped in dismay. Right in the middle was a big stain. Now how in the world did Mom's best tablecloth—the one that had taken her so many months to finish—end up with a stain? Oh yes, that's right. We'd all been here for Christmas, and one of my brother's kids had accidentally knocked over a glass of soda pop. The sight of her grandchild sobbing with remorse had been more important than the table-cloth, and Mom had said she was sure the pop would come out when she washed it.

All right, so it looked like I'd have to forget the tablecloth, too. Maybe I'd be better off attending to the big things right now, anyway, like vacuuming. Satisfied that I was finally going to make some progress, I got out the vacuum cleaner. Except—why did it sound so funny? And why wasn't it picking up those bits of paper on the living room carpeting? I pulled out the attachments hose and flipped the switch again. A ha. That's why. No suction. The hose was plugged. Well, of course the hose was plugged. I couldn't find the new dish towels. Mom's best tablecloth had a big stain. Why wouldn't the vacuum cleaner hose be plugged?

And right then and there, I started to cry. Now what was I going to do? Would a wire hanger fix the vacuum cleaner? No new dish towels and no tablecloth was bad enough, but I absolutely could not let guests come to the house without vacuuming. I went to my mother's closet, found a wire hanger and straightened it out. Thirty min-utes later, however, the vacuum cleaner was still plugged.

Where was Dad? I knew he'd gone outside and that, because it was mid-April, he was probably puttering around in his garden, but why wasn't he in here when I needed him? After being a farmer for more than fifty years, he could fix absolutely anything. And besides, I had plenty of other work to do. Just at that moment, my father came into the house. "What's wrong?" he asked, noticing my tear-streaked face.

Although it had been years since I called him "Daddy," it just sort of slipped out, and along with it came fresh tears. "Oh, Daddy—I can't find the new dish towels. The tablecloth has a big stain. The vacuum cleaner is plugged. And—and. . . ." I stopped and swallowed hard. ". . . I miss my mother." There. I'd said it. And in that instant, the whole world seemed to stop while Dad drew a deep breath and let it out slowly.

"I know you do," he said. "So do I."

You see, only three weeks earlier, my mother was diagnosed with advanced gallbladder cancer. Mom had died Saturday night, and this was Monday. My father's niece and her husband were driving 275 miles to attend the funeral, and they would be staying at the house. As Dad gazed at me, I noticed how much he seemed to have aged in the last few weeks. His face was covered with silvery stubble, too. It was a rare morning when my father didn't shave, but then again the past couple of days had been far from ordinary. "And you know what?" Dad continued. "You always will miss her. In fact, it won't ever go away completely. Not even when you're as old as I am."

After the funeral was over and my father's relatives had gone home, I found the dish towels. Mom had put them in her dresser drawer. And with several washings, the stain finally came out of the tablecloth. Dad had been able to fix the vacuum cleaner, too. But nothing could fix the fact that my mother was gone. And now all these years later, I realize Dad was right—I am always going to miss her.

But I've also figured out what else he was trying to tell me on that April day in 1985—that missing my mother keeps her alive in my heart.

LeAnn R. Ralph

Things I Never Told My Mother

Do not wait for ideal circumstances, nor the best opportunities, they will never come.

Janet F. Stuart

One day while I was dusting a shelf, a china canister almost slipped out of my hands. The canister, with a picture of a windmill on one side and the word "Barley" underneath, is one of a set given to my parents as a wedding present in 1920. As a young child, I remember learning to read the words—"Rice," "Flour," "Oats" and "Barley"—just above my head on the kitchen shelf. The one canister I have left is now, it shocks me to realize, a family heirloom. That day when it almost slipped from my hands, I felt a wave of grief—the momentary anguish I still feel about my mother's death.

For many years my mother felt the need to tell me what she would be leaving behind when she died. She wanted to be reassured that I would care for the things that were important to her. I always refused to take her seriously—in an unconscious struggle to deny her mortality, I suppose.

Her own mother had brought a beautiful glass bowl

back from Czechoslovakia, and my mother tried many times to give it to me. I always said that *things* did not interest me.

The last time I saw her, my husband and I were about to leave on a month's trip. "I wish you'd let me give you some of my jewelry," she said. "I have so much more than I need. And with all those television interviews you do, you could use some different beads and pins." She was so persistent that I finally—grudgingly, I'm afraid—accepted a gold chain. A week later, flying back to New York for my mother's funeral, I held that chain to my cheek and wept, caressing it, the whole way home.

I now realize that what my mother had been trying to tell me was that things are important if they evoke memories of the people we love. I wish I'd been more sensitive to her unspoken questions: "Will you miss me when I'm gone? Will remembrances of our life together speak to you of my love?" I wish I could tell her how much her jewelry, canister and bowl mean to me now. And they do help me remember.

Recently as I put on her gold chain and went to meet an old friend, I thought about my mother's gift for human relationships. She kept in touch with hundreds of friends—often by writing long letters. None were more special than those of her childhood with whom she laughed a lot. How I loved to hear that laughter! I, too, cherish old friends—some of whom I've had for sixty years. I wish I could thank my mother for teaching me the enduring value of friendship.

Another unspoken bond we shared was our love for writing. My father, now ninety-three, still gives me yellowed sheets of paper on which his young bride wrote passionate poems—afraid perhaps, to express her deepest emotions any other way. On one faded sheet she had carefully penned:

I could not weave a story
When laughter filled my heart
But I can write an endless tale
Since my soul's been torn apart!

She gave up writing poetry to become a parent educator. I wanted to write plays when I was young, but my
father told me that was a nice hobby—not a secure pro-
fession. I became a parent educator, too. I wonder if my
father told my mother that being a poet was just a nice
hobby. I wish I'd let my mother know that I'd seen the
poet in her.

When Valentine's Day or Mother's Day approaches, I
am saddened to remember how I scorned my mother's
pleasure in any excuse to celebrate love. If I could, I'd send
her ten valentines now!

I wish I'd had more fun with my mother, gone to more
matinees and taken more trips with her. Those were
things we both loved to do, things she taught me to
appreciate. Every time I go to the theater and the lights go
down, I remember my mother squeezing my hand and
whispering, "Magic time." I want to thank her for that gift
of joy. I wish I could say, "Mama, oh, how I loved you!" My
hope is that some daughters reading this will do just that
before it's too late.

Eda LeShan

Is It Asking Too Much?

Family faces are magic mirrors. Looking at people who belong to us, we see the past, present and future.

Gail Lumet Buckley

At my high school graduation, the awards were presented for achievement, contribution to the school, the community, scholarship and more. I sat patiently through them knowing they were not for me. The Chaplain's Award was given to the student who most embodied the school motto, "The Way, The Truth and The Life." I loved that motto and knew it would define my life, though I didn't yet know how.

The Headmaster read the list of qualities this year's candidate had—most giving, contributed most to civic activities, most, most, most. I cannot even name all the things that were said. I sat thinking *"Why are they talking about my mother, why would my mother be getting an award at my graduation?"* I knew her this way. Our community knew her this way. These words described her perfectly.

When I heard my name called, I began to cry. I walked

to the stage to receive the award that my mother, inside of me, had won. Without noticing, I had taken her in and standing on the stage I knew I had found myself as well. I thought I would never ask for anything other than the joy of this moment.

"Am I asking too much?" I wondered, years later.

My heart was set on getting into Yale Divinity School, the school I wanted more than any other, the career that I knew I was called into, the path that had begun at my high school graduation. When the letter of acceptance came, I guessed that maybe it wasn't too much to ask. But how could I pay for it? It would surely be too much to ask, to even hope, that my mother could pay my way. But even as I doubted, I knew the answer. There was nothing that was too much to ask of my mother. And so, I went to Yale Divinity School.

Years later, an Episcopal priest myself, married to another one, I wondered again, after years of trying to get pregnant, *"Is it too much to ask that I have a child?"* I had so much already: love, a congregation, my parents, my grandmother, my sister, my health and my husband. I deeply wanted a child, but was I asking too much?

Soon after, we had a son, and again I thought that was all I would ever ask of life.

But I knew deep in my heart that I would treasure a daughter. I prayed for guidance and found myself thinking from time to time, *"Is it too much to ask to have a daughter?"*

Within months I was, blessedly, answered. "Yes," the doctor said as I entered his office, "you are about two months along in your pregnancy. Do you want to know the sex of your next child?"

"I already know," I smiled. Once again I uttered a silent prayer of thanks and knew that I would ask for nothing more of life.

My daughter was born, healthy and beautiful and I now know it's not too much to ask for what I am about to get. In the next few moments, the eighty-five years that separate my grandmother from her great-granddaughter will melt away. I realize in a startled moment, that as I took my mother inside of me, so my mother had taken her own good and generous mother inside her and that my daughter, if I could ask for just one more thing, would take us all into her own being.

Waiting for this late plane, I ask for nothing and I say from deep in my heart "Thank you."

The Reverend Melissa Hollerith

$\overline{3}$

MEMORIES

It is only possible to live happily-ever-after on a day-to-day basis.

Margaret Bonano

The Magic Jar Years

I love these little people; and it is not a slight thing when they, who are so fresh from God, love us.

Charles Dickens

One day a mother brought home a small jar and gave it to her little girl on her birthday. She told her little girl that the jar was magic, and she could write to her mommy about anything in the world, put it in the jar, and later, in its place, there would be a note for her. Soon the jar became a special part of their lives.

The little girl loved to get letters from her mommy. They always told her how special she was and had lots of XXXXs and OOOOs on them. Often there were reminders of something special they had planned together the next day, or a good luck letter if there was a dance recital coming up. Sometimes, too, there would be a little gift in the jar and a note telling her how proud her mommy was of her. She kept all of her mommy's letters in a pretty box by her bed.

The mother treasured each of her little girl's letters, too.

There were crayoned "I love yous," tea-party invitations, requests for ballet slippers, and even some Mother's Day cards that had been folded and folded and folded just to fit in the jar. Those always made the mother smile. There was one where her little girl told her she was afraid of the dark, and that very night a small light was placed in her room, and all was well. Another favorite came when their dog Muffin was expecting puppies; there in the jar was a little note that read, "You're going to be a grandma!" The mother kept all of those very special letters safely tucked in a chest at the end of her bed.

As the years went by, that little girl grew into a young lady and then got married and started a home of her own. For the first time, the jar sat empty. The mother dusted the jar every day and sometimes looked inside, remembering—sad that the magic jar years had to end.

One day the young lady came to visit her mother. She went straight to her mother's room, opened the chest at the end of her bed, and found what she was looking for. She folded the piece of paper and put it in the jar, and handed it to her mother. The mother opened the magic jar and there was that note from so long ago, "You're going to be a grandma!"

And when that baby boy was born months later, there was the jar sitting in his nursery with a blue bow tied around it, and a note that read, "Magic jar years never end; they are always just beginning."

Cassie Marie Moore

The Best Day Ever

We've all had one or more of those life-changing phone calls.

"Mom, I'm in the hospital."

"Mom, I'm pregnant!"

"Mom, I really need to borrow a thousand dollars right away."

Sometimes those phone calls stop your heart with anguish and fear.

Sometimes they're downright joyous. Other times they make your head spin. I received a head-spinner on a hot day in July 2002.

"Mom, Canyon and I have decided to get married—in three days. We want you to come!"

It was my oldest daughter, the one armed with a master's degree in fine arts from Yale University, the one whose college loans surpass the entire annual budget for a medium-size state. The one who had been living with her Jewish boyfriend for twelve years, the boyfriend our entire family rated a ten on the scale of great catches.

When you get one of those phone calls you suddenly feel like a trapeze artist for Ringling Brothers. Your heart does a few wild swings back and forth while you desperately wonder if this is going to be a regular wedding, and if so how on earth are they going to pull it off in three days. Then your mind grabs the trapeze, does a giant flip and catches the bar at the last possible second when your daughter tells you it's going to be a simple civil ceremony, a do-it-yourself spiritual event at a park afterwards, then lunch and a boat ride.

Ah, they've made all the plans, you think to yourself. *You're off the hook. And it sounds like fun! Just go and enjoy.*

"We were going to elope, but then a few of our friends found out, and well, I think there will be about a dozen people now, including you."

This is the place where the mother begins to stammer and stutter, "Uh, well, where are you getting married exactly? Will there be a reception? Is it a dressy event? When should I come? You say it's this Thursday? I could be there day after tomorrow, Wednesday morning. Is that okay?"

As my heart continued the flip-flops, my mouth asked more inane questions. Jeanne finally interrupted, "Mom, we're getting married at City Hall in lower Manhattan, not too far from Ground Zero. Then we're going to Riverside Park next to the Hudson River to have a religious ceremony. Then we'll have a late lunch in an outdoor café near the river. And then we're all taking the Circle Line Harbor Lights cruise around lower Manhattan."

"Sounds wonderful, my dear. See you Wednesday!"

At that moment, I thanked God for my daughter's common sense and her organizational skills. I also breathed a sigh of relief for my airline pilot friends who'd given me some inexpensive standby friend passes.

I'd be flying to New York in two days for pennies on the dollar. I especially thanked God that Jeanne, like me, had not inherited any big-wedding planning genes. Big weddings with their outlandish extravagances and mega-stress give me the heebie-jeebies. Imagine, a New York wedding, and all I had to do was get there, try to be a little useful, and enjoy the day.

The best things about Jeanne and Canyon's wedding? The pure, delicious unrehearsed fun of it all, for one thing. Watching Jeanne get dressed in the lovely, handmade, unpretentious, midnight-blue, fitted street-length dress from the fifties that she bought at a resale shop for $15. Being asked by the bride and groom to make a chuppah (Jewish wedding canopy) the morning of the wedding. Just give this Christian mama a hot glue gun, lots of ribbon, an umbrella and I'm in heaven. It was a grand chuppah.

What else did I love about that day? The three of us taking the New York subway to get to the courthouse and on our way to the subway, stopping in a small restaurant to ask the owner if we could have one of his starched white dinner napkins to wrap around the wine glass that Canyon planned to smash at the end of the ceremony in the park, and the startled Middle Eastern owner smiling, finally understanding our need, bowing, handing over the napkin as she said in broken English, "Congratulations, congratulations!"

It was a day of giggling absurdity at the very crabby magistrate and her forty-five-second civil ceremony; then profound spirituality as Canyon and Jeanne exchanged rings again and read prayers in the park in what seemed like much more of a wedding than the courthouse event. It was a day of lighthearted wonder, perfect weather and smuggled champagne onto the Circle Line tour boat.

Best of all, it was commitment before God and state. A wedding, pure and simple. A day blessed with spontaneity, the laughter of friends, the deep love of husband and wife, and the awe and joy of one very happy, very proud mother.

Patricia Lorenz

The Nicest Thing
My Mother Ever Said to Me

The mother's heart is the child's schoolroom.

Henry Ward Beecher

When I was about twelve my mother was recounting some clever thing I did when I was three. Her memories, undoubtedly edited by the years, painted me as the perfect preschooler. I compared myself unfavorably with the golden-haired charmer she recalled. Not quite a teenager, I was awkward with horn-rimmed glasses and hair frizzed from home permanents. (Frizz was not the style then.)

Other girls were teased by the "obnoxious" boys at school and clustered in happy groups. My romances were all imaginary, my friends few. "When was I the best age?" I asked a trifle hesitantly.

Mother looked at me in surprise. "Right now," she told me. "You're the best age you've ever been."

At a luncheon the day before my college graduation, Mother was talking about how fast time flies. It seemed only a month ago she was a Brownie leader, and I was a

Brownie. In college, I hadn't been a cheerleader. The hairstyles were now bouffant, but my hair was in a skinny ponytail.

Most nights I'd been at the dorm desk ringing the rooms of other girls as their dates arrived. I had no grad school or Peace Corps applications in the mail. I commented to my mother that I supposed she missed her little girl.

"Heavens, no," she said emphatically. "You're the best age now you've ever been."

Three years later, I was living with my parents again, this time with two babies in the spare room. I'd married my high school sweetheart, and he'd left me. Only for two months until we could join him at the air base in Okinawa, it's true, but there I was with diapers and rattles and baby powder.

Coping with infants who woke at dawn, spurned their oatmeal, then nibbled on the newspapers, I turned my parents' well-ordered home into a nursery.

I ate a bit too much, slept a bit too much and crabbed a bit too much. Apologetically I told my mother I was sure she'd be glad to get back to normal—kids were fine, but I was a bit old to be her child.

"Oh, no," she said. "I enjoy those baby boys, but right now you are the best age you've ever been."

Suddenly my "babies" were teenagers with vacuum-cleaner appetites. My house was never entirely clean, and I was all too inclined to start planning dinner at 4:45. "Frizz" was finally in style, but my hair was straight as a string. Nevertheless, during a holiday visit, my mother said, "You're the best age ever."

The very next week my sixteen-year-old son and I were having a discussion. Although I've forgotten the subject, I remember it was somewhat, um, heated.

We often held heated discussions since we held

vastly differing views on the redeeming benefits of TV, the definition of a clean room and whether the just-under-a-quarter-full gas tank he left me had quite a bit left or was darn near empty.

"Brother," he finally said in exasperation. "I bet you wish I was two years old again and you could boss me."

But looking up (!) at him, I only paused a moment before saying honestly, "No, Dan, that's not true at all. Right now you are the best age you've ever been."

And with those words I passed on a gift of acceptance, a feeling of worth and worthiness and security. I handed on my mother's gift of love.

Marilyn Pribus

The Queen Of Coleslaw

Love has nothing to do with what you are expecting to get—only with what you are expecting to give—which is everything.

Katharine Hepburn

To my mother, the four basic food groups are meat, dairy, grain and coleslaw. She thinks if it's not used in coleslaw, it's not a vegetable, it's a nuisance, and not worth growing in the first place. In our house, the slaw goes on the table in a bowl that—well, let's just say if we made a batch of punch we'd have nothing to put it in. Poking out of the top is a huge stainless steel cafeteria-style spoon, dubbed the "institution spoon" by my brother, who often acted as if he belonged in one.

I love my mother's coleslaw, but I remember a time when it provoked absolute panic in me.

Early on in first grade, I raced home from school at lunchtime with a collection of papers handed to me by the teacher. As I burst through the front door I immediately ran to the kitchen where my mother stood at the stove stirring a pot of chicken noodle soup. Pulling on her apron with one hand and holding a fist full of papers in the other, I pleaded with her, "Read them to me, Mom—please!"

Mom took the papers as we sat at the kitchen table. Slowly she started reading aloud. I listened intently to every word, paying no attention to the bowl of soup in front of me. I squealed with delight as she read to me what seemed an almost endless list of exciting adventures awaiting me in the coming year.

And then it happened.

"It's customary for mothers to bring a homemade treat for the class to share on each child's birthday," she read. "It needn't be anything fancy, just something you enjoy making."

The words floated through the air in agonizing slow motion, hovering over my head in the mist of the steamy chicken soup.

"Just something you enjoy making . . . enjoy making . . . enjoy making." The phrase echoed loudly inside of me, conjuring up the same stomach churning feeling that accompanies the ominous phrase: "You have a cavity . . . a cavity . . . a cavity."

My mother's standard response to anyone who paid her coleslaw a compliment was this: "It's nothing fancy, it's just something I enjoy making." Oh, how those words wreaked havoc with me.

Until my birthday in April, I lived in dread that mother would show up at school pushing a wheelbarrow full of her famous coleslaw for everyone to share. I pictured that old stainless steel spoon protruding out of a mountain of cabbage while she navigated the wheelbarrow up and down the aisles. As she maneuvered, a stack of "Happy Birthday" Dixie cups would be dangling from her wrist in a drawstring plastic bag.

When I left for school on the morning of my birthday, there were two large heads of cabbage in the refrigerator and a curious grin on my mother's face. Full-blown panic swept me into its sturdy grip.

Much to my relief, Mom showed up promptly at 1:30 in the afternoon with a tray full of yummy chocolate cupcakes. Each one had two M&Ms for eyes and a string of four or five more in a semicircle to make a smile. All except mine. On mine, one of the "eye" M&Ms was cut in half so that my cupcake was winking at me. To this day Mom says it was just a coincidence but I am not convinced.

I owe my mother a thank-you for the cupcakes and the coleslaw. But mostly I owe her a thank-you for the memory of her standing at the kitchen table with her apron tied in a big old bow in the back. Mom always shredded the cabbage in time to the tune playing on the radio. I wonder if she knows I noticed that. I did, you know. My mother not only makes the best coleslaw, she makes the best memories, too.

Annmarie Tait

The Magic Pillow

With every deed you are sowing a seed, though the harvest you may not see.

Ella Wheeler Wilcox

Valentine's Day had arrived, and like every other day of the year, I was very busy. My romantic husband Roy planned a date like we had never had before. A reservation at an expensive restaurant was made. A beautifully wrapped present had been sitting on my dresser for a few days prior to the heart-filled holiday.

After a hard day at work, I hurried home, ran into the house, and jumped into the shower. When my sweetheart arrived, I was dressed in my finest outfit and ready to go. He hugged me just as the sitter arrived. We were both excited.

Unfortunately, the littlest member in our household wasn't so happy.

"Daddy, you were going to take me to buy Mamma a present," Becky, our eight-year-old daughter said, as she sadly walked over to the couch and sat down beside the babysitter.

Roy looked at his watch and realized that if we were to

make our reservations, we had to leave right away. He didn't even have a few minutes to take her to the corner drugstore to buy a heart-shaped box of chocolate candy.

"I'm sorry, I was late getting home, honey," he said.

"That's okay," Becky replied. "I understand."

The entire evening was bittersweet. I couldn't help being concerned about the disappointment in Becky's eyes. I remembered how the joyful Valentine's Day glow had left her face just before the door closed behind us. She wanted me to know how much she loved me. She didn't realize it, but I already knew it very well.

Today, I can't remember what was wrapped in that beautiful box from my husband, but I'll never forget the special gift I received when we arrived back home. Becky was asleep on the couch, clutching a box. When I kissed her cheek, she awoke. "I've got something for you, Mamma," she said, as a giant smile covered her face.

The box was wrapped in newspaper. As I tore the paper off and opened the box, I found the sweetest Valentine gift that I have ever received.

After Roy and I left for our date, Becky got busy. She raided my fabric and cross-stitch box. She stitched the words "I Love Ya" on a piece of red fabric, cut the fabric in the shape of a heart, stitched two mismatched pieces together, adorned it with lace and stuffed it with cotton. It was a lopsided heart-shaped pillow, filled with love, which I'll cherish forever.

My wonderful Valentine gift has a special place in my bedroom today, over thirteen years later. As Becky was growing up into a young woman, many times I held that pillow close to my heart. I don't know if a pillow can hold magic, but this pillow has surely held a great deal of joy for me over the years. It has helped me through several sleepless nights since Becky left home for college. I not only cherish the gift, but the memory as well.

I know that I am a very lucky mother, indeed, to have such a wonderful girl, who wanted so desperately to share her heart with me. As long as I live, there will never be another Valentine's Day which will be any more special to me than that one.

Nancy B. Gibbs

"This drawing is for my mom. If I'm ever famous, her fridge will be worth a bundle!"

Monkey Bar Courage

All things are possible until they are proved impossible—and even the impossible may only be so as of now.

Pearl S. Buck

You stand daredevil high on metal monkey bars, oblivious to danger. "Don't," I warn, "It's not safe." And you grudgingly oblige me and hang down closer to the earth. I stand guard anyway, but glance away for a moment, distracted by twilight.

I turnback toward you, only to helplessly watch you fall to the ground.

You get up gasping, your nose and mouth already bleeding. Horrified, I hold you tightly and try to absorb the hurt. You cry loudly from your pain, and I cry for all the ways I cannot protect you.

But in a few moments, you collect yourself. With a long, quivering sniffle and a brave, shaky breath, you brush away the remaining bark mulch that I have missed and give me a slightly teary-eyed, crooked smile.

"Mommy, I really want to get back on. And this time, I

want to do a back flip." You say this even though your lip is still bleeding.

And in this minute my surprise co-mingles with awe, respect and pride, and I see more than my tear-stained three-year-old daughter standing before me. I see the raw material of courage. I see the makings of perseverance and determination. I see a girl with something that I didn't put inside her, a girl who has something that nobody can take away. I see you, my daughter, a child who falls down but gets up and keeps dancing. And I see once again that I am the student, and you are the inspiration.

As I hoist your small body up to the bar my thought is a prayer, for you and for me, *Don't ever let go of this.*

Karen C. Driscoll

Nothing but the Truth

Suzy was always an imaginative, verbal, excited child. When she was very little she never saw just one dog but, throwing her arms out wide, she'd say, "There were a zil lion dogs out there." I feared that she would soon lose the ability to distinguish what was real from what was fantasy. So we talked about lies and the truth and God's commandments about telling the truth. As the time approached for her to enter school, I thought that I should take some firmer steps to teach Suzy about truth. I determined the next time she came in with a huge fib I'd find a way to really teach her.

That very afternoon, she was playing in the backyard and came running in excitedly yelling, "Mother, there's a bear in the backyard. A big brown bear!"

"Suzy, what have I told you about telling the truth? Now go up to your room and you talk to God about this."

Suzy disappeared to her room and was very quiet for a while. I went in to see how she was feeling, and with a beatific smile, she said, "I talked to God and he said he thought it was a bear at first, too."

Winfield Firman

Cinderella

The love you take is equal to the love you make.

John Lennon & Paul McCartney

My mother committed suicide when I was thirteen, four years after my father died. So my sister Alyce, a battered spouse and mother of two, became my guardian and the only mother I would really know. Within two years, we fled to Los Angeles to escape from her abusive husband.

One day in our second year in L.A. as I thumbed through college catalogues, Alyce asked, "What are you doing about the prom?"

I shrugged. "Who would I go with?"

"We'll see about that." She gave me a June Cleaver smile. "Every girl needs to go to her prom."

I felt more an outcast not being asked to the prom than I had on my first day in the L.A. high school. That day I was noticed because I was a farm girl who looked like one of the Beverly Hillbillies. And as a teenage girl, getting good grades didn't get many points, so I, with my straight As, was out of luck finding a prom date. I hid behind a proud smile and told Alyce, "The prom is nothing special."

I held up the stack of schoolbooks I was carrying. "I'd rather study. You know how important getting a college scholarship is to me."

Alyce ruffled my hair. "You're going to the prom."

The rest of that semester I studied extra hard to be sure I got a scholarship. Alyce, on the other hand, apparently was beating the bushes for my prom date. One day she came home from work and announced, "I've found him."

"Who?"

"Your prom date." Alyce's face was lighted by a smile that sprawled from ear to ear.

"What? You can't be serious. I have no intention of going to some dumb prom with a guy you bribed."

"I didn't bribe anyone. He's a colleague's son."

"I can't believe you're doing this. I'm not going."

Then she produced a gold satin tea length dress that I could only imagine Princess Grace wearing. The dress had cap sleeves, a scoop neck and a bodice that would hug my torso. The full skirt gracefully flared from the waist, which was accented with a matching gold satin sash. "What's that?" I pointed at the gown.

"Your prom dress. That is if you like it."

It was beautiful, and after a lifetime of inheriting hand-me-downs, the thought of wearing my first truly elegant dress almost melted the horror of being escorted to the prom by a store-bought guy.

"Try it on." Alyce pushed the dress towards me. I didn't take it.

"Go ahead. Just see how it looks."

I knew what she was up to. She believed once I had the dress on, I would change my mind. She was right. I was caught off guard and should have remembered her stubbornness once she had her mind set on something. Yet standing there with that gorgeous dress held in front of my face, I temporarily forgot my sister was an expert in obstinant persistence.

I knew better than to fight Alyce's determination so I grabbed the dress from her and retreated to my bedroom to try it on. As I slipped the dress over my head and down my body, I shuddered with delight at the luxurious softness of the satin. I closed my eyes and caressed the gown's silky bodice and skirt. Then I twirled around so I could listen to the rustle of the new material.

When I came back to the living room to model the dress, Alyce pulled out matching high-heel satin pumps and bag. I shook my head in disbelief. When she held up the new white wool coat, I surrendered.

"You've thought of everything," I said.

"Almost. I've got to make an appointment to get your hair and nails done. You're going to stun them at this ball."

"Hmmm," I said and escaped to my room with my bounty. I sat on my bed fingering each item laid out before me and dreamed about the prom. But then I thought: *What if I hate my date?* I yelled out to my sister, "What's my date's name?"

"Troy Marvel."

"Ah, the marvelous Troy," I chuckled, wondering if she had invented the name, just as perfect as the dress. Later that evening, I discovered Troy was a student at UCLA and he drove an MG. Not only did I have a date, but he was an older man, a college man.

On the day of the prom Alyce kept her promise and dragged me to Michael's Salon to get my hair and nails done. "I'll have to work a miracle," Michael said as he rubbed his hand in my hair. "It's so fine and no body."

Michael scrubbed my hair with a fragrant shampoo that made my head tingle. I began to feel the transformation taking place from a charwoman to Cinderella. While I sat under the hair dryer, a manicurist turned my hands—raw cuticles, shaggy nails and all—into ones that I'd only seen the likes of in magazines.

As I admired my new pearl nail polish, a woman in a pink lab coat approached me carrying a suitcase and grabbed my newly perfect right hand. "My name is Bobbie," she said and pulled me toward a bar stool in front of a mirror. "Sit," she said, pointing to the stool. I did as I was told. She placed the suitcase on a shelf beneath the mirror that faced me. She opened the case and produced layers of colorful makeup.

"Oh no," I screeched and scowled at Alyce. "It's bad enough I'm going through this date thing, but this?" I pointed to the container.

"This won't be painful," Bobbie laughed. "Besides you need a little color." Bobbie winked.

I groaned but gave in when Alyce hovered nearby.

When Bobbie finished her task, I didn't recognize the girl in the mirror. Michael had created a soft, yet sophisticated upsweep hairstyle and Bobbie's magic gave my skin a glow which looked completely natural. I had never imagined looking like this.

"It's not bad," I said, tilting my head from side to side. Secretly I felt like a swan rather than the ugly duckling I thought I was. For once, I didn't stick my tongue out at the image staring back from the mirror.

Promptly at seven that night, Alyce and I heard a knock at the door. I wanted to bolt from the room, but Alyce was too quick. She flung the door wide and produced Troy, a drop-dead handsome twenty-one-year-old with black curly hair and perfect white teeth. "What a dream boat," I mumbled to myself.

Troy handed me a corsage of white baby roses held together by gold satin ribbons that matched my dress. Then in one fluid motion he helped me on with my coat, took my arm and led me out the door. I was charmed.

Troy's MG sped into the school parking lot. He walked around the car to open my door as I sat like a queen waiting for him. Several students stopped to see who he was. He reached his hand toward me and helped me out of the car seat. I tried to remember Alyce's lesson about swinging both legs out at the same time. You could hear the gasps from the group when I rose out of the car and they recognized me.

Troy and I strolled into the gym, transformed for this night into a Hawaiian resort complete with miniature waterfalls, fountains sculpted like fish, potted palm trees, flaming torches and non-alcoholic punch served in coconuts. A hush filled the room, and with everyone staring at us, Troy circled his right arm around my back to dance. Then, as though someone had ordered an attack, the same girls who had ignored me for the past two years surrounded us and greeted me, their new best friend.

Prince Charming had rescued me and completed the metamorphosis begun by my sister. For one night I was a swan, Cinderella touched by her fairy godmother—and it was wonderful. Yet like all fantasies, that one came to an abrupt end. All too soon I was home again, pulling off the beautiful dress and stepping out of the matching shoes.

When Troy discovered I wasn't the glamorous woman manufactured by Alyce, Michael and Bobbie, he moved on. Unlike the real Cinderella story, Alyce wasn't a wicked stepmother, and the glass slipper didn't fit my foot. Yet that one evening will forever be special to me, because I learned about the love of a sister—my mother—and to what lengths she would go to make my life magical.

Tekla Dennison Miller

Thirsty

When you're in your nineties and looking back, it's not going to be how much money you made or how many awards you've won. It's really what did you stand for. Did you make a positive difference for people?

Elizabeth Dole

"I'm thirsty," my little girl, Becky, shouted many nights when she couldn't get to sleep. Like all good mothers, I got up and accompanied her to the refrigerator to get her something to drink. Together we sat down at the kitchen table over a glass of water. We talked about the things that were important to her. Since everyone else in the house was fast asleep, those few minutes served as quality time together.

Sometimes we laughed, while at other times we shed a few tears. The conversations always ended with great big bear hugs and, as soon as the glass was empty, a good-night kiss. Then Becky contentedly skipped off to bed while I quietly slipped back into my bed and thanked God for the blessing of my little girl and for our quiet moment.

The years went by very quickly. Before I knew it, Becky was a teenager. We shopped together and watched a few movies, but unfortunately our time together was often short. She was busy playing in the high school band and twirling flags when she wasn't studying. I missed having her home during the day and always looked forward to her return each night. Those were the times that I became thirsty for her. But luckily, many nights, still over a glass of water, she shared her adolescent concerns with me. I discovered that she wasn't always seeking my motherly advice. She simply needed me to listen to her. And so our quiet moments continued, on and off, even through her teen years.

I realized that my life was about to change drastically after Becky finished high school. My twin sons were already living on their own. Becky was our last child. I was very proud of her and knew that she needed to gain a sense of independence, even though her absence would leave a great void in my life. The first few days after she moved out, I couldn't bear to go into her room. Finally, when I opened the door about a week later, I saw her face on everything. The familiar squeak of her door made me cry. I could still smell the heavenly scents of her perfumes and powder. Her empty room left an even bigger vacancy in my heart. I discovered how much I missed our nightly discussions. I truly thirsted for her now that she was gone.

Three weeks after she moved away from home, I had to laugh as I was reminded of the many nights from the past. Shortly before midnight, right after I went to bed, I heard the back door open.

"I'm thirsty," Becky shouted, as she came inside. I jumped up from my bed, went into the kitchen, and together, just like old times, I got her something to drink. We sat down and shared the humorous events of her day. Again, she did the talking while I listened intently.

Just before she left, she gave me another big old bear hug. I went back to bed, laughed again about her stories, and this time thanked God for the blessing of my grown daughter. Even though our lives are very different now, I'm convinced that our quiet moments and midnight bear hugs made certain that the love between us will never grow old.

And after momentarily fearing that our private late-night ritual ended when she moved, I now believe Becky will come home thirsty many more times in the future, especially when she needs a bear hug to get her through the night.

Nancy B. Gibbs

Don't Close the Door

When I was a freshman in college I received in the mail a bulging envelope from my mom. It was a card of encouragement—with a brown, plastic doorstop in it.

"Don't 'close the door' yet," she wrote.

I hated college when I first got there . . . and not the way many freshmen hate it for the first half-hour. They all got over it at the first frat party. I didn't get over it for a year. I wanted to go home, sleep in my own room, go to a state school I could drive to, and only endure minimal amounts of change. The doorstop stayed with me throughout that year, a constant reminder to persevere. I made it through, with the support and encouragement provided from home. I embraced school after that.

During my junior year, Mom asked me to block off a chunk of time during a visit home over a college break. A family meeting. They were common for some families, but not in my house. I don't think we were ever called for a family meeting. I was excited and thought it was good news to be shared with all three kids all at once. Remarried, perhaps?

But when I went home I learned that not only was Mom

not getting remarried, but the news wasn't good at all, and my brother and sister already knew. My mom was sitting in front of the fireplace, John next to her, my sister on the couch, and my brother on the love seat. I was in a chair.

Cancer.

I was at her side, crying on her. It had returned after five years of hiding, just when she was about to throw her arms up in triumph. The magical five-year mark dangled just out of reach as doctors told her of a recurrence.

It was Thanksgiving and her birthday, and I was bound and determined not to go back to school. When we found out five years earlier, my aunt picked me up from school, and I spent the ensuing days taking Mom water and soup and clearing away tissues and stroking her hair back as I had done as a child to coerce her into falling asleep so I could stay up past bedtime.

This time, I wanted to go with her to Boston as she gathered second and third opinions. She wouldn't let me, though, telling me not to throw away a semester of work; she'd be fine, she'd call me with any news . . . but there wouldn't be much news to report anyway, and I'd be home for Christmas in no time at all.

I went back to school, as detached as I'd been that first year, halfheartedly going through the motions and longing to be home by her side—as I'd been through the first attack on my mother's body from the inside out. But I knew I had to stay, if not for myself, then for her. I knew the last thing she needed was the added worry of me wasting an academic year.

That year I had also been trying to define a senior honor's thesis and was discouraged at my lack of inspiration. I was jealous that students with other majors had noble purposes to explore: a public relations campaign to increase organ donation; a scientist working on a cancer-related treatment. What in the world could a photographer do that would make a difference? My world was defined by art, not finding cures.

Finally it came to me one day. My two problems shared a common thread.

I embarked on a project for my mom. It was a photographic tribute to cancer survivors. Through words and pictures I journeyed through the struggle of cancer survivors—anyone courageous enough to fight that fight is a survivor in my mind—and the inspiration they focused on to endure the debilitating and excruciating treatments. I went to support groups and asked for volunteers. Most everyone was willing.

Mom visited while I was studying in London, and I took her to the Vidal Sassoon school for her "first" haircut after radiation and chemotherapy. I photographed her soon after that in the new daring cut she had wanted for years but was afraid to get. She was the centerpiece of my thesis. At graduation she came up and saw her photograph hanging in an exhibit. It was called "Survivor's Instinct," and she embodied it. She, along with the others pictured, define perseverance. The lesson she gave me years earlier had come full circle.

We recently had a surprise party for my mom's fiftieth birthday. I found out afterwards that she didn't think she'd make it to fifty. She's healthy now, and younger than ever. She just might make it to 100.

As for the doorstop, the funny thing is that I don't know where it is anymore, but I can picture it: brown, plastic and triangular, with scratches and scuffs. The object is missing, but the memory of that envelope and everything it meant is forever a lesson to persevere and to keep my heart open. It is the greatest lesson I learned from my mom.

Christie Kelley Montone

Happy Birthday, Baby

People tend to become what you tell them they are.

Dorothy Delay

It took me a while to realize what day it was. I awoke to gray skies and the chance of snow in the forecast for Wednesday, January twenty-eighth. My birthday. I was thirty-five. I turned away from the clock radio and wished I'd taken the day off from work. I wanted to stay in bed and snuggle up to my self-pity about being alone—yet again—on this significant day. My most recent attempt at romance had crashed and burned two weeks earlier, and the wounds were still fresh. It hadn't been a long relationship, and it wasn't even that much of a relationship, but it had refueled my hopes and dreams about having someone to come home to. As I lay in bed, I remembered blowing out last year's candles and wishing for the man of my dreams—sure that my luck would change this year. "What the hell is it gonna take?" I asked my walls, angry and terrified at the same time. When the phone rang, I expected to hear warm wishes from my parents or brothers. Instead, it was a man that I once cried over, calling to say hi and completely forgetting my birthday. My sister-in-law called next, updating me on her happy life with my brother, and putting my two-year-old niece on the phone to sing to me. I hung up, fed my cat, and tried to remember what I loved about the glamorous single life when I was twenty-something.

Adding to the gloom was the fact that I no longer liked my job as a news reporter. I was dragging myself into the radio station every day, trying to figure out where else I belonged and what else I should be doing. *Today would be bearable,* I thought, because they'd probably have a party for me at work, or maybe my recent ex would do the unexpected and send flowers. I was also looking forward to interviewing a favorite jazz musician whose saxophone and sense of humor were typically delightful. Little did I know that he'd be cranky from a recent root canal, and so uncooperative that I wanted to shout, "Screw you and your attitude—I shouldn't even be here today!" To add insult to injury, my co-workers forgot my birthday, and I went home in a snit, empty-handed, slipping in the snow and cursing myself for wearing boots with heels and no tread.

A dinner party with a great circle of women was the bright spot in my day, as my friends made me laugh and look on the bright side of my latest romantic disaster. But after they left, the sadness returned. I didn't want to be alone at the end of the day, I didn't want to be alone at age thirty-five, and I didn't know where my life was going. My parents had left me a birthday message, and I was glad that I had missed the call, because I didn't want to talk to them when I felt like such a miserable failure as a daughter and as a woman. I questioned my choices in life, and wondered just what I had passed up marriage and motherhood for. What was so great about my independent life?

I poured myself a glass of wine and sat down to seek comfort from birthday cards that I'd grabbed from the mailbox after work. One envelope reached out to me with the familiar, feminine script of my mother, whose handwriting echoed my grandmother's. I pulled out a pink card that read, "The only thing better than having a delightful daughter is watching her become a beautiful woman." Inside, were these unexpected words.

"As I write, it's snowing outside—just like the day you were born, thirty-five years ago. I'll never forget the moment they placed you in my arms, and I knew what I was meant to do with my life. I was so thrilled to have a baby girl—it was a dream come true! Through the years, you continue to be a delight to me—so sweet and thoughtful, and smart and talented. I am so grateful for our friendship, and I admire your courage and adventurous spirit. You are a warm and beautiful woman, Kim Childs, and you are my best friend. Know that I wish you a wonderful year ahead—filled with everything you desire and deserve! I love you, XXOO Mom."

My teardrops hit the paper as I read those powerful words of love. I cried for the deep connection I had to this woman who considered me a gift, a success and an inspiration. Her message stirred my soul and breathed new life into me. I knew, as I lay down to sleep that night, that I was treasured, and that my life made a difference and brought joy to someone I cherished. It was my mother's second-greatest birthday gift to me—thirty-five years after the first.

Kim Childs

Making Memories

After eating breakfast, my little girl says, "Mommy, will you watch this show with me?" I look at the breakfast dishes in the sink and then at her big brown eyes.

"Okay," I say, and we snuggle together on the couch and watch her favorite show.

After the show, we put together a puzzle and I head for the kitchen to wash those dirty dishes when the phone rings. "Hi," my friend says, "What have you been doing?"

"Well," I say, "watching my little one's favorite show with her and putting together a puzzle."

"Oh," she says, "so you're not busy today."

No, I think to myself, *just busy making memories.*

After lunch, Erica says, "Mommy, please play a game with me." Now I am looking at not only the breakfast dishes but also the lunch dishes piled in the sink. But again, I look at those big brown eyes and I remember how special it felt when my mom played games with me when I was a little girl.

"Sounds like fun," I answer, "but just one game." We play her favorite game, and I can tell she is delighting in every moment.

When the game ends, she says, "Please read me a story."
"Okay," I say, "but just one."

After reading her favorite story, I head for the kitchen to tackle those dishes. With the dishes now done, I start to fix supper. My willing little helper comes eagerly to the kitchen to help me with my task. I'm running behind and thinking about how much faster I could do this if my sweet little one would just go play or watch a video, but her willingness to help and her eagerness to learn how to do what her mommy is doing melts my heart, and I say, "Okay, you can help," knowing it will probably take twice as long.

As supper is about ready, my husband comes home from work and asks, "What did you do today?"

I answer, "Let's see, we watched her favorite show and we played a game and read a book. I did the dishes and vacuumed; then with my little helper, I fixed supper."

"Great," he says, "I'm glad you didn't have a busy day today."

But I was busy, I think to myself, *busy making memories.*

After supper, Erica says, "Let's bake cookies."

"Okay," I say, "let's bake cookies."

After baking cookies, once again I am staring at a mountain of dishes from supper and cookie baking, but with the smell of warm cookies consuming the house, I pour us a glass of cold milk and fill a plate with warm cookies and take them to the table. We gather around the table eating cookies, drinking milk, talking and making memories.

No sooner have I tackled those dishes than my little sweetie comes tugging at my shirt, saying, "Could we take a walk?"

"Okay," I say, "let's take a walk." The second time around the block I'm thinking about the mountain of laundry that I need to get started on and the dust encompassing our home; but I feel the warmth of her hand in mine and the sweetness of our conversation as she enjoys my undivided attention, and I decide at least once more around the block sounds like a good idea.

When we get home, my husband asks, "Where have you been?"

"We've been making memories," I say.

A load in the wash and, my little girl all bathed and in her gown, the tiredness begins to creep in as she says, "Let's fix each other's hair."

I'm so tired! my mind is saying, but I hear my mouth saying, "Okay, let's brush each other's hair." With that task complete, she jumps up excitedly, "Let's paint each other's nails! Please!" So she paints my toenails, and I paint her fingernails, and we read a book while waiting for our nails to dry. I have to turn the pages, of course, because her fingernails are still drying.

We put away the book and say our prayers. My husband peeks his head in the door, "What are my girls doing?" he asks.

"Making memories," I answer.

"Mommy," she says, "will you lay with me until I fall asleep?"

"Yes," I say, but inside I'm thinking, *I hope she falls asleep quickly so I can get up; I have so much to do.*

About that time, two precious little arms encircle my neck as she whispers, "Mommy, nobody but God loves you as much as I do." I feel the tears roll down my cheeks as I thank God for the day we spent making memories.

Tonna Canfield

$\overline{4}$

CHALLENGES

Remember, we all stumble, every one of us. That's why it's a comfort to go hand in hand.

Emily Kimbrough

A Second Chance

To feel that one has a place in life solves half the problems of contentment.

George Woodberry

I grew up as a foster child from the age of eight. Unlike most children I knew, I never really had a biological mother. I never got to experience the unconditional love and wonderment a mother gives her child. So growing up was a bit harder on me than on most other children. A drastic change came suddenly when I was in the eleventh grade. I was now in my second foster home and had been there for the past five years. I was surrounded by a warm and caring family. But still something pained me deeply. I felt "out of place." I wasn't her birth child, so I remained distant, not allowing myself to love her as much as I could.

In one night, things changed for the better and forever. I was doing homework while waiting for the rest of the family to return home from their events. It was a daily routine. I spent most of my nights by myself finding things to keep me busy. As I was reading a paragraph for English I heard the closing of the back door and my foster mom calling for me. I walked into the kitchen where she was holding a hardcover children's book that she had borrowed from work. "I want you to read this," she said excitedly. "It's absolutely wonderful." She handed me the book, and I glanced at it with curiosity: *The Kissing Hand* by Audrey Penn. I was just about to question her when she smiled at me. "Trust me. You'll love it!"

Reluctantly I grabbed a stool and made myself comfortable at the counter and began to read the book. I thoroughly enjoyed it. It was a touching story of a raccoon mom who places a kiss in the palm of her child's hand to remind him that if ever he should get scared he just has to press his Kissing Hand to his cheek. That way he can always remember that his mommy loves him. I wondered why my foster mom asked me to read it. But I shrugged off the unknown answer and headed back to my room to complete my unfinished homework.

Later that night, I was sitting at the same spot where I had read the book and talking with Mom when suddenly she did something totally unexpected. She ever so gently took my hand and put a warm loving kiss in the center of my palm. She then quietly closed my hand and held it between hers and spoke words that I had dreamt of hearing for so long. "Whenever you get scared or sad, remember that your mommy loves you."

As the tears began to form in my eyes, I began to understand, and so I smiled a smile that touched the very depth of my once-wounded heart. I truly do have a mother. No, she wasn't biological, but she was mine just the same.

Cynthia Blatchford

Little Dolly

Every mother has the breathtaking privilege of sharing with God in the creation of new life. She helps bring into existence a soul that will endure for all eternity.

James Keller

I wish now that I could say I'd loved my daughter wholeheartedly right from the beginning. But when I first glimpsed Elisheva, born six weeks early, my first thought—God forgive me—was *chicken.* She was a scrawny chicken baby, the kind of baby I'd always sneered at when one was born to other parents. I couldn't help it. My first child, a boy, had been a golden, healthy baby who cooed and smiled almost straight out of the womb, teethed painlessly, talked in full sentences, read early and—at six and a half—will probably be up for that Nobel any year now.

But my daughter was different. The first time I saw her, I literally passed out. It didn't help that there was an IV line straight into her forehead and what looked like a Lucite Tupperware cake cover over her head supplying oxygen, but it might have just been from the long labor and the fact that I'd insisted on walking rather than riding in a wheelchair. I recovered to find three neonatal pediatricians staring helplessly down at me, probably trying to puzzle out what to do for a full-sized patient.

But if I thought her ruddy-yellow-skinned scrawniness was appalling, all thoughts of chicken quickly crossed the road when, the next morning, I first heard her cry. My only thought then—I admit, there's probably a special level of hell for mothers like me—was *seagull*. When the nurses paged to tell me she was awake and hungry, I heard a screeching, squawking seabird off in the distance, and as I walked toward the ICU, I realized that the noise must be emanating from my tiny bird baby. I couldn't imagine how any sound could pierce the walls of her plastic isolette, around the corner and down the hall, but she'd managed it. I walked a little slower, dreading my first physical contact with a creature who only two days earlier had been smashing my ribs from inside and parking herself on my bladder, sending me running to the bathroom every ten minutes.

Still exhausted and post-partum six weeks before I thought I'd even be feeling the first labor pangs, I didn't want or need a hungry scavenger in my life. Blearily, I made my way into the ICU. I pinpointed her by the noise rather than by any kind of visual recognition—I figured she'd gotten her looks from somewhere else on the evolutionary ladder altogether.

"Go and get comfortable," the nurse called, directing me to a rocking chair in a private playroom off the ICU. I sat in the chair, piled my lap high with pillows, and waited in dread for the baby. Soon enough, the nurse was there in front of me, carrying a pink-wrapped bundle with what looked like a sock on its head.

"What's that?" I asked.

"Stocking cap," she explained. "The volunteers made them for the New Years' babies." She showed me the glittering pompoms and gold ribbon tied around in an attempt to make the preemies' shaven heads look festive. I just braced myself to take the baby from her.

I held out my arms. "Are you ready?" she asked me. I must have nodded. "Here you go," she said, leaning over, and then, in an enchanted half-whisper, added, "Here's your little dolly." Her gentle words jarred me out of my daze; suddenly, the phrase "chicken baby" was gone. All I could hear, over and over in my mind, was "little dolly." I took a long look at the baby, brought her closer, and—unlike my son, who had always been too busy to nurse properly—she latched on immediately and began to drink.

My heart melted; I imagined I could feel its tears of relief flowing out into those first rich drops of colostrum, the early milk that welcomes a newborn after the shock of getting born. This was the milk, I realized, that would fatten her up so others, too, would recognize in her what only that nurse and I had glimpsed—a perfect dolly; my very own little baby girl, cuddling tight, a sparkling stocking cap cradling her sparse, vulnerable hair.

Some time during her first summer, as my mother and I were watching her lying on the rug kicking her legs, just for the thrill of seeing her double knees jiggle and her plump thighs wobble, my mother turned and asked, "Where did this fat, happy little girl come from?" I looked at my daughter and shrugged, pretending I'd never doubted, that, like that heaven-sent nurse, I'd been able to see through to her beauty all along.

Jennifer M. Paquette

Pantyhose Hair

*Happiness is a butterfly, which, when pursued,
is always just beyond your grasp, but which, if
you will sit down quietly, may alight upon you.*

Nathaniel Hawthorne

When I was six, I donned my mother's pantyhose and wore them . . . on my head. They were my very own long, luxuriant pantyhose hair. What necessitated my resorting to this was the fact that my mother kept cutting my hair into one of those "cute little pixie cuts." I got expert at layering several pairs, so that I could braid and style my many-legged pantyhose hair. I was never allowed to wear my beautiful hosiery hair out in public, but at home I gloried in it. I promised myself, with all of the fierce determination of my six-year-old self, that if I ever had a little girl, I would never, ever cut my little girl's hair.

So, when I found out at thirty-two years of age that I was pregnant with a little girl, I felt two things. First, I felt an absolute feather-tickle of joy all throughout my body. Second, I was suffused with a fierce maternal protection toward my little girl's unseen tresses.

Imagine with what joy I looked forward to my little girl's Rapunzel-like ringlets. All of my thwarted longings for flowing tresses, all of my impeded desires for an enviable mane would be made right, accounted for, sublimated by my own daughter's inviolate strands. I went into a veritable frenzy of buying hair accessories. Hair bows, hair bands, hair clips, hair scrunchies, little hair bows that attached by Velcro, I bought them all. I bought every color of the rainbow and every pattern that I could find. My little girl actually had more hair accessories than she could ever hope to wear, unless of course I adorned her head with four or five at a time, which I did not consider out of the question or in any way extreme.

I was only mildly discouraged when Jasmine Rain was born with very little hair—just a light vanilla fuzz. I took to proudly adorning her fuzzy little head with those headbands for newborns that look like garter belts (despite the rude discouragement I received from one of my brother-in-laws to the effect that I was squeezing her little brain and the fact that he would surreptitiously remove them when I wasn't looking—like I wouldn't notice—and the fact that he kept trying to convert my husband to his "no headband" philosophy).

I received hope from nature. Kittens, puppies, bunnies, all are born hairless. All of these, in no time, sport thick, luxurious growths. I wasn't worried. I waited patiently through the first, second and third months. Of course I was always brushing and lavishing unstinting attention on the little bit of encouragement that was there in the form of blonde dandelion fluff.

Then in the fourth month, there was still no hair. I started to worry. I read every article I could get my hands on regarding hair growth and developmental expectations. I quizzed friends and coworkers about their experiences and stared forlornly at the heads of all the thickly haired babies that seemed to accost my stricken eyes everywhere I went. What was I doing wrong?

The ribbons, bows and assorted hopefuls sat dusty on her closet shelf—a sad testament to my optimistic expectations of just a short time ago. I was horrified to hear the same words uttered in regard to my Jazzy that had so mortified me as a child ("What a cute little boy!") always offered in the heartiest and most jovial of manners. But still I maintained my hope. Every little tuft of growth was greeted with excited enthusiasm and happy pleasure.

Finally, when Jazzy turned two, I was rewarded for my patience and faith. Jazzy's hair began to grow (whether it was just time for it to grow or whether the naked-with-a-carved-wooden-mask-ceremonial-hair-growing dance I did accomplished it, I just don't know). Whatever the reason, it was now my supreme pleasure to contemplate the appropriate adorning of Jazzy's hair.

Unfortunately, contemplate it is all I've been able to do. Would you believe that every time I try to put her hair in pigtails Jazzy squeals a high-pitched scream and will absolutely not allow me to do it? Would you believe that every headband that I put lovingly on her head is yanked off immediately in the most annoyed manner? Can you credit the fact that now that her hair is at the right length to finally utilize her extensive hair fashion wardrobe that she vehemently refuses to do so?

I've read that asserting her opinions and preferences is the first step on the road to her developing independence. I've read that it shows a healthy level of self-confidence and incipient autonomy. I'm trying to look on the bright side and I am happy that she has a very opinionated little mind of her own. But still, it has been a bit disillusioning for me. And frankly I'm starting to worry that Jazzy will be the exact opposite of me and hate long hair and feel like I forced it on her and end up shaving her head just to get back at me. I hope by the time she is old enough to do that, I will be peacefully accepting of her in whatever guise she chooses to coif herself. Maybe I'll have shaved my head by then too—in utter frustration!

At least, for now, I have my own long hair to console me. And one other thing, Jazzy does, sometimes, allow a stylish hat.

Annette Marie Hyder

"I have great looking hair 'cause my Mom's
a hairdresser! It's cut with love!"

Reprinted by permission of Stephanie Piro.

An Angel in Disguise

First keep the peace within yourself, then you can also bring peace to others.

Thomas à Kempis

"I wouldn't be your daughter if you paid me!" I vehemently declared to my new stepmother, in response to her introducing me as her daughter to a man fixing our windows. That was one of the many conflicts we had throughout my high school years. In my rebellious youth, my insecurity compelled me to lash out, to hurt people before they hurt me.

Imagine a divorced woman, living in Colorado with two small children, ages three and five, who meets, falls in love with, and decides to marry a man who lives in New Mexico. To do so, she must sell her home, give up the teaching job that she loves, and go to court against her ex-husband, in order to be allowed to move her children out of the state. After all this, she is confronted with two unruly teenagers, my brother and me, who are convinced she is the enemy and the source of all their problems. When she secures a job as a history teacher at their high school, they inform friends and students that she is a "bitch." They pick on her children with a relentless cruelty. They embarrass her, insult her and ignore her. How does she respond?

With pure, unconditional love. Out of instinct, Mary Jo exercised tough love long before the term was mainstream. She laid down the rules. Dinner was at 6:30 P.M. I had to call by 6:00 if I wouldn't be there. In addition to family dinners, there would be family nights and family vacations.

I was used to being independent, basically coming and going as I pleased. Mary Jo wanted to know what my schedule was and who my friends were. The minimal rule was to say "Hello" when I came home and "Good-bye" before going anywhere. I tried to avoid even this, sneaking in the house, up to my room with friends. She would appear instantly, "Hi, I'm Mary Jo, Alice's stepmother. What's your name?"

When she tried to talk to me, I yelled and walked away. When she tried to hug me, I pushed her away. She said, "I know you don't like it, but I'm going to hug you anyway." She wrote me letters and signed them, "I love you! Mary Jo." I tore them up and threw them in the garbage where she could see them. The next letter said, "I know you're going to tear this up. I love you, anyway! Mary Jo."

On my sixteenth birthday Mary Jo and I got into an argument because I was picking on her daughter. I was sent to my room. I called my friends to meet me on the corner and climbed out the window. I got home around 6:00 that evening, afraid to go in the house. As I pushed the door open and stepped in, I heard, "Surprise!" Six of my girlfriends were sitting around the table, which was full of food and presents. Mary Jo had planned the party and cooked for me. She treated me like a princess in front of my friends. I felt so special, yet so guilty. When the party was over, Mary Jo said, "Happy birthday. I love you. You're grounded."

One day I was walking past my dad and Mary Jo's bedroom. I heard her crying. I don't remember what she was saying, but it was about me and how she never knew how tough it all would be. To say I stopped acting out or that we never fought again would be an exaggeration, but listening to her pain invited me one step closer to her.

Most of my anger and hurt was about my father, his past actions and the walls we had built between us over the years. Mary Jo was often caught in the middle. Over time, I came to love and respect her. Since the day my father had introduced her, I thought she was beautiful. I used to sincerely question, "What do you see in him?" She would tell me all the good things about my father I was desperately trying to forget in an effort to hate him. I asked that question and heard the answer so much that I began to see the good that she saw in him. I began to take the love and acceptance that Mary Jo had poured into me and practice it on my father. After a while, there was a bridge where there used to be a wall.

When I was in trouble, Mary Jo dealt with my behavior directly. She told me what I had done wrong and what the punishment was. She didn't make a big production. She made it clear what she would and would not tolerate. In the midst of it all, she built my self-esteem by saying things like, "You're better than that" and "I expect more from someone like you." After hearing, "You're always doing things like this" and "Are you going to be a permanent problem?" for years, I walked away from Mary Jo's lectures feeling two inches taller.

More important than how she dealt with my unruly behavior was that she taught me positive alternatives and introduced me to things I could feel good about. To an outsider, playing cards, cooking and family dinners may be casual events, but these events were like shots of joy and self-worth to me. They were medicine for a sickness that could have lasted a lifetime.

One of the strongest medicines I have ever tasted is running. That, too, was a gift from Mary Jo. She ran a ten-mile race the day she married my father. I had never run before, but I figured if she could do it so could I. I walked almost as much as I ran. However, I have run, and won, many races since that day. Mary Jo and I have run through mountains and neighborhoods together. In high school, I ran track and cross-country. I acted as if I didn't care if Mary Jo came to my races or not, as well as ignoring her when she did. Sometimes I wouldn't even tell her if I had one, but she'd find out through the school. Before I'd start, I'd scan the crowd. When I saw her face, though I told no one, comfort surged through my body.

To say Mary Jo made a positive difference in my life is an understatement. She made a pivotal difference in my life. She served as a role model, a mother and a friend. She taught me what it means to be a family and created events that make up some of my most cherished memories. She made every holiday a celebration. She passed down the gift of running, which has given me strength, peace, privacy, a place to cry, to pray, to evolve. She taught me the manners that have allowed me to excel in business and in life.

Above it all, Mary Jo taught me about love. She showed me that love cures; love softens; love sees beneath the tough exterior; love changes people; love is the creator of metamorphosis. Today, I am proud for Mary Jo to call me her daughter, and I am privileged to call her my friend.

Alice Lundy Blum

Clothes Closet Reflections

Angels can fly because they take themselves lightly.

C. K. Chesterton

All mothers of teenage daughters know what it's like. Clothes shopping with that age group is a test of patience, physical endurance, restraint and basic human kindness.

"Mother, give it up! These pants are way too baggy!"

"They're skin tight!"

"Well, these shoes are okay and they look just like the name-brand ones and they fit okay, but Mother, they don't have that little aardvark on the label and everybody will know! I'll pay the twenty-dollar difference myself for the name-brand ones, okay?"

"When donkeys fly, you will."

"Mom! Do you actually think I'd be caught dead in a dress like that?"

"No, I was thinking more in terms of the homecoming dance, but if you keep talking to me like this . . ."

Oh Lord, give me patience. Direct me out of this store and over to the place where they sell warm chocolate-chip cookies. Quickly.

After a few dismal, distressing shopping trips with my daughters, trips that practically brutalized me with teenage logic, I decided to let them shop alone from then on with money they earned themselves.

Thanks, Lord, for that brilliant idea. I may survive single motherhood, after all.

Then one day, a few years later, it happened.

"Mom," Julie asked sweetly, "may I borrow your yellow blouse to wear to school tomorrow? And maybe that brown print skirt?"

"Sure, honey!" I practically fell off the stool at the kitchen counter. At last my daughters were growing up. Our taste in clothes was starting to meld. I suddenly felt ten years younger.

A few minutes later, Jeanne passed through the kitchen.

"Mom, could I try on some of your clothes? I might like to borrow your plaid skirt and one of your scarves."

"Help yourself, my dear," I smiled smugly.

Either I'm getting really hip when it comes to clothes, or they've finally discovered sensible fashion, I mused.

Single parenthood was suddenly fun. Instead of fighting over the cost of clothes and the styles my daughters chose versus those that actually made sense in the real world, suddenly visions of new, exciting mother-daughter shopping sprees danced in my head. I saw the three of us lunching together after our shopping adventures, discussing our bargains and look-alike fashions, while dining on quiche and croissants.

Right then Jeanne and Julie emerged from my bedroom dressed practically head-to-toe in fashions from my wardrobe, including jewelry and accessories.

"Thanks, Mom! These are great!" they bubbled.

I wasn't so sure about the combinations they'd chosen, but I certainly wasn't about to criticize. After all, I didn't want to ruin this special moment, this tender passage from teendom to adulthood.

"Yeah, they're perfect Mom," Jeanne nodded. "It's nerd day at school tomorrow . . . you know, everybody dresses up like the fifties, real dorky-like. These things are perfect."

"Oh . . ."

Lord, are you there? I need more patience. Lots more. Right this minute, Lord. Are you listening?

Patricia Lorenz

"I see strange things in your future . . . shoes disappearing, blouses missing from the closet. . . . You wouldn't happen to have a teenage daughter?

Certificate of Graduation from Childhood into Adolescence

Let us be grateful to the people who make us happy; they are the gardeners who make our souls blossom.

Marcel Proust

For My Daughter, Sarah, on Her Thirteenth Birthday. A Statement and Some Promises

I hereby recognize that you are no longer a child, and that your new self needs a new and different kind of mother, and a new way to belong to this household. To this end, I promise:

To have faith in your good sense, intelligence, ability to make good decisions in your best interest, and your good heart, no matter what you do. I will interfere sometimes because I also trust my own good sense, and I know that you are not yet grown, but I will never doubt that you are doing the best you can. Deep down, I trust you.

I will respect and love whoever you are at any given

time, knowing that you are doing what you need to do. You can count on me to support your growing, learning and discovering who you are in any way that I can. I know that you will be changing many times before you can discover who you are, that it may be painful for both of us, and that there will be joy in it, too.

I will not rely on you for friendship, for sharing my life with, or for being a child when I need one around, although I will always be glad to spend time with you when you want to. Thank you for being a wonderful buddy for the last twelve years. I look forward to being buddies again sometime in the future. In the meantime I will not burden you with my needing you—you have enough to worry about on your own.

You do not need to take care of me, feel guilty about how you feel about me or lie to me to make me feel better. I don't want to add to your pain or confusion. Any doubts I have about how well I did as the mother of a child, I will keep to myself. I can't make up for the past, but I can try to do the right thing in the present.

When you were a child, I tried hard to help you become self-reliant and resourceful, and it may have seemed to you that I refused to help, to give rides, make arrangements, etc., when I could have. Now I think you have become a self-reliant, resourceful person, and I will help you whenever I can.

I will require that you be as honest as you can be, that you will ask for help when you need it, that you tell me what is going on with you as much as you can, that you take responsibilities that you are ready for and that you not take the ones that you are not ready for, and that we never lose sight of the fact that we are just two human beings trying to play this game as well as we can. I'll be the mother, you be the daughter, and we'll do our best.

As you travel through these next six years, you can

count on me to be here, to love you, respect you, to guide you whenever you need it. I will be available to talk about anything, any time, without condemning you. I will not act like your therapist or your teacher. I will try to talk more about things that should be talked about in case you don't quite dare ask. If I do something stupid, or break any of these promises, you can tell me. Good luck!

I am looking forward to knowing the beautiful, intelligent, capable, loving woman that you are becoming.

Rebecca Reid

And Baby Makes Two

The relationship between a mother and her daughter is as varied, as mysterious, as constantly changing and interconnected as the patterns that touch, move away from, and touch again in a kaleidoscope.

Lyn Lifshin

I was not quite twenty years old when I gave birth to my beautiful daughter, terrified of the responsibility of raising her properly. Before she was placed in my arms, I wondered if I would ever bond with this little stranger. Halfway into our first nursing time together, she had requisitioned the rest of my life for the purpose of loving her. She stretched me beyond what I thought were my limits of patience, brilliance, creativity, endurance and capacity for love—especially during her adolescent years!

In the summer of her twelfth year, my daughter Tiffany and I went to Virginia Beach. I wanted to attend a week-long conference on ancient Egypt for a book I was writing. This was also my vacation time, and I was eagerly looking forward to combining my participation in the conference with an oceanside vacation with my daughter. She was enrolled in a program for teens while parents attended the conference. We would have meals and evenings together. We settled in at the motel on the beach. Tiffany was not very sure she wanted to be there, even though she always loved being at the ocean. She kept wondering what she was missing at home. What were her friends doing?

When I became a single parent in my daughter's sixth year, I had made a decision to keep the dynamics of our communication very real—not to pull rank, as in "... because I said so," or " ... because I'm your mother." I tried to make any and every topic of conversation permissible. I had opted for communication based on trust, fairness and a clear discussion of issues. That option, however, didn't seem to be working very well, and I had begun to wonder if my approach needed revision. My daughter was sulky, belligerent and non-communicative. She had been like that for almost a year. My February 6th Aquarian daughter, who finds it imperative to do everything years before others do, had decided twelve was the year of her independence. She was trying to experience her entire adolescence in as short a time as possible. There was a new crowd of friends to hang out with in the neighborhood. She tried smoking, then quit smoking. She experimented with marijuana, and she assumed a defiant attitude about contact with boys. As she became more secretive and withdrawn, our communication suffered. This was a departure from our usual way of relating to each other. We had always been quite close.

As the conference began, she and the other young people formed a tightly knit group. Their activities during the day were organized, and in the evening they were left to their own resources. Tiffany chose to spend as much time as possible with her new friends. We didn't see a great deal of one another except at meals, and at night in the motel. I would ask her about her day, whether or not she was enjoying herself. She would answer in monosyllables. This was the stuff of sitcoms, so I attempted dealing with it humorously by answering my own questions in great detail in what was ostensibly her voice. Her looks were withering! Composure cracking, I alternated between patience and exasperation. This was after all, my only vacation for the year, and I sorely needed the rejuvenation. Yet here I was with a sour-faced twelve-year-old who didn't wish to be there and certainly didn't wish to be with her mother, of all people.

One evening toward the end of the week, I was sitting alone on the beach thinking about our relationship. I was feeling frustrated and sad. My daughter was slipping through my fingers while I felt powerless to stop her from doing so. I heard voices and laughter coming toward the beach from behind me. A group of "barely" adolescents were crossing the street to walk on the beach. They were so occupied with themselves that they didn't notice me. Especially occupied were Tiffany and Thomas, a sweet and charming boy a few years older than she. They were walking closely together, he with his arm around her. I watched them from the distance, seeing the circle of boisterous energy the little group made.

The others noticed me first. I heard them squeal, "Tiffany, your mother . . ." elbowing her and pointing in my direction. The alarm was out. She quickly slid out from under Thomas's easy embrace. I watched all this happen and then I called her over to me. The group split apart not knowing quite where to go, but apparently relieved they were not the ones being called on the carpet. Everyone, especially Tiffany, was certain she was in big trouble.

She stopped a few feet away from me, looking sullen and ashamed at the same time. This had to be nipped in the bud right then. I said, "Tiffany, did Thomas have his arm around you just now?"

"Yes," she replied in a challenging, if somewhat shaky voice.

"Did you want him to put his arm around you?"

Again, "Yes."

"Did you think there was anything wrong with his putting his arm around you until you saw me?"

"No." She wondered what I might be getting at. These questions were not what she expected.

"Did you want him to stop doing it?"

"No."

"Then don't ever let me catch you, no matter who is involved, going against what you believe in. Not even if it's me."

She stared at me in disbelief, trying to reconcile my stern tone with the grace of my message. Tears filled her eyes, as she stared hard, seemingly right through me. In that instant, my daughter had a moment of truth. She would never again close herself off from me and make a travesty of our relationship. I was no longer just mother, an authority figure to be challenged! Tiffany realized she could count on me to truly love her, no matter what she did. She felt herself give way to the truth of that, and the trust that emerged poured over all her hostility and rebellion like balm. She just melted, right into my arms, where I kissed away her tears. That night the floodgates opened and she began to talk to me. This was definitely a turning point in our relationship. She never treated me like a stranger again.

Cie Simurro

Who'll Water My Teardrops?

I don't believe that life is supposed to make you feel good, or to make you feel miserable either. Life is just supposed to make you feel.

Gloria Naylor

My daughter's tears started as we drove out of our driveway and down our neighborhood streets toward the highways that would take us over nine hundred miles to Colorado and her first year of college. These were the streets she and I had traveled hundreds of happy times, going here or there, many times sharing thoughts and laughter. How perceptive she is, I have often thought, at reading people and situations, getting to the core of any matter, and putting into words the clarity of her thoughts. She is so much more capable of this than I was at her age.

Now she could not find the words to say why she was crying on an occasion that should have been mostly happy. I thought she should be feeling the excitement of beginning a life for herself away from home—that she would be exhilarated at the prospect of being on her own and free from her parents' constant scrutiny. What went wrong?

Was she crying because she would be away for an extended period for the first time, because she would be leaving her friends, familiar places and faces, and her family or because she was leaving her best friend and first love, a young man she met months ago? This was the loss that seemed to have the greatest impact on her at this time.

I hoped the long trip would be another happy time for the two of us when we could talk freely and deeply for the two days we would be on the road. Her sorrow made it difficult to converse about the good times of the past and the new experiences she could look forward to. Though the tears eventually subsided, there would be no bonding on this day, and my chance to impress her with my best worldly advice had passed. Mostly we shared silence.

The next day when the mountains came into view and loomed larger so, too, did the reality of her future in this beautiful country. As the mountains grew, so did her anticipation and her spirits. We exchanged superficial talk.

Finally, we were on campus, and she was moving into her room, unpacking and settling in. She and her roommate seemed to hit it off right away. Both liked thick, gourmet coffee and country music; both were messy and had to set the alarm clock on the other side of the room to get out of bed in the morning. I never thought I'd see these habits as positive traits.

The orientation schedule was informative but grueling and kept both of us tuned into surviving the present. There were meetings for parents only, for students only, and for both parents and students together. I learned that this university is one of the top-ten party schools in the nation, that sexually transmitted diseases are epidemic and that two-thirds of the freshman class is on academic probation after the first midterms. Why did we agree to let her go to school here?

It was difficult for us to find our way around a six-hundred-acre campus where most of the buildings looked the same and where I needed my glasses to read the building names. Our differing methods of finding our way caused more friction between the two of us than anything else. I was into map reading, and she was into following her nose on the random chance that it would take her to the right building.

On the final day of orientation, registration was thoroughly frustrating, even maddening. It seemed as though none of the classes she wanted to take were open, and there were long lines for every step of the registration process. There was one advisor for approximately fifteen students. Only through her perseverance and willingness to wait for hours the next day to meet alone with an advisor did she get the classes she wanted.

With a gentle nudge she made it clear that it was time for me to leave her on her own. Now the excitement was hers, and a lump settled in my throat and tears came to my eyes. If I was going to impart any great new wisdom, it would have to be done in the few minutes of our leave-taking. What could I say that hadn't already been expressed?

I told her of a time when she was very young. She and I went shopping at a large department store, and I was trying on clothing. She walked out of the dressing room leaving me in a state of undress and unable to go after her. By the time I got my clothes back on, she was gone. After frantically searching for what seemed like an eternity, I found her sitting quietly in the mall security office. It was a nightmare that seemed to describe this moment aptly. When she leaves me today, I will want to run after her. I still want her to stay with me, safe and secure. Now I am emotionally undressed; I cannot chase after her. She will be more content without me than I think she should be.

As I gave her a final hug, I could not hold back the tears.

"I love you," I said.

Out of nowhere she said, "Will you water my teardrops?" This is our name for the plants she has sitting in the windows of her bedroom. The delicate vines cascade to the floor nearly covering one wall; the small, circular leaves and the fragile, lavender flowers resemble teardrops. We both knew what she was asking. Would her room be there when she returned, the same as she left it? Would her family be there for her as we always had been in the past? Would we drive and laugh and confide on the same familiar streets that surround the only home she has ever known?

Yes, we'll water your teardrops.

She turned toward her new life, and I turned toward home. As the mountains diminished in my rearview mirror, so, too, did her presence. I became lonelier and emptier until the plains flattened my emotions. I managed to hold myself together for nearly twenty-six hours until the familiar sights of home brought cascades of tears.

Without her our streets are silent; our house is empty; my stomach is hollow.

Who'll water my teardrops?

Win Herberg

"I promise to write you from college, Mom. And I'll call, e-mail and even send telepathic messages!"

Reprinted by permission of Stephanie Piro.

The Nightgown

People become really quite remarkable when they start thinking that they can do things. When they believe in themselves they have the first secret of success.

Norman Vincent Peale

In the bottom drawer of my mother's walnut veneer dresser lay a Joan Crawford–style nylon and lace nightgown. It was blue and wrapped carefully in white tissue with a tiny flowered lavender sachet tucked into its folds.

I was ten or eleven when Mother first showed me the nightgown. I thought it was the most beautiful, most elegant thing I'd ever seen. "Your father gave this to me; I'm saving it for when I go to the hospital some day," she would say quietly, as if to herself. Every now and then if I happened to be around when the dresser drawer was open, she'd let me look at the gown. I would run my fingers over it lightly, and we would joke about the slim chances of its ever being worn.

"You're never sick, Mom. You'll never wear this nightgown if you wait for the hospital," I would scold gently.

She would smile and say firmly, "It's too good for every day."

In truth, there was no occasion special enough—in or out of a hospital—for her to have worn such a nightgown. I eventually learned that it was not because the gown was too good but rather that my mother did not feel entitled to wear it. That kept her from ever knowing its elegance next to her skin.

I think there must have been a time, before I was born, when she might have believed otherwise, when she was a "heartbreaker," according to her high school yearbook. I imagine that in 1936 she might have danced and swirled in a filmy, blue nightgown to seduce my handsome teenage father, as she flirted with her wide brown eyes and sweet smile. I imagine she might have sung him a love song in her rich alto voice or sat quietly holding his hand and sharing dreams. She was young and seemingly invulnerable, even to her alcoholic father's rages and her mother's sudden death in that same year. And she had my father, who was suffering his own pain, his parents' divorce and the humiliating poverty that followed. They had each other back then, and I doubt that entitlement entered her mind.

The nightgown remained in the bottom drawer for the next thirty-some years, disturbed only when it was packed up and moved a few times. Finally, it was moved to a small apartment and into the bottom drawer of an early-American dresser, taken from my parents' bedroom. By now, my mother had long since stopped dancing and flirting. Years of betrayal and conflict had dimmed the light in those brown eyes, and divorce had left her alone, depressed and bitter. She functioned well enough—found a job, developed a small circle of women friends, traveled occasionally to visit my sisters, even remarried briefly. She loved her grandchildren and the Pittsburgh Steelers and her devoted cat Poppy. But she had clearly given up caring deeply about her life and her dreams. It was in this resignation and unresolved grief that my mother's cancer was born.

I want to write about the times my mother did go to the hospital and wore only regulation gowns, about the horror of watching the IVs of crippling medicine flow into her veins, medicine that would prolong her deteriorating life by only six months. I want to write complaint after complaint about how indifferent and incompetent her doctor and the nursing staff seemed, how insensitive I believed the entire world was being to my dying mother. But that would take me away from the story that matters more, the one about my mother's lost and then found sense of entitlement.

It happened one night early on in the series of chemotherapy treatments, which were fairly routine but required an overnight hospital stay for observation. By now my mother's body had become weakened by days and nights of severe nausea and vomiting. When we got to her room, we found a team of doctors and nurses tending to her roommate, who was in apparent cardiac arrest. While the medical staff ran back and forth past Mother's bed, I helped her settle in to wait for the chemo IV. Occasionally, a nurse would stop by to verify why Mother was there; occasionally, still another nurse would stop by to see if someone had stopped by yet, presumably to set up the IV. Three hours passed. Our shared abilities to find humor in bad situations were tapped. Although the woman in the next bed was now stable, this good news had no positive effect whatsoever on the level of care Mother was getting. Then a nurse came into the room to say that Mother's chart had been lost and they were waiting for her doctor to call back. Again, we waited. At last, a different nurse came into the room. She said to Mother, "We still haven't heard from the doctor. Do you happen to remember what color the medicine is that goes into your IV?"

The question hung in the room for a moment. Mother stammered, "Well, I think it was blue . . ."

I jumped from my chair.

"What color is it?" I said, "What *color* is it?"

Mother patted my hand, a clenched fist. She looked so tiny and frail in that oversized bed. It broke my heart. I turned to the phone and started dialing the doctor's answering service. I handed the phone to mother to wait for a connection and left the room, furious, looking for anyone who resembled a doctor on duty. I approached two residents in the hallway and launched into my problem. Before I could finish, one of the residents put his hand on my shoulder and said, "Look, dear, I'm not your mother's physician; you'll just have to wait . . ."

I jerked away from him as if touched by a hot wire.

"Don't you *dare* call me dear!" I said, feeling faint with outrage.

I returned to the room, shaking. Mother was talking to the doctor on the phone. She said, "What do you mean, my values are misplaced?"

I watched her brown eyes flicker with anger. She sat up on the edge of the bed. In that moment, something in each of us seemed to click. I went to the closet and got Mother's clothes and began dressing her, first the socks, then slacks, then the blouse. She moved her legs and arms cooperatively and shifted her butt when needed, still holding the phone to her ear. The flicker in her eyes began twinkling, the hint of a smile forming. I packed up her few toiletries and got her coat, as she slammed down the phone.

"He told me my values are misplaced," she said. "He said I should be willing to go through a little inconvenience to prolong my life. He told me I'm being childish. Can you believe that?"

"Easily," I said.

It was well past midnight and we had been in the hospital for hours. "Mom," I said, "let's get the hell out of here."

I held her coat as she put her arms through the sleeves. "I'm ready," she said.

I found a wheelchair in the hallway and helped Mother into the seat. I tucked my coat around her legs and piled the overnight bag and our purses on her lap. She gripped the handles of all three bags until her thin knuckles turned white. She looked up at me, her face illuminated by a full smile. "Let's go," she said.

Halfway down the hall, the nursing supervisor stepped in front of the wheelchair. "Where do you think you're going?" she demanded of us both.

"I'm going *home*," my mother said quietly and firmly.

"You're going home? And just why are you going home in the middle of the night like this?" the supervisor demanded even more loudly.

Mother locked glares with the nurse for a moment. Then she said, just as quietly and firmly as before, "Because I've had enough of this crap."

For the second time that night, a sentence hung in the air. The nurse stepped aside. I patted Mother's shoulder approvingly, and we flew to the elevator door and into the chilly April night.

Following my mother's death a year later, I found the blue nightgown in her bottom drawer. The lace felt stiffer than I had remembered, and the tissue had yellowed some, but the lavender scent was still strong as I held the gown to my face for a long time. Then I placed it into a plastic trash bag designated for Goodwill. I did not want a keepsake that my mother had seen as too good for her. I thought back to those wonderful moments after we left the hospital that April night.

When we had gotten a safe distance away, I pulled into the parking lot of a fast food restaurant, and we collapsed into tearful, hysterical laughter. While I stuffed myself excitedly with french fries and Mother tried to swallow a milkshake, we relived the night, minute by bizarre minute, and savored our triumph—over the system maybe, maybe even over death and, although neither of us spoke it, I think we knew we were also savoring, for this brief, shining hour, my mother's triumph over resignation and depression and bitterness, and over all of the unresolved pain of generations before her.

Alicia Nordan

Climb On

Accept challenges, so that you may feel the exhilaration of victory.

George S. Patton

At a workshop recently I was asked to make a list of all the gifts I had received that made a difference in my life. What a task! To sort through my past for the many wonderful gifts of encouragement, of understanding, of real physical or financial assistance, of listening, and of good advice, is to acknowledge the many people who have given me a hand along the way. A gift I received from my daughter Lacy last summer stands out as especially heartfelt.

It was a soft June morning when she called me and said cheerily, "Hi, Mom, you want to go rock climbing?" I longed to go rock climbing. I was just a few months past abdominal surgery for cancer and still regaining my physical strength and emotional equilibrium. I was not sure I could climb a small hill, let alone a big rock. Because I trust her so deeply and because she made it seem fine to go along, I decided to do it.

We ordered picnic lunches and drove to the base of our

climbing site. We loaded up with gear—big, impressive-looking blue and purple climbing ropes, harnesses, an assortment of carabiners, special climbers' shoes, helmets, the lunches, water and insect repellent. We hiked up a road and cut into the woods along an overgrown trail. It was hot, and I was working hard—harder than I dreamed I could. I stopped often to catch my breath, but it felt great to be out in the early morning sun, tramping through woods that echoed with birdcalls. I was glad to be alive.

Rose Ledge is a beautiful site deep in the woods and perfect for beginning climbs. The ledge looked awfully high to me, but Lacy and Connie set up the climb with great energy and efficiency. Lacy anchored our ropes to trees above the ledge and dropped them straight down where they landed at my feet. She set up the safety system known as belaying and tested it out. I watched and ate a cookie.

To ready ourselves for climbing we stretched a bit, then did "bouldering" on smaller rocks. This meant clambering around on rocks while Lacy "spotted" me, standing close to break my fall if needed. Bouldering was hard for me and scary, too, even though I was only a few feet off the ground. I did love the feel of the solidness of rock as I wedged a toe here and found a hand-hold there.

I stepped into the big black harness, tightened the waist, and donned a helmet. I was then fastened to Lacy by a rope that could be loosened or tightened as I climbed. Lacy, the belayer, was tied in and anchored at the bottom tree and, because of this system, I could not fall. *At least that is the theory,* I thought, as I struggled to get my breath.

"Ready to climb, Mom?" Lacy chirped. I wanted to shout out a resounding "Ready!" but what came out was more like the pathetic meow of the cat when he wants his breakfast. "Yeow," I said in a hoarse whisper.

Then came the series of questions and responses

between climber and belayer, me and Lacy, to make sure we were communicating and the safety system was working. When it is all secure, the climber says, "Climbing," and the belayer says, "Climb on!"

The first few steps weren't that hard, and I was well off the ground and mighty pleased with myself when I stopped the first time. I was safely wedged into the chimney we had chosen as a first effort. As I climbed higher, the footholds became toeholds, the hand-holds finger-holds, and I was suddenly scared. I stopped.

"I'm scared. I can't go any higher," I called down.

"That's fine, Mom, just rest right there. Remember I've got you," she called back. I took some deep breaths and snuck a look. Oh goodness, I was far from the bottom and nowhere near the top. I wanted to complete that climb so badly I could taste it. "Now what?" I yelled out.

"You're doing great, Mom, just great," Lacy said. I blinked back tears and swallowed hard. Lacy gave me specific instructions and with my heart hammering away, I did just what she said, and before I knew it, I was up further than I ever imagined I could go. Elated by this realization, I scrambled up the last of the climb using feet, knees, elbows, hands, back and sheer determination. I let out a loud "Eeeee haaaa!" when I got to the top. Lacy was laughing and yelling, "You made it, Mom, you did it!"

I was euphoric and giddy with achievement—but wait: I realized with a nasty jolt that I now had to get down again.

There were two ways to go down. I could climb down: hard and slow but safe. Or I could rappel down: glide down while gently bouncing off the wall of the rock. That required a leap of faith because I had to lean back into the harness and let myself go. I had to trust the system we created totally.

It is a heart-stopping thrill to fall backwards into space, let me tell you. After a few mini-falls, I was back on the ground and said loudly and with great confidence, "Off belay!" And Lacy, my beautiful daughter, responded as quietly as a prayer, "Belay off."

Eating lunch, I was famished, exhausted and exhilarated all at once. Through the rest of the warm summer afternoon, I rested and watched Lacy and the others climb. We walked back to the truck in companionable silence as the accomplishments of the day sank in. That day Lacy took such good care of me. She provided for me: lunch, safety, cheer and an opportunity to have what I have always loved best: an adventure. She taught me everything I needed to know about climbing that rock, she provided my physical and emotional safety and she cheered me on. Something deep inside my chest shifted as I experienced a powerful turning of the cosmic coin. Lacy was giving me what I had always worked to give her.

It was months later when I felt another piece of this experience settle into place. At the same workshop, I was asked to discover what the gifts said about me. If the gifts were a kind of mirror, what did they reflect?

This gift reflected a mother who provided safety while encouraging my daughter to climb higher. Since Lacy always has, I must have done my part. Now when either of us faces a difficult challenge we say to the other, "Climbing," and know the response will be, "Climb on."

Judy Henning

Heave Ho

Changes are not only possible and predictable, but to deny them is to be an accomplice to one's own necessary vegetation.

Gail Sheehy

Well, I'm not a lot of the things I used to be, but I'm sure of a lot of things I didn't used to be. Some of those things are good, some bad, some are just what they are, different. Like they say: nothing ever stays the same.

MS (multiple sclerosis) has become a part of who I am, just a part. Having lived with the culprit for over half of my life, I'm getting used to the adversities presented to me. I've learned that laughter can go a long way in dealing with hardships and difficulties. It seems as if my life is becoming quite a comic routine!

The other day my daughter came to get me. Driving is one thing I don't do anymore. Since she had no lift in her SUV, it was determined I would take my wheelchair instead of my motorized scooter. That wasn't the problem. The problem was her vehicle.

We'd recently moved into the neighborhood and had

not gotten acquainted with our neighbors. Of all days, the neighbors across the street were out in the front visiting with company. They are a young couple with two little girls. And I am an old lady. I don't feel like an old lady, but that's beside the point. To a young couple, I'm an old lady. Well, really to be truthful, a fat old lady.

My daughter has an Eddie Bauer Ford Expedition, whatever that is. It looks like a green tank when you're an old lady, especially when you're an old lady in a wheel-chair. She pushed me up next to that monster, and I eye-balled it and knew that this was going to be one gigantic challenge. "Now, Ronda, this is not going to be easy," I comment.

"We can do it," she says.

Oh sure, I think to myself, *what is this we stuff?*

"Just put your foot up here, and get a hold of that."

"Oh yeah, sure!"

"Come on, I'll help you," she assures me.

She takes my foot and places it on the running board or whatever in the world they call them these days—that's what they called them in my day.

"Now get a hold of that strap up there, Mom, and pull!"

This is where I begin to snicker and my foot slips off whatever that dang thing my foot was on. She lets out a giggle behind me, and we start all over again. Now my daughter is a petite little thing and I am, well—old. We get my foot up on that thing again, I grab hold and holler, "Shove!" She gives me a nudge, and I holler again, "I said shove!" She starts laughing and down I come! By this time, we are both laughing and creating quite a scene.

"Now, Ronda, you have to butt your shoulder to me and shove hard, like your dad does," I say between my laugh-ter and her giggles. "Don't be afraid to push hard."

I have plenty of padding so it's not like she was going to hurt herself on my bones or anything. A big part of my body is numb so it wasn't like I could feel her bouncing off my blubber either. So we began again.

"I don't want to hurt you, Mom," she giggles.

"Don't worry; you're not going to hurt me; your dad does it all the time," I assure her. My comments don't bring any sympathy, just more giggles. As we start again she gets serious and so do I, as I become aware that I am making quite an impression on our neighbors.

"Now shove!" I scream.

"Heave ho!" she shouts.

We both break out in hysterical laughter as the steering wheel gets acquainted with my face, leaving my feet and legs sticking out the door. I'm prone on the front seat and the neighbors are getting free entertainment. By this time my face is in excruciating pain, not from the steering wheel, but from the muscles being strained from so much laughter. Ronda helps me, and I finally get pushed, pulled and tucked into my seat, and we drive away leaving my neighbors wondering about the circus act that has moved in across the street.

Yeah, things have changed, I've changed; nothing ever stays the same, not even circus acts. I hope my neighbors are prepared, because I've become a three-ringer!

Betty A. King

Fifteen-Minute Rule

When my mother and grandmother moved in with me, I believed with all my heart that we could make whatever sacrifices were necessary, for I loved them both dearly. They were both widowed within six months of each other and it just seemed the natural thing to do. Being divorced and raising a young daughter by myself, I thought it would be nice having the extra family around. Maybe ours wasn't a typical family setting, but it was our family, and there was much love and laughter in our home.

There were concessions to be made and boundaries to be outlined, but by far our biggest obstacle has been—the laundry. Four women don't have too much laundry unless one of them is thirteen. Mother was "in charge" of the laundry, as we each had our own assigned household chores and responsibilities. As my daughter, Sara, entered her teens, she picked up the belief of most teenage girls that she needed to change her attire at least fifteen times a day. Now, this wouldn't have been such a problem except for laundry day.

Mom went on a rampage and tried to explain to Sara that it was okay to change clothes so often, but followed with these instructions: "If they aren't dirty, don't put them in the laundry room. Just hang them back up." Every laundry day I heard the same shriek from the washroom: "I'm not washing clean clothes!"

Weeks went by, and the problem escalated with each load of laundry, until Mom finally laid down the law with her official definition of "dirty." "If you didn't wear it more than fifteen minutes, it isn't dirty! So hang it back up!" she screamed.

As crazy as it sounds, this declaration seemed to work. Laundry day was no longer a shouting match. The piles of clothes in the washroom became smaller each week, much to my mother's great satisfaction.

One morning after a teenage slumber party, I arose early to meet Mom in the kitchen for coffee. I found her leaning over the cabinet laughing so hard the tears were streaming down her face.

"What's so funny this early in the morning?" I grumbled. I'm not a morning person, so it has to be pretty good to get a chuckle out of me this early in the day. Yet, here was my mother, holding herself in stitches with uncontrollable laughter. She was laughing so hard, she couldn't even answer me. Every time she tried to speak, she got tickled all over again and finally she just handed me the bowl that had been sitting on the kitchen cabinet.

Inside this very large stainless steel bowl was a note in my daughter's handwriting that said simply, "Memaw, is this dirty? It only had popcorn in it for about fifteen minutes."

Ferna Lary Mills

You Have to Try, Mom

*Everyone who has ever done a kind deed for us,
or spoken one word of encouragement to us, has
entered into the make-up of our character and
of our thoughts, as well as our success.*

George Burton Adams

Krista didn't suspect anything at first. After all, her elderly Korean mother had survived the death of her husband five years before. Krista missed her father, too, yet she thought Mom had done pretty well. But her hardworking mom had never mastered English in the twenty-plus years she had lived in the United States. When the police pulled her mom over and took away her driver's license, Krista wanted to attribute it to her mother's poor English. However, when her mom threw "the fit" in the bank, she knew things were bad. Then the convalescent home kicked her out after two weeks because she fought with other patients. With Krista's husband's reluctant consent, her mom moved in with them.

"Honey," said the husband one day, "Your mother is losing it. She glued the kids' school papers on the wall today."

Krista didn't know what to say. As the honorable daughter it was her duty to take care of her mother as the mother had done for her all these years.

Now and again the mom even forgot Krista's name.

"Mom, you have to try," an exasperated Krista pled. "You have to try to remember things."

The elderly mom's slow decline took its toll on the family. Nerves frayed, arguments arose, tempers flew and Krista's two small children cried frequently. Slowly Krista's mom withered away until one day she breathed her last breath. The family picked up the pieces of their lives. But one thing bothered Krista. Maybe it was a strange thing, she thought, but she didn't want the bed her mother died in to be in the house. When her husband went off to work and the kids to school, Krista decided to take the bed apart. As she pulled the mattresses off the box spring, she found a child's red notebook inside, a notebook that had been reported missing for some time.

What the heck is this doing here? she said to herself as she opened the book. Inside it, written in beautiful Korean, every page from top to bottom read the same:

Krista is my daughter's name.
Krista is my daughter's name.
Krista is my daughter's name.
Krista is my daughter's name.
Krista is my daughter's name.

Paul Karrer

The Death I Shared with My Mother

There came a time when the risk to remain tight in the bud was more painful than the risk it took to blossom

Anaïs Nin

It was very hard for me to explain why I spent so much time in psychotherapy. In my thirties and forties, I was successful and mostly happy. I had wonderful parents, a fascinating career, a terrific marriage, a lovely child. I lived comfortably, although we never seemed to have enough money—but we never let that interfere with theatre, travel, buying paintings and records. And, how remarkable, I had a happier childhood than most of my friends and colleagues. When I met my future husband, he wrote me, "Your parents sound fascinating. I picture a dinner party at your house, with Madame Chiang Kai-shek and Churchill having a heated discussion in the living room." Slightly exaggerated, but not far off. My parents were socialists, had dozens of interesting friends, worked for improving the world at important jobs. My father was a gentle philosopher, my mother a turbulent poet. Most of the time they understood me, being part of the first generation to be studying Freud.

What was wrong with this picture? Every so often I would feel depressed, dying for chocolate, feeling unattractive, unpopular, self-conscious. When I look back now I marvel at how many good friends and loving teachers there were. I was nominated for president of the student council, almost valedictorian (only boys won in those days) and editor of the school magazine. My closest friends today, I've had for seventy years!

In many years of therapy, with several therapists, I discovered the roots of my problem. Because I'd been truly loved, I could dare to face my childhood, and what I discovered was that I was profoundly tied to my mother, and that I had been getting a message from her all my life, that she was and had been a very bad child and a failure as an adult. I began to understand that her feelings of unworthiness were as crazy as mine. She was a pioneer. She wrote two books and dozens of articles helping parents to understand their children. Although she and my father had a happy marriage, enjoying traveling, the theatre and music together—she also had occasional rages; times when she criticized me unmercifully—screaming at me to clean up my room, nagging me constantly about my appearance. I began to understand the confusion of feelings and how my mother was transmitting some strange and profound double messages.

And then I wrote a book to help children deal with the death of a parent. Having become a child psychologist, I understood many of the special problems—the irrational feelings of having been a bad child, intense feelings of rejection, anger at the dead parents, enormous portions of guilt and anxiety.

I mentioned this project to an aunt who had been almost a sister to my mother. She was the family historian.

She presented me with a few pages of a diary kept by my great-grandfather. They were written the day my grandmother died in childbirth. My mother was four years old. The family gathered all day in great sorrow. My grandmother was twenty-seven years old, adored by my grandfather, passionately devoted to her little girl. She was desperately ill for a week, and then she died.

My great-grandfather's diary spoke of his anguish at his daughter Eda's death, of her husband's terrible suffering, and then he wrote, "All the family is here, grief-stricken. But Jeannette and Irene [my aunt] are playing so happily, oblivious."

The next day's entry; "Jeannette cried all night with a toothache. My wife told her that her mother was very tired and needed a rest so she was taking a vacation."

The mystery of our two lives—my mother and me—was solved. No one explained Eda's disappearance or talked about her. My grandfather and my mother moved into the home of the great-grandparents. A year later Jeannette was playing on the stoop of the brownstone house and she heard two neighbors talking about her, "poor little orphan." She raced screaming into the house and was finally told the truth. For a year she had thought her mother "left her for a vacation." (From her, of course.)

I knew that no one had ever told my four-year-old mother, but what she came to believe was that people leave you when you are bad. If she had been good, and really loved, her mother wouldn't suddenly disappear. It was also very naughty to be angry.

By the time I had enough insight, my mother and I had a hard time talking about it, but she liked my book. She was aware of her suffering. She even wrote about it. I had great compassion for the bright, lovable little girl whose world had suddenly caved in. I understood our feelings of unworthiness—she had fed it to me by emotional osmosis!

Now I am seventy-six. My mother died at seventy-eight. For the first time I understand another dimension of her deprivation. I look like my mother before she died. I have thin hair, but it's not white. My hands are exactly like hers—age spots and all. My teeth came out from the same areas as she lost hers. All my various diseases of aging are exactly like hers. Our talents are the same as well as our feelings. As I look in a mirror, I see her face. The comfort of old age is I am still so much a part of her. I knew her, saw her, all my growing years. And then it came to me. She never really knew what her mother looked like, how she spoke, how she loved her. There are very few pictures—Eda was so young. My mother grew old without any sense of connection, without ever knowing what I know, that my mother and I were connected in appearance, personality and that the closer I will come to my own death, the more I feel my mother is with me. And she's an adorable four years old, an emotionally wrecked child, an adult who created a marvelous life in spite of her suffering. How I wish we could sit down together, talk about her triumph over pain. I'd tell her that if her mother had lived she'd probably have looked like Aunt Carrie and Aunt Irene, both talented writers, creative women, one a playwright. And she surely would have loved her mother as much as I did.

Eda LeShan

5

LESSONS

Never grow a wishbone, daughter, where a backbone ought to be.

Clementine Paddleford

A Cup of Coffee

You cannot plan the future by the past.

Edmund Burke

I heated up a cup of coffee today in the microwave. I wasn't sure if I should laugh or cry as I stood there holding the steaming cup for the second time this morning. My son woke up crying, and it took nearly an hour of singing, consoling and rocking to get him back to sleep. In the meantime, my coffee got cold. So, I heated it up in the microwave.

I grew up vowing never to be like my mother. She is a wonderful, strong woman, and anyone would be proud to be like her. But I wasn't going to be. No one in town seemed to know her name. To the teachers and students at the various schools her children attended, she was simply known as ____'s mom (fill in the blank with any one of her five children's names). At the grocery stores and around the auto parts stores and hardware places, they affectionately called her "Mrs. Dale" after my father's first name; and the folks at the bank, utility companies and other such important places addressed her with Dad's last name, as Mrs. Keffer. Mom answered to all of these with a smile and kind words.

I, on the other hand, was never as gracious about it. Often, I would tell the bagger at the grocery store, "Her name is Joyce, by the way," as he handed her the bag and told her to have a nice day using one of the aforementioned names. Mom would always smile and say, "You have a good day, too," as she shot me the mind-your-manners-I-taught-you-better-than-that look. When we would then get to the car, I would bicker at her for not standing up for herself. "You are your own person," I would retort. "You're not just an extension of Dad."

"I could be called a lot worse," she would always reply. "Besides, everyone knows your dad."

Everyone in this small town did know my dad. He was a friendly, hard-working man who liked to flirt with the checkout girls and give car advice to anyone who needed it. He could charm his way out of a speeding ticket and talk his way into a better deal with ease. He would not think twice about fixing a broken part on one of the neighbor kid's bikes. Or leaving in the middle of a cold winter night to change a frightened teen's flat tire.

But everyone knew my mom, too. While Dad was a great man in the community, Mom was equally special. She had her own way of talking herself into a good deal, and she loved to give friendly advice to people she met. When she would wake up on cold, snowy mornings to a house full of college kids who had been stranded in town, she would weave her way through the sleeping bodies and fix enough pancakes for all. If anyone was in need, my mom was right in the thick of the fight to help. She would collect items for a family who lost all in a house fire, canned goods for the church pantry, and clothes for a teen mother's baby when no one else would help.

As a teen, I never understood my mom. How could

someone with so much to offer the world be content to stay home and be known as an adjunct to her husband or as someone's mother? Why wasn't she proud of who she was? Once upon a time, she wanted to be a nurse and join the Peace Corps. How could anyone give up her dreams for washing out dirty diapers and packing my father's bologna sandwiches?

All I knew was that this was not going to happen to me. I had big dreams of making a difference in the world—but with a bang, not a whimper. People would know me. I planned on working my way up through the ranks of the YMCA with a busy writing career on the side. My husband, if there was one, would be right behind me and, as for children, they would be cute and at their nanny's side. I would not be like my mother—I would be me. And people would know me as someone important.

Now here I was heating up my cup of coffee in the microwave for the second time. Just as I had watched her do a million times after setting it down to pack a lunch, feed the cats, tie a shoe, retrieve a towel from the dryer, find a paper that needed returning to school, answer the phone and a million other possible interruptions. I dreamed of downing a good café latte for breakfast before another busy day at the office, and here I was drinking instant mocha from a "Happy Birthday" mug with colored balloons all over it.

I understand now. I understood eight months ago as I held my son for the first time. I understood when his tiny little hand wrapped around my finger and his big blue eyes looked into mine as he drifted off to sleep. I understood when the love I have for my husband tripled as I first saw the little body cuddled in his big, strong arms and saw the tears streak down his face. I understood it all instantly.

I look forward to the day that I will be known as Andrew's

mom to the people in town and the children at school. Every day, as my husband returns home from work and his face lights up as his son holds out his hands, I am proud to be Mrs. Frank Huff. Just like my mom is proud to be called Mrs. Dale Keffer. Just like my mom. Those are four words that I thought I would never say proudly.

By the way, if you see her, her name is Joyce.

And now I need to heat up my coffee again.

Barb Huff

"You don't need a job, Mom. I'm your career!"

Perfect Vision

There are two things to aim at in life: first, to get what you want; and after that, to enjoy it. Only the wisest of mankind achieve the second.

Logan Pearsall Smith

My twin daughters have finally reached the age of two. And this means two things. First, they have control over language. Second, they have control over their bladders. In light of these latest acquisitions, one of their favorite pastimes recently has been to insult each other employing a combination of these newfound skills.

My darling girls now run around shouting, or just stating conversationally, "I pee on you!" followed by an illustrative, higher pitched, "PEE!" I honestly don't know where the seed that sprouted into this less-than-charming behavior came from. (Unless it was the isolated incident where an undiapered baby brother spritzed one of the girls in the head with, well, maybe you can guess. To say the least, it made quite an impression.)

Mostly, they say this to each other when they're bickering. Or sometimes when they're just plain bored. It is, happily, an idle threat unaccompanied by any action other than thrusting one's stomach out at the insulted party during the "PEE!" part.

In the privacy of our own home, and behind their backs, my husband and I are gently amused by our daughters' urinary shenanigans. However, this isn't exactly the type of conversation I'd say we encourage. Aside from the obvious objections, this one's got a high parental embarrassment factor. A public exhibition is bound to raise a few questioning eyebrows.

But it seems as if there are many things that two-year-olds do that don't need a lot of encouragement, and in my experience, they are frequently the very things that you would rather not have your offspring doing or saying in public. And with two two-year-old daughters, plus a one-year-old son, being the current equation of my life, I have ample opportunity to experience this particular phenomenon firsthand. Further, I'll have to admit that there are days when it feels as if the sum of this equation will be the loss of my desire to venture ever again into a public space.

Yes, with three kids under three years you greatly increase your odds that any given excursion into the public domain will involve loud conversations about bodily functions, declarations of nasal contents and the canvassing of total strangers to ascertain their anatomical correctness. This verbal barrage will likely serenade the complete devastation of at least one display or teaser table, and the attempted consumption of the (non-edible and expensive) merchandise displayed thereon.

It is also extremely likely there will be whining, followed by a smattering of biting and hair-pulling, and a diaper bypass (or two or three), which will then be combined with excessive trips to the potty, leading to the need for new "big girl" pants anyway. These will have been accidentally left at home by yours truly. Hold the applause, please.

And that's all on a good day.

Believe me, I receive more than my fair share of stares, unhelpful comments and looks from passersby. So, my plate's full. And I try to limit the accretion of potentially embarrassing additions to it, such as shouts about voiding one's bladder on a sibling. But, of course, my kids have other ideas. And sometimes, it's these other ideas that teach me most about what being a parent is really all about.

Take, for example, last week at the drug store. Busily engaged seeking shampoo, it suddenly filters into to my brain that my twins are once again having their little "conversation." And have been for some time.

"I pee on you. Pee!" is countered by, "NO! I pee on *you!* Pee!"

They go back and forth and back and forth, as only two-year-olds can manage. It was actually a quiet discussion, and relatively civil, but I looked around furtively to see if anyone was eavesdropping.

It was then that I noticed two little old ladies staring at me. Lovely ladies, quintessential grandmotherly women, proper, upright pillars of the community they were. Ladies you'd like to drink tea and eat crumpets with, not offend by exposure to your overly bladder-minded toddlers.

They started slowly walking toward us purposefully and I could tell they meant to say something. *Oh great,* I thought, inwardly cringing, *just what I need.*

The oldest lady, a dear woman with a frail gray bun and a sturdy walker, reached me first. She bent over, peered at my daughters, and stuck a crooked finger out at them. My heart sank. Embarrassment aside, I rallied to defend my children from the onslaught of a stranger.

But she looked up, beaming. "I just wanted to tell you," she said "you have the two *most* precious little girls in this stroller! They are just beautiful, and so well-behaved!"

Her friend was nodding in agreement.

It was then that I noticed their hearing aids.

I was actually blushing, thinking, *Ladies, if you only knew what these precious girls have been discussing for the past ten minutes.* But then I smiled, and agreed, and thanked her because, of course, what she had said *was* true. I thought of the many times that my own "deaf ear" would serve my children and myself well.

"Oh, and look at the beautiful baby in the backpack!" They cooed over my son for a second.

Then one of them asked, "Are they all yours?"

I get this question a lot, but it is frequently worded more like "Are *all* these children *yours?*" and asked in a tone that implies that if the answer is "yes," then I should have my head examined. I nodded my head in the affirmative, or maybe my son nodded it for me, as he was, at that moment, ripping out handfuls of my hair.

Both their faces lit up at my answer, "Oh! What a blessing to have *such* a beautiful family!" one said.

"Yes, you're very lucky indeed," the other added.

They both smiled and sighed.

"Enjoy them. They grow up too fast."

Despite the day I'd been having, I knew I had just experienced great wisdom from women who knew a thing or two; women with impaired hearing but perfect vision. These women didn't need to see (or hear) the nitty-gritty sometimes-less-than-pretty details of life with toddlers. They had very likely been there themselves. And what they now saw was the forest, where I sometimes still only see the trees.

They saw the truth.

And that truth has become my four-sentence mantra, my reminder that the "I pee on you" days will not last forever. It's a bittersweet benediction.

"I am lucky."
"I am blessed."
"Enjoy them."
"They grow up too fast."

Karen Driscoll

A Fib and the Matinee

Faultfinding without suggestions for improvement is a waste of time.

Ralph C. Smedley

I was six years old and my sister, Sally Kay, was a submissive three. For some reason, I thought we needed to earn some money. I decided we should "hire out" as maids. We visited the neighbors, offering to clean house for them for a quarter.

Reasonable as our offer was, there were no takers. But one neighbor telephoned Mother to let her know what Mary Alice and Sally Kay were doing. Mother had just hung up the phone when we came bursting through the back door, into the kitchen of our apartment.

"Girls," Mother asked, "Why were you two going around the neighborhood telling people you would clean their houses?"

Mother wasn't angry with us. In fact, we learned afterwards, she was amused that we had come up with such an idea. But, for some reason, we both denied having done any such thing. Shocked and terribly hurt that her dear little girls could be such "bold-faced liars," Mother then told us that Mrs. Jones had just called to tell her we had been to her house and said we would clean it for a quarter.

Faced with the truth, we admitted what we had done. Mother said that we had "fibbed." We had not told the truth. She was sure that we knew better. She tried to explain why a fib hurt, but she didn't feel that we really understood.

Years later, she told us that the "lesson" she came up with for trying to teach us to be truthful would probably have been frowned upon by child psychologists. The idea came to her in a flash . . . and our tender-hearted mother told us it was the most difficult lesson she ever taught us. It was a lesson we never forgot.

After admonishing us, Mother cheerfully began preparing for lunch. As we munched on sandwiches, she asked, "Would you two like to go to the movies this afternoon?"

"Wow! Would we ever!" We wondered what movie would be playing. Mother said "the matinee." Oh, fantastic! We would be going to "the matinee"! Weren't we lucky? We got bathed and all dressed up. It was like getting ready for a birthday party. We hurried outside the apartment, not wanting to miss the bus that would take us downtown. On the landing, Mother stunned us by saying, "Girls, we are not going to the movies today."

We didn't hear her right. "What?" we objected. "What do you mean? Aren't we going to the matinee? Mommy, you said we were going to go to the matinee!"

Mother stooped and gathered us in her arms. I couldn't understand why there were tears in her eyes. We still had time to get the bus. But hugging us, she gently explained that this was what a fib felt like.

"It is important that what we say is true," Mother said. "I fibbed to you just now, and it felt awful to me. I don't ever want to fib again, and I'm sure you don't want to fib again either. People must be able to believe each other. Do you understand?"

We assured her that we understood. We would never forget.

And since we had learned the lesson, why not go on to the matinee? There was still time.

"Not today," Mother told us. We would go another time.

That is how, over fifty years ago, my sister and I learned to be truthful. We have never forgotten how much a fib can hurt.

Mary Alice Dress Baumgardner

The Littlest Daughter

The proverb warns that, "You should not bite the hand that feeds you." But maybe you should, if it prevents you from feeding yourself.

Thomas Szasz

They were a happy family: four Pogue daughters all in the same school in different grades. They were talented and friendly girls. The youngest, Janice, who was in my class, seemed to be glued to her mother's skirts. The three older girls took the bus to school every morning and gaily rushed to their classrooms, but Janice was always driven to school by her mother, arriving just in time for the kindergarten morning song. Her mother usually stayed around until Janice seemed to be content and was involved in some activity, and then she would tiptoe out. But she would return in time to take Janice home.

One Friday, Janice's mother called and asked for a conference with me. She entered in an agitated and fragile way. She almost seemed to wring her hands in distress. She said in a too-soft voice, "My husband is going to Europe on business for two weeks, and he insists that I go with him. I have tried to explain over and over that Janice needs me here. But he is equally adamant that she will be fine without me so I have no choice; I have to go. I have told the babysitter that she is to drive her every morning and watch her until she is settled into the classroom. She has explicit instructions about picking her up and getting to school early so Janice won't worry. Will you please give Janice special attention and help her during this time of our separation? We have never been apart a single day since she was born five years ago. She is so young and fragile, and I want to be sure everything goes well for her."

She stopped for a quick breath, but I stepped in and assured her that we would make every effort to support Janice and see that she was happy and healthy while her mother was away. I even volunteered to meet Janice at her car so she would see a familiar face. Janice's mother thanked me for our understanding and reassurance. As she left we talked about the logistics of watching for Janice and agreed that it would present some extra effort on my part but was worth the time it might take.

Monday morning, anticipating a tearful, anxious child, I planned a special program of fun and games. I waited outside to greet Janice, but just then the bus arrived and not three, but four Pogue girls got off of it. Janice skipped along joyfully, yelling "good-bye" to her sisters as she ran with two friends into the classroom. I walked slowly into the classroom and called Janice over to ask how the bus ride went. Impatiently she said, "Oh, I always wanted to take the bus with the other kids, but Mother needs to be with me. You see there won't be any more babies, and so I have to be a baby a little longer. While she is away, I'll just ride the bus every day. I am five, you know."

Julie Firman

Chasing Butterflies

The best way to secure future happiness is to be as happy as is rightfully possible today.

Charles W. Eliot

I remember the day well—the turning point in my relationship with my daughter. It began on a hot July morning, the sun beating down upon our small country home. Outside, sitting in the shade of a maple tree, I sketched pictures of my five-year-old daughter, Abigail, as she chased butterflies. Moments like these kept me safe in her world. She was rapidly changing—becoming more and more like the butterflies she'd chase—always in motion. Today, however, I relished being the center of her kingdom and stifled my growing concern that the future would lessen our closeness.

"Look, Mama!" she shouted, waving toward the dirt road. "It's Rachel. Hi, Rachel!" Our neighbor's daughter waved back, and I gasped in disbelief. What had happened to that cute eight-year-old girl selling Girl Scout cookies on my doorstep six years ago? Surely, she isn't this tattered-looking teen sporting an eyebrow ring and purple hair! I watched as Rachel rounded the corner of our yard to head onto a path leading into the woods. She stopped only once to light a cigarette. Even though rumor had it that Rachel and her mother hadn't spoken to each other for two years, I had dismissed the gossip as just that—gossip. Now, after seeing Rachel, I gave it more credibility.

Abigail watched her, too, before turning to me. "Mama, was that a cigarette Rachel had?"

I explained that it was, answering as many questions as I could, but seeing Rachel in her rebellious teenage persona had soured my mood. Insecurities about what the future held for my own daughter and me surfaced. Had I been equipping Abigail with what she'd need to survive in the world? Had I been laying the foundation in these formative years to ward off a relationship disaster such as Rachel's?

"How about if we go swimming?" I suggested, wanting to avoid seeing Rachel again. Abigail shouted in agreement and danced around the yard. Little things made her so happy, and my heart became a camera—freeze-framing every inch of her. At the public pool, she was timid of the water and barely ventured from the baby pool.

"Okay," I told her. "I'm Ariel the Mermaid, and you're Melody, her daughter. We need to go over to the big pool and save Atlantica from Ursula." She hesitated, but then the promise of an exciting new game overcame her apprehension and she galloped toward me.

"Let's go!" she giggled, entwining her petal-soft fingers in mine as we entered the pool.

We played for an eternity, and as she relaxed, I inched her closer to the deep end. Soon, I began to see our lives as that intimidating body of water ahead. If I could teach her to swim, we could stay afloat through life's rough seas.

"Mama!" she cried when she couldn't touch the bottom

any longer. "I don't want to go any further!"

"Trust me," I whispered into her ear, soothing away her fears. "Hold onto my neck and you'll see how much fun we can have together." Her tiny fingers choked me but I continued calming her and soon she relaxed and shouted in glee.

"This is fun, Mama! I'm floating! Whee!" I held on to her waist and spun her around. The water cascaded over her as she imagined herself a real mermaid.

"Mama!" she exclaimed, watching as other children jumped into the pool. "I want to do that. Can you catch me?" I moved her to the pool's concrete edge and lifted her out. She stood there, scared.

"I don't want to do it now," she told me, her face full of anxiety. "What if you don't catch me?"

"I *will* catch you, Abigail," I said, knowing that this was a monumental minute in our lives. "You must trust me." Our eyes locked and in a split-second, both of our different fears became one. She was so much like me. From the way she ate a Snickers bar to the way she comforted her dolls—I'd witnessed so much of myself in my daughter.

"Honey, I know that you're scared. Even Mama gets scared sometimes."

"What scares you?" she blurted, her tone suggesting that mothers were never afraid of anything.

"Well, right now, I'm scared that you won't trust me," I confessed. A flurry of emotions crossed her beautiful features as she digested my words. And then, in a moment frozen in time, she closed her eyes and jumped off of the ledge. I hadn't expected it so soon, but then I seized the God-given opportunity and reached out for her. My hands clasped around her wet body, and I pulled her toward me—safe and secure.

"Mama! You did it!" she shouted, kissing my face. "I trusted you, and you caught me! Now we both don't have

to be afraid anymore." Her excitement bubbled over.
"Mom, I think we went on an adventure today!"

Her words sparked tearful promises of hope to my soul.
Like the butterflies she would chase—never knowing
which way they'd travel—I realized that an old adage still
proved true. Life is an adventure to be lived and not a
problem to be solved. Somehow, some way, she and I
would get through the difficult seasons of life.

Later, after we'd pulled into our driveway, Abigail
jumped out of the van and squealed in delight. Running
over to the bush her father had planted to attract butterflies, she giggled and waved at me.

"Mama! Do you see them?" she asked, pointing at the
brightly colored insects fluttering over the bush's blossoms. I nodded, capturing her enthusiasm and tucking it
safely inside my heart. *We're going to be just fine,* I thought,
smiling as my daughter turned away from me to begin
chasing butterflies.

Karen Majoris-Garrison

The Rag Doll

Recently, my ten-year-old daughter Holly was enrolled in a course given by the local historical society. It was called "Colonial Mornings" and was offered to young ladies between the ages of eight and twelve. Each Saturday morning, the girls assembled at an old restored colonial mansion to learn about the everyday lives of girls of the 1700s. Week by week, they were exposed to sewing and cooking, music and dancing, and arts and crafts of the period. Holly enjoyed the program tremendously and also the friendships she developed, and she hated to see it end.

For the grand finale, the teachers arranged for an expert to set up and conduct a formal English high tea, to take place in the old mansion. The girls would be seated at tables properly set with fine bone china and silver flatware characteristic of the time. They would sample different teas and enjoy traditional pastries. For an extra measure of charm and fun, they were encouraged to bring one of their dolls to tea with them.

On the morning of the "tea party," Holly and I made our way to the mansion one last time. We walked up the gravel path that was once a thoroughfare for horse-drawn carriages and entered the stately Georgian brick structure, along with the other girls in her class and their parents.

As we stepped into the dining room, we entered another era. It was resplendent with vases of flowers and colorful china plates and cups. Sunlight filtered through the lace curtains onto lavishly embroidered tablecloths and napkins. Each table showcased a unique teapot, and sparkling crystal bowls held tea bags and brown sugar cubes. The visual impact of the room brought "oohs" and "aahs" from the girls as they eagerly took their seats with their dolls.

Then I noticed something that surprised me somewhat. Each of the other girls at Holly's table had come with a very fancy, expensive-looking doll. They had handmade dolls with creamy, porcelain faces and hands, or collector dolls I'd seen in catalogs and specialty shops. Their starched dresses were trimmed at the necks and hands with lace and tied at the waist with velvet ribbons. They had long, sleek, jet-black hair, golden curls or perfect auburn ringlets. Deep brown and vivid blue eyes shone from rosy-cheeked faces, upon which even the freckles were flawlessly placed. As I surveyed this scene, apprehension crept over me and my throat tightened.

My daughter had brought her rag doll. It had been made from some linen I'd sewn together and stuffed with filler. It wore a little nightgown of calico left over from the curtains I'd made for Holly's room and was cinched at the neck with string. The hair consisted of strands of brown yarn that Holly had painstakingly glued in place to resemble mine. Finally, she had applied the face with Magic Markers, carefully drawing big almond eyes and a slightly crooked smile like my own. Now that face was faded and smeared from many days of sunlight and nights of cuddles and kisses. I was terrified that Holly might feel that her beloved doll was inferior, unworthy, compared to the others.

But with one look at my daughter's face, my fears evaporated. The sparkle of pride never left her eyes as she clutched her treasured toy. In that instant, I had a privileged glimpse into the core of her character. To her, that rag doll was lovelier than any of the others, and why not? The beauty of her own labor and love was cast back at her through that crooked little Magic Marker smile.

Once the girls were all seated, Holly blissfully introduced her doll to the glassy-stared *objects d'art* in her company. She did not show one glint of regret or embarrassment that she had invited her "Mommy Doll" to high tea.

Sandra Schnell

More Than a Pair of Gloves

Character is the architecture of the being.

Louise Nevelson

Albert Einstein once said, "Only a life lived for others is a life worthwhile." These words eloquently describe all that my mother was. She loved and gave unselfishly, despite turmoil in her own life. Struggling to maintain a marriage to an alcoholic and to raise four daughters practically on her own, she still found time to give to others. Life was never easy, but our home was filled as much with laughter and fun as it was with tears, if not more. She passed this love of life, laughter and people on to her daughters and grandchildren.

I recall an incident in grade school when Mom noticed my classmate and her siblings did not have any mittens, hats or scarves. The next day, a package was on the desk of each of the six kids, containing two hats, two sets of gloves and two scarves. I can't forget the joy in my classmate's eyes upon receiving such a simple gift, and the pride with which she and her siblings wore them. It seemed like such a simple gift but meant the world to those kids.

Mom bought those gifts without thinking twice. She told me it was because when she was a child, she and her siblings were always the ones with the flimsy jackets in the cold winter and with chapped gloveless hands. No one helped them. She couldn't bear to think of that happening to any more kids.

Whenever I see a child without a jacket or gloves, I don't see a stranger; I see my mother, aunts and uncles. That is what she taught me to see: It may not be you or a loved one right now, but it may have been you yesterday and could be you tomorrow. Use your knowledge and experience to make a difference in someone's life. This difference can be as simple as a pair of gloves.

In 1990, my mother's life was cut short by the selfishness of a drunk driver. I was sixteen, and had so much left to learn from Mom, but she had already taught me her greatest lesson—loving and caring unselfishly.

I've always realized how important my mother was to our family, but it has taken seven years since her death to learn what she meant to others. Recently, I received a letter from a long-time family friend. It told me so much I already knew about Mom, but never knew others had seen in her, too. This friend told me she thinks of Mom almost every day and will never be able to put into words how thankful she is for having known my mother.

This is perhaps the greatest gift I have ever received, knowing that my mother wasn't a gift only to me, but was precious to everyone who was blessed to have known her. It was a pair of gloves, but it was my mother's own simple gift to me.

Julia A. Doyle

The Gift

The willingness to accept responsibility for one's own life is the source from which self-respect springs.

Joan Didion

When I was a child, Mom taught me to question everything. She was a mother who never minded the eternal "why." She made me consider the possibilities myself, jumping in only when my maturity or knowledge couldn't encompass the entire issue.

When I wanted to do something, I had to review all possibilities within my limited scope. "What would you feel like if someone did that to you?" was a question always asked when I reacted to an issue or event. She guided me, made certain I attended church and Sunday school and had a solid background of character and morality.

On my thirteenth birthday, all that changed. Entering my teens was heady in itself but attained an even higher ranking when Mom called me into her room after school.

"Anne," she told me, patting the bed beside her, "I want to talk to you."

"What's up?" I asked easily, self-assured in my new-found teen status.

"I've spent the last twelve years giving you a sense of values and morals," she began. "Do you know the difference between right and wrong?"

"Yeah, sure," I replied, my grin slipping slightly at this unexpected opening.

"You've now entered your teens, and life, from this point, will be much more complicated," Mom told me. "I've given you the basics. Now it's time for you to begin making your own decisions."

I looked at her blankly. What decisions?

Mom smiled. "From this time on, you'll make your own rules; what time to get up, when to go to bed, when to do your homework, and who you select as companions and friends will be your decision now."

"I don't understand," I told her. "Are you mad at me? What did I do?"

Mom put her arms around me, hugging me close. "Everyone has to begin making her own decisions in life sooner or later. I've seen too many young people let loose from their parents make horrible mistakes, usually when they're away at college and no one is there to give them guidance. I've seen them go wild, and some have ruined their lives forever. So I'm going to give you your freedom early."

I stared at her, dumbfounded. All sorts of possibilities occurred to me. Staying out as late as I wanted, parties, no one to tell me I had to do my homework? Super!

Mom smiled again as she stood and looked down at me. "Remember, this is a responsibility. The rest of the family will be watching. Your aunts, uncles and cousins will be waiting for any possible misstep. You'll have only yourself to blame."

"Why?" I asked, elated that she trusted me so much.

"Because I'd rather you make your mistakes now, while you're at home and I can advise and assist you," she replied, hugging me. "Remember, I'm always here for you. If you want advice, or just to talk, I'm available any time."

With this she ended the conversation and the birthday proceeded pretty much as the previous ones had, with cake, ice cream, presents and family. I knew quite well she wasn't stepping out of my life entirely, merely giving me space in which to stretch my wings and prepare for the flight I'd someday be taking.

During the coming years, I made my share of mistakes, the same ones all teenagers do. I neglected my homework periodically, stayed up late occasionally, and once attended a party I had reservations about. Mom never berated me for them. When grades slipped, she quietly pointed out that my chances for the university I wanted to attend would slip as far as my grades did, the lower they were, the poorer my chances of acceptance. If I stayed up late, she cheerfully chided me for my sour mood. After the party she simply asked me what I would picture those friends doing in ten years. Did I wish to share this future with them? Undoubtedly, I did not. When I saw this, I invariably altered my behavior to compensate. She was always ready with advice on how best to mend the tears in the fabric of my life. I never resented her as so many teens do. In fact, this brought us much closer.

A few years ago, I took my daughter into my room on her thirteenth birthday. We had a similar talk. We, too, have remained close during her teens. My son had a similar discussion with his dad at the same age. My children made many of the same mistakes that are the milestones of growth and maturity, but many others they passed by because they thought about it and came to us to discuss it first. They looked at us as mentors rather than jailers, and we've all been better for it. The continuity of life and wisdom has remained unaltered in this family for years and if I'm not available, my children will seek out my mother for advice.

Honor, love and respect for the wisdom of experience are valued in our family because of the wise words of my best friend, my mother.

Anne Lambert

Running Role Model

For me it is the challenge—the challenge to try to beat myself and do better than I did in the past. I try to keep in mind not what I have accomplished, but what I have to try to accomplish in the future.

Jackie Joyner-Kersee

I admit it—I did it purely for myself. Well, at first I did it because I'd lost a bet. After my best friend completed her ninth Tufts 10K, I bet her that if she would run the Boston Marathon, I, a non-runner, would run Tufts next time. I posed this idle bet because I never thought she'd really do it. Guess what? She did it!

Preparing to make good on my wager, I began my training in earnest, and I quickly fell in love with the solitude, the fresh air and sunshine, the singing birds, and the capabilities of my thirty-eight-year-old body. During those first few runs, however, I couldn't shake feelings of guilt about pursuing self-gratification. Wasn't I supposed to be home taking care of my family?

My guilt crescendoed when, after one particularly long

run, I returned home to soak sore muscles in a leisurely hot bath and left my "off-duty" sign posted a while longer. Lying in my Epsom salts, I heard Melissa, my three-year-old, whimper, "Where's Mommy?" My husband distracted her—while I gritted my teeth and grasped the sides of the tub, torn between the desire for time by myself and the urge to comfort my child. In that moment, I understood that with each run, I needed to train not only my body, but my mind—to allow myself this private time to seek the selfhood I was entitled to! Besides, if I were reenergized, I'd be better able to handle the demands of motherhood.

Indeed, my two daughters quickly adjusted to my long weekend runs. They'd casually acknowledge that I was leaving. "Going running, Mom?" Gina, my eight-year-old, would ask as she watched me lace up my running shoes. "Have a nice run," Melissa would add.

I'd kiss them and leave, and they'd be all smiles, knowing this was a chance for them to be alone in the house, while Dad worked in the garden, one ear on them. (Mother Nature programmed men with far fewer guilt genes, and women are finally taking heed.) Moreover, I think they recognized that I came back from my runs nicer than when I left!

Finally, it was time for my first practice race—a 5K. Off I went with a number pinned to my chest—my heart pounding behind it. My family cheered me on from the sidelines, and when I finished the race, they lunged to hug me, despite my sweaty body.

"Did you win?" asked Melissa. (I couldn't believe she hadn't noticed that four million people crossed the finish line before me.)

"Sorry you didn't win, Mom," said Gina. (She'd noticed!)

"Girls, I *finished!*" I proudly announced, briefly explaining that this was a *personal* victory. Yet even in the excitement of my own triumph, I noted with pride that my daughters, at such a young age, accepted as quite natural that women can—and should—be winners. When I was a child, the message I got was that nice girls don't compete.

Months later, I successfully completed the Tufts 10K, and instead of abandoning running with this fulfilled obligation, I surprised myself and continued.

Not too long ago, I ran my third Tufts 10K. Each has been as triumphant as the one before. But that year, the scene was more magical than ever. Melissa, then six, wore a running suit her sister bought her with her own money. Gina, then eleven and nearly my size, wore my commemorative shirt from my first Tufts 10K.

As I ran alongside six thousand other women, I thought of my two most loyal fans—my daughters—awaiting me at the finish line. With them was my adoring husband, who admits he gushes with pride when the starting gun fires and I run past with the pack. And that year, my best friend, sidelined by an aggravated injury, watched the race with my family. No bets necessary: I was running for *all* of us.

As I approached the finish line, my daughters jumped off the curb and ran to meet me. Holding hands, we raced the final tenth of a mile together.

Afterwards, I stretched my tired legs, wiped my sweaty face and chowed down on snacks. Meanwhile, my daughters animatedly and repeatedly announced that several children, including a seven-year-old, had run the race. I suspected what was coming.

"Can I run with you next year? Can I start training with you now? Can we? Can we?" I heard over and over again as I slipped out of my sweaty T-shirt into a dry one.

I considered their request: Training with them would mean giving up my time to rejuvenate and be alone amid fall leaves, nature paths and singing birds. Training with them would mean being a teacher, as usual, instead of, for a change, the one being taught. Training with them would mean sharing the hot water three ways at the end of each run. However, training with my daughters would also mean that I have helped these two future women tackle an obstacle, learn a skill and take pride in their own accomplishments.

"Of course," I announced. In part, I waged this idle threat because I never thought they'd really do it, but I knew if they would it could only be a positive step for all of us. So we went home and attempted our first mile run together. Guess what? They did it!

Mindy Pollack-Fusi

"I want a training bra, and my mom
needs a sports bra."

Reprinted by permission of Donna Barstow.

The Stick

What helps me to go forward is that I stay receptive. I feel that anything can happen.

Anouk Aimee

It was an unusual Mother's Day. I was thirty thousand feet in the air, flying from Texas back home to Hartford, Connecticut, where my daughter Beth was waiting for me in her college dorm. I had spent the last five days in Big Bend National Park in Texas as part of the base camp support for six individuals who were making a Vision Quest: a three-day solo fast in the desert in order to seek inner vision and guidance from God for the next season of their lives. On the way to Big Bend I had found a three-foot stick that I slowly and carefully sanded smooth. On top of the stick I carved my name, and I tied a lavender bandana at hand height to make the wood easier to grasp. It would be my walking stick, my prayer stick . . . even my defense against snakes, if necessary. During the following days the stick became an appendage. It symbolized all I was learning and the unique path that beckoned me.

Flying home with such a long "carry-on" was a

challenge. It was too long for the overhead compartment. For two connecting flights I had to rely on the goodwill of fellow travelers who allowed me to thread my cumbersome stick underneath our seats and between their feet. If nothing else, I was determined. From the airport in Hartford I called Beth to say I had arrived. I picked up my car, found Beth at her dorm, and we were soon in deep conversation at a nearby restaurant enjoying my Mother's Day dinner. Midway through the trading of our stories I realized that I had set the stick beside me when I called Beth from the airport and never picked it up again. We called the airport lost and found, baggage claim, even the cleaning services. Sympathetic airline personnel searched for me, but every call was a dead end. The stick was gone.

That night Beth and I drove to our small cottage on the Connecticut shore. Beth planned to spend the next several days there preparing for final exams. I had only the following day before I returned to Boston and my work. As we walked the beach the next morning my eyes were searching the sand and looking behind any bushes which covered the sea wall, searching for a piece of wood with potential. Eventually I spotted a suitable piece of driftwood and set to work. As Beth read and outlined her texts, I sanded and shaped my new stick. Again I engraved my name. I no longer had a bandana, but found some leather rope and twined it around the stick's circumference. On the beach I found long seagull feathers to tie to the end of the leather. Beth watched me as I worked. When we bent our heads to inspect my completed project, she said, "I love your stick, Mom. It's cool." I placed it in a corner of the cottage and smiled at her. "Use it as often as you wish. It can belong to both of us." With that, I was reluctantly off to Boston.

I returned to the cottage alone the following weekend. Arriving just minutes before sunset, I quickly unlocked the cottage door and reached inside to grab my walking stick from the corner, ready to walk the shoreline. But my fingers were circling more than my stick. I turned on a light and walked inside. Then I looked. Standing next to the stick I had so painstakingly created several days before was a second stick about three-quarters the height of my own. It, too, had been sanded smooth, and on the top, in my daughter's careful hand, was printed Beth. Childhood hair ribbons were twisted around the wood at hand height, and at the end of the ribbons were tied the small, soft feathers which often dotted the beach, shed from the underbellies of young gulls.

I don't remember how long I stood in that corner. I know I missed the sunset, but a different light was trying to illuminate my heart. I stood still until the strong message from my daughter invaded every corner of my being. I replayed our conversation. "Use the stick," I had said. "It can be ours." And Beth, without words, was speaking what was true. "Mom, I cannot borrow your stick or your journey. Every person has her own way to walk. As close as we have been or will ever be, my path is separate from your own. There must be two sticks, not one."

Years later, the sticks still stand in the cottage side by side. I eventually moved to Texas, and my daughter went on to New York City where she pursued a career in theatre. Sometimes we meet at the beach and still take long hikes at sunset, but never with our sticks. I'm not sure they were ever meant for walking.

Paula D'Arcy

What a Grandmother Is

A mother becomes a true grandmother the day she stops noticing the terrible things her children do because she is so enchanted with the wonderful things her grandchildren do.

Lois Wyse

A grandmother is a lady who has no children of her own, so she likes other people's little girls. A grandfather is a man grandmother. He goes for walks with boys, and they talk about fishing and tractors and stuff like that.

Grandmas don't have to do anything except be there. They are old, so they shouldn't play hard or run. It is enough if they drive us to the market where the pretend horse is and have lots of dimes ready. Or if they take us for walks, they slow down past things like pretty leaves or caterpillars. They should never "Hurry up."

Usually they are fat, but not too fat to tie the kids' shoes. They wear glasses, and they can take their teeth and gums off. It is better if they don't typewrite or play cards except with us. They don't have to be smart, only answer questions like why dogs chase cats or how come God isn't married.

They don't talk baby talk like visitors do, because it is hard to understand. When they read to us they don't skip words or mind if it is the same story again.

Everybody should try to have one, especially if you don't have television, because grandmas are the only grown-ups who have got time.

Patsy Gray
age 9

Reprinted by permission of Donna Barstow.

Thoughts on Being a Grandmother

Never be afraid to sit a while and think.

Lorraine Hansberry

I lie on the sofa and cuddle with the baby. My first grandchild! My daughter has gone on a quick outing alone and I have the honor of being the first babysitter. I watch his big brown eyes study my face and his tiny hands reach out in an effort to coordinate and touch what he sees. "Soon," I tell him. "Soon you'll be reaching and grasping everything in sight."

But I am in no hurry. I remember how I was constantly awaiting and anticipating the next new experience with my daughter. Her first smile, her first clumsy effort to sit up alone, that exciting first step, first word, first day of school. And then, suddenly, before I really had time to enjoy each of those special times, they were gone. I will not make that mistake again. With the wisdom of age and the experience, I will enjoy each precious moment.

His eyes become heavy and begin to close. I ease myself into a more comfortable position and he stirs and looks up at me for just a moment. With that glance, I recall another time, so many years ago, in another room on another sofa. I was cuddling with another child, my eighteen-month-old daughter. As she drifted off to sleep, she looked up at me and, in that one unique moment, I was able to envision for just an instant the woman my child would become. I recall the shivers that ran up my spine and the tears that appeared in my eyes and slid unchecked down my cheeks.

I recall saying a silent prayer for my little girl's future. I didn't think in grandiose terms of fame and fortune. I just prayed that someday a worthy (such an old-fashioned word, and yet so appropriate!) young man would look beneath her outer beauty and see the loyalty, the kindness, the determination that I had glimpsed so briefly and would cherish for so long.

Once again, I feel tears slide gently down my cheeks as I watch the sleeping baby boy. He is the representation of the fulfillment of all those prayers and dreams I carried in my heart for my daughter over the years. This tiny child, who fills me with such overwhelming love I can barely believe it, is my daughter's child.

I am thrilled for my daughter and all that awaits her as she watches this child grow and learn and become his own little person. Like me, she will experience great joys and survive major disappointments. She will rejoice in successes and regret more than a few mistakes. There will always be some guilt. But it isn't the important part. Love is the important part. You can't love too much. Perhaps there are psychologists and sociologists who would disagree with me. But as I watch my sleeping grandson and think of that little one who is now his mother, I know deep down inside that the one thing I will never be guilty of is not loving enough. Love is the drive for every feeling I've ever had, every action I've ever taken and every decision I've ever made with regard to my child. The results have not always been perfect because the situations were not in line with my motivation. But the end results have been worthwhile; the mistakes more than justified. I will continue to love my daughter with this unconditional love for as long as I live.

And now I am a grandmother. I feel the same emotions toward him, but there is a subtle difference. I can't quite put my finger on it. I draw him nearer to me and feel the warmth of his tiny body as he nestles contentedly in my arms. He feels safe and loved right where he is, but in a few minutes his mother will appear and I'll see in her face that, though she was gone less than an hour, she missed him. She can't wait to pick him up, to hold him, to take him home.

And then I realize. That's the difference. She will take him home. As I stand by always with arms open as the ready caretaker, the willing supporter, the hopeful advisor, he will go home with my daughter. She will nourish him physically, emotionally and spiritually every day of his life in ways that I am not meant to do. I have a new role. I am his grandmother. I will watch his face light up in recognition when he sees me as he grows older. I will bake his favorite cookies and we'll sit together in a rocking chair sharing a favorite book. I'll listen lovingly as his mother shares the little stories that shape his growing up years. I will to be at his school plays or his softball games or his piano recitals. I will be a part of his life because I am his grandmother.

And I will never, ever be able to love him too much.

Donna M. Hoffman

6

LIKE MOTHER, LIKE DAUGHTER

The truth is that when one woman gives birth to another, to someone who is like her, they are linked together for life in a very special way.

Nancy Friday

Reprinted by permission of Donna Barstow.

I Am My Mother

*All women become like their mothers. That is
their tragedy. No man does. That is his.*

Oscar Wilde

I swore it would never happen. In fact, I spent most of
my life trying to make sure it wouldn't happen. And yet it
crept up on me when I wasn't looking.

I am now officially my mother.

Don't get me wrong: My mother is a wonderful, smart,
funny, loving, sweet woman, and I love her dearly. But I
swore I'd never be like her.

How could I ever be so cruel as to not let my five-year-
old child eat sugared cereal every morning for breakfast?
How could I even think about banning cartoons from my
children's lives? And how could I ever be so heartless as
to not allow my child dessert until she had eaten something healthy first?

Then there were the teen years. What kind of mother
imposes a curfew on her teenage daughter, I asked. Didn't
she trust me? And what was the idea of making the boys
I went out with come inside to meet her and Dad before I

could leave? They weren't going out with my parents so why should they have to meet them?

Never would I subject my children to these atrocities.

My children, I vowed, would be allowed to survive on chocolate bars and, of course, sugared cereal. They would watch TV until their eyes popped out if that is what they so desired. Curfew? Not in my house! My children could stay out all night, and the next day, too, if they wanted, and I would applaud their independence and trustworthiness.

My children would have such a cool and hip mom that they would probably invite me to their parties, and all of the other kids would say, "Cool! There's that awesome mom! Boy, are her kids lucky!"

I also planned on never worrying. I watched my mother worry about me, about my sisters, about everything it seemed, and I knew I would never be like that. I told her often that she had no need to worry about me—I'd be home by midnight, maybe 1:00 A.M., and everything would be fine. There was no need to worry—the car has only a few dents in it, and nobody was hurt. What's to worry about? Why worry about my friends? They are very nice people who simply happen to have spiked hair, tattoos and pierced body parts. No need to worry. I could handle myself.

I planned on never worrying like that with my children. I planned on being hip and cool. I would, of course, always dress in the most recent fashions, and never, ever, wear "mom" clothes. I would be so hip that my children's friends would think I was one of them.

Yes, that was my plan. To be the coolest, hippest mother around. To enforce only one rule in my house—there are no rules. I was planning on a complete revolt from my upbringing; I was planning on giving my children everything I was so brutally deprived of.

But something happened along the way.

I had a child of my own.

On the day I brought my little girl home from the hospital, I made my husband throw out all the remaining sugared cereal. When she started eating solid food, I never gave her anything sweet until she had something healthy first.

And she has yet to see a cartoon on TV.

She hasn't hit the teen years yet, but I shudder to think of all the things she will want to do, and all of the things I won't let her do. I've already decided she'll have an 8:00 P.M. curfew and not be allowed to date until she's eighteen. Of course, I reason, this is all for her own good, and so she'll understand and meekly go along with my rules. Or not.

I'm already worried.

But she will always be showered with love, affection and adoration. She already loves to read books, and she has a penchant for broccoli and other vegetables. Okay, maybe not the veggies, but the rest is true.

As for me, I've finally admitted that my mom was pretty great after all. Even though I was deprived of so many wonderful, glorious things as a child, I turned out okay. And I have a feeling that my little girl will, too—although she'll probably grow up planning all her life not to be like me. I only hope I can be as good a mother to her as my mother was, and is, to me.

Anne Tews Schwab

The Baby Book

If you count all your assets, you always show a profit.

Robert Quillen

When I was a little girl, I loved looking through my baby book. I would sit nestled on my mother's lap, while she carefully turned the pages for me. She read my name out loud. She read her name, my father's name, my grandparents' names. She read the date and time of my birth. She let me look inside the little envelope with a lock of my baby hair in it. My favorite part of the book was at the very end. It was three pages of photographs, and I was in every single one. The photos were slipping behind the clear plastic that refused to hold them in place and the plastic on one page was torn. This did not bother me in the least. I loved to look at the pictures of my mother holding the newborn me. When one photo slid behind another, my mother would pull it out, and I laughed in excitement as the hidden treasure was revealed.

Now I am a mother with a daughter of my own. As I put together a baby book for my daughter, I keep looking back into my own book. However, my baby book no longer looks the same. When I look at the photo of my mother bathing me, I notice that she looks tired—as I feel now. When I look carefully into the background of the photos, I see that my mother's kitchen had cluttered counters—like my kitchen has now. I see photos of my smiling, happy face in a bathtub, oblivious to the clutter and my mother's fatigue—just as my baby smiles now.

And I notice one other change in the book. There was always a section of pages in the middle of the book that were never written in. These are the blank pages that I hear my new mother friends complain about. I hear mothers guiltily complain that they have not filled in all of the pages of the baby book yet. I hear mothers criticizing themselves, saying that it will be depressing if their child sees blank pages in her baby book. But as I look back in my baby book, I see that all of the blank pages have suddenly disappeared. Where the blank pages once lay, I now see my mother cooking me warm, nourishing meals and giving me hot baths. I see my mother reading me books and taking me sledding in the front yard. I see my mother tucking me into bed and bandaging my skinned knee. I see pages full of love.

Julie Bete

Reprinted by permission of Vahan Shirvanian.

Beach Talk

None of us knows what the next change is going to be, what unexpected opportunity is just around the corner, waiting to change all the tenor of our lives.

Kathleen Norris

It's countdown time. In a month, more or less, my daughter is due to give birth. "Do you think I'll stay like this forever?" she asks as we walk the beach.

"The condition isn't permanent," I assure her.

She feels as if she's going to explode, as I felt back in August of 1965 when my due date came and no baby arrived. Six days later, Elizabeth bounced red-faced into the world, and my stomach, which had gotten as huge as my daughter's is now, began to deflate.

Elizabeth parades her pregnancy proudly. Clad only in a two-piece black swimsuit, her belly protruding over the bottom half, she reminds me of photos one might see among the pages of *National Geographic*.

The last two days have been special for us, our time, my daughter's and mine. She has invited me to her summer house, where we put our busy lives on hold for a mother/daughter mini-vacation. Now, we walk the beach, filling in the blank spaces of our lives, usually relegated to brief, late-night phone calls assuring each other we are both well.

This morning we have time to linger as we savor that rare gift of togetherness. Walking along with my child who is carrying her child in utero, I note silently that our lives, as if by magic, will change in a heartbeat.

Soon, these lazy summer days that run smoothly into each other will be interrupted by the demands of a new-born, and knowing this, Elizabeth has invited me to Fire Island to share in these few remaining quiet moments. Aside from an occasional seagull and a few early morning walkers like us, Liz and I are alone.

Our talk turns to practical matters that have to do with her pregnancy: Lamaze classes, Liz's work schedule, and how she plans to combine her job with motherhood. We discuss breast-feeding, the intricacies of the labor process, her fear of the pain and the security of knowing if it gets too difficult there are positive alternatives. Her doctor from Manhattan also has a house on Fire Island. "If you go into labor on the island," he joked, "I'll simply throw you in my boat and deliver the baby on board."

"You call me the minute a contraction hits," I remind her, "so I can get to the hospital. That's part of the deal."

"You also promise to behave," she warns me. "You promise to sit in the waiting room and not bug anyone."

I agree to be the model mother, waiting patiently until my grandchild arrives. If it were up to me, I would be with her every step of the way. I even offered to be her Lamaze coach.

"Really, Mom!" she said. "That's why God invented husbands."

We talk about motherhood, and I recall my pediatrician

telling me thirty years ago, "The best thing you can do is enjoy your baby. Have fun. Everything else will fall into place."

It sounded good even though it wasn't always possible. New parents are bound up in tending to the needs of their infants. Fun takes a back seat to new responsibilities. Sleep-deprived and edgy, parents respond to every cry, every nuance, walking through these early days in a zombie-like trance.

"Will I be a good mother?" Elizabeth asks suddenly. "How will I know what to do? How do I know if I'm doing it right? What if I make mistakes?" Her barrage of questions comes pouring out as a last-minute, urgent attempt to gather up my secrets of mothering, and the fact is, even now, I don't have the answers.

"You will make mistakes," I say. "You won't always know what to do, but it won't matter. All you need to do is love your child." I echo my pediatrician's words: "The rest will fall into place."

I feel a bit smug as I offer these words of wisdom, but they are the only ones I have. The rest will follow on their own. Liz and her husband, Noel will find answers through their own parenting techniques, and years later, they may be as stymied as I am now when their children seek for the responses she looks for from me this morning.

What I do tell her is that I was more unprepared than she is and: "It's the loving that always makes it work." She seems satisfied with that. We walk back holding hands and looking forward to breakfast.

"The baby just kicked really hard!" Liz says.

I reach out to touch the fleshy belly that houses my grandchild. Today I think it's a boy. Yesterday I was convinced it was a girl. The suspense is killing me.

"Whatever it is, I think I'm going to explode," Liz says.

I brush a strand of hair from her eyes. "I love you," I say.

"Me, too, Mom," she whispers.

The clouds part, giving birth to sunshine as a new day stretches out before us. We walk the rest of the way arm in arm, alone together, mother and daughter in one shadow.

Judith Marks-White

The Bentwood Rocker

One must learn by doing the thing, for though you think you know it, you have no certainty until you try.

Aristotle

I was pregnant with my first child when my parents gave me a bentwood rocker. The rounded body of the rocker seemed to perfectly represent cuddling and nurturing and all of the wonderful things I expected parenting to be. Staring at the curled wood, I envisioned myself wearing a pristine lace gown peacefully swaddling my sweet cherub while humming a soothing lullaby. I'm embarrassed to admit that my vision even included songbirds circling overhead. It was a dream I often envisioned, and before me stood the rocker that would make my dreams come true.

When I looked from the rocker to my mother, I recognized similar maternal feelings reflected in her eyes. But I saw something unfamiliar there as well. Although I didn't fully recognize the wistful look in my mother's eyes, I knew our relationship was about to change, because, although I would still be my mother's child, I would also be my child's mother.

Now, many years later, I come much closer to seeing what my mother saw in the rocker and me that day. She saw my innocent anticipation and shared my hope for and belief in the future. But she also saw much more. In her mind's eye, my mother saw a much clearer picture. Less radiant perhaps, but certainly more realistic. The infant she saw was squalling with colic and the mother was crying in exhausted frustration at her inability to quiet the tiny intruder.

She saw an older mother rocking a sobbing toddler who had just had a rude run-in with a doorknob. And she saw an even older mother rocking broken spirits, much slower to heal than bruised knees or skinned elbows. In my mother's eyes was also a bit of grief. Grief for her own losses and mine. Loss of childhood and of innocence. Loss of the pure love and unwavering trust of youth.

But even more than that, my mother must have grieved for the naiveté she saw in me. She knew the guilt and disappointment a child can elicit in a mother which, no matter how undeserved, are unexpected feelings for which she could never prepare me. My mother gave me many things over the years: a sense of humor, a sense of confidence and a strong sense of pride in my own mothering skills. But no matter how clear the picture in her mind, no matter how much she knew, there was only so much she could tell me. The rest, I would have to learn in my own hours of rocking.

In one instant, she saw my dreams and knew the reality was something she could not communicate. In that moment, she gave me her silence. She allowed me my dreams and my independence. She let me live my dream. Between that act of unselfishness and the rocker, I do not know which was the greater gift.

Cindy Phiffer

Lullaby for My Mother

Let me kiss away the frowns
as you kissed away the fears.
When rolling thunder flung me to your lap,
your breast became my haven.
Now it's my turn to snuggle you into sleep.
Sleep, *Mamele*, sleep.

These gnarled hands spoke of love
more eloquently than words—fed, diapered,
braided ribbons into my hair,
made dolls out of rags, cookies of dough.
Unfurl them, like flowers to the sun.
Sleep, *Mamele*, sleep.

Feel safe with me, I'll protect you
from sharp breeze or impatient eye.
Close your eyes, my aged child
and when you no longer can see
you'll hear me softly croon
Sleep *Mamele*, sleep.

Bella Kudatsky

Mamele—Yiddish endearment ("little Mommy")

The Deep "Well!"

Your diamonds are not in far distant moun-
tains or yonder seas; they are in your own back-
yard, if you but dig for them.

Russell H. Conwell

My house is in sight. I am racing home from school, my book satchel banging against my leg, catching on my Girl Scout knee socks, chafing me with every stride. My cheeks are burning, and I taste a trickle of salty sweat from my forehead. The Jones boys are in hot pursuit, each trying to outdo the other on their stingray bikes. Each trying to be The One, who catches up, catches me. It's the same thing, every day.

I shortcut up the alley, throw open the back gate, burst through the screen door and hurl myself into the kitchen, screaming "MAMA!" She feigns concern, hides a smile, crooks a sassy arm on her hip then looks straight at me, her eyebrows climbing into her hairline, crinkling her forehead as they rise. "We—ll?"

For those of you who don't speak East-Texas-Depression-Era-Salt-of-the-Earth-Grade-School Principal, it means, loosely translated, "If you don't run, they can't chase you. And apparently, you ran. Again."

She then pops the top off a Coke bottle and hands it to me. "But Mama—," I whine. She raises her hand. "Not till I get my coffee. And my glasses. I can't listen without my glasses." I'm wiggling all over the chair, anxious to spill my day. She sits down, and over the brim of her favorite cup, her eyes lock in on mine. "We—ll?" That one means, "What are you waiting for? I can't draw breath till I know your every move."

So, I spill. The girl who wrote the F-word on the bathroom wall. How I *have* to run when the Jones boys chase me because there are six of them, and it scares me. That we saw two dogs on the playground stuck together, which is why the girl wrote the F-word on the bathroom wall. I breathe and take a gulp of my Coke. About the spelling bee that I almost won, but lost on account of the word "independent." A wise and gentle smile spreads across her face. "We—ll?" That means, obviously, "Learn to spell it. And then become it."

It wasn't that she didn't talk. Oh, she talked all the time. But not while she was *listening*. She listened with her whole body. She was one big ear. And it always began the same way: her hand in the air, eyes wide and round, as if I were going to announce the winning bingo card, and then, "Wait, let me get my coffee. And my glasses; I can't listen without my glasses."

The non sequitur was lost on me. But then she would become one with my eyeballs. And I would spill.

The older I grew, the deeper the "We—ll" became. At fourteen, I was voted Miss This or Most That. The "Well!" rushed from her mouth, carrying the word "proud" right behind it. Until the next week, when I ran home in tears because the same kids who adored me on Monday, enough to crown me Miss This or Most That, whispered about me in the halls, plotting against me by Friday. Across the kitchen table, my mother lowered her cup, cocked her head, and slowly removed her glasses. Only one eyebrow slid up her forehead, then arched stiffly. Bad sign. But she held my hand at the same time. Quietly she said, "We—ll?" In other words, "There is a difference between being popular, and being loved. One means you're a trend; the other, a friend. Which were *you*?"

Oddly enough, when I most needed her listening eyes, her silent comfort, her practical advice, I could not reach for it. At seventeen, my heart was shredded and discarded by the boy to whom I had given every inch of myself. I could not turn to my mother. How could she possibly know what it is to lose that kind of love? To offer one's self in moonlight, tucked between sand dunes, to listen to the murmurings of "forever" and "always." How could I bear to expose myself twice, to be naked, raw, porous, then risk being cast aside again, this time by her?

After two weeks of my slithering through the back door, muttering a mumbled, "Fine" in response to her query about my day, she brought her coffee cup and her glasses into my bedroom and shut the door. Though it was just the two of us who lived in this house, her shutting of the door signaled a sense of privacy, importance and safety. I began to spill. And shake, and finally, to cry. There was no "We—ll," no sage advice, no migrating eyebrows or steady gazes. Wisely she cast her eyes down, to give me my dignity. Kindly, she nodded periodically in empathy. Finally she scooped me up in a ball, and held me like a child, and simply cooed, "There, there, now. There, there . . ."

Class alone, or perhaps a mother's love, made her bite her lip, I know. She could have said, "We—ll, what the hell do you think it was like for me when your dad left? I don't know love and loss? Try losing a son; try losing a mother at an age younger than you, Toots, try starting over at forty in a strange town, working two jobs, with a child to raise." But she didn't.

Over the years, my children, my friends, even my friends' children, have adopted the same language of listening. "We—ll" is the vernacular of our hearts. We cajole, comfort and question each other with that simple Southern two-syllable word; our conversations are punctuated with the lift or knit of an eyebrow, with the crook or wave of an arm, with a giggle or sigh from our lips. We both listen and feel heard through my mother's tongue.

I am forty-five now. Soon I will be sitting at my mother's kitchen table, elbows propped up, drinking coffee and returning the favor of rapt attention. My mother's life is full, rich, exciting and occasionally in need of my listening eyes. And so, I will hold up my hand, and make her wait till I fish the glasses out of my purse. Then I'll listen. I'll bore a hole right through her eyeballs, and delight in the lilt of my own honed delivery of "We—ll . . ."

Karen O. Krakower

Yeah? Well . . . Whatever!

It's a funny thing about speech habits. You fall into certain patterns without realizing it. You know, there are those people who say "you know" all the time. (If you knew, they wouldn't have to tell you!)

I remember my high school English teacher, Miss Braswell. Whenever we'd start a sentence with "Well," she'd snap, "Three wells, and you could be a well digger."

Which brings me to my point . . . I was talking to my daughter Linda on the phone the other day.

"I'm really upset with Leslie," she complained about her sister. "Ever since she moved to England, she's become such a snob about the English language. I feel like Eliza Doolittle with Henry Higgins."

"Really?" I asked. "What's her problem?"

"Well," replied Linda, and a picture of Miss Braswell flashed through my mind, ". . . well, she said she hoped I wouldn't be offended, but she noticed I'd been using the word 'yeah' a lot. Have you noticed me doing that?"

"Yeah?"

"Yeah, you've noticed?"

"No, I was asking a question."

"Well, do I?"

"Well, yeah. So what did you say to her?"

"I said I'd watch it."

"So what did she say?"

"She said, 'Whatever.'"

"Whatever? What kind of answer is that?"

"Yeah, well, I guess it means forget it."

"Yeah? Well, whatever."

"So did I tell you I was attacked by a pit bull last week?"

"Yeah?"

"Yeah. He opened up quite a gash. I didn't get a shot or anything. I hope I don't get rabies or something. Do you think I'll have any bad results?"

"I don't know. Do you find yourself saying 'yeah' a lot?"

"Yeah!"

"Get a shot!"

"Yeah?"

"Well, whatever."

Phyllis W. Zeno

The Look

It happens to the best of us. We plan for a baby and for a few blissful months, that is exactly what we have—a soft and usually sweet-smelling baby who looks adorable in eyelet and ribbon and who endearingly dampens the shoulders and laps of those enslaved by the dimpled wee knuckles and the gentle gurgles. That's how it all begins.

At some point, however, the baby which we had planned for, all sweetness and light, becomes a person with complex thought processes and with means of expressing herself. This is something we had not planned for.

A few days ago, I answered a question from my daughter with what I thought was a terribly clever and witty remark. I turned to see the reaction from my beloved eldest and was met with The Look. Those of you who have never had the unique privilege of living with a nine-year-old girl may not be familiar with The Look (this may be viewed as a sexist remark, but I find that my daughter is ever so much more accomplished at giving The Look than my eldest son).

The Look involves a slackening of the jaw, a downward tilt of the head and a 180-degree roll of the eyes. The Look is often accompanied by a forceful exhalation of breath indicating: a) disgust, b) disbelief, c) exasperation, d) embarrassment, e) all of the above. The Look occurs more frequently in public, where the youngster must never be seen to approve of anything the parent does, says, likes, thinks or is.

And so I had been fixed with The Look. It was meant, of course, to indicate the extreme disapproval of the actions of the parent (me) on the part of the child (my daughter). It was meant to whip me into line, to check my inappropriate behavior, but I thought it was really quite funny. My laughter brought on another Look and the icy comment, "*Not* amusing, Mother."

Now the child's grandmother finds this is all very humorous. She sarcastically says that things will only get better. She says she can hardly wait until my daughter turns thirteen. She says she is most delighted to see that the Ultimate Mother's Curse ("I hope you have a child who is just like you!" which was first cast over me when I was, perhaps, three) has finally come true. The child's grandmother offers no sympathy. Instead, she laughs gleefully and begins to point out the many ways in which my daughter and I are alike.

I fix her with The Look and try to pretend she's not my mother.

M. M. English

Kathy Shaskan

"No offense, Mom, but I reject your
entire system of beliefs, values and ethics."

Reprinted by permission of Kathy Shaskan.

Mom SAID/She MEANT

I think it started with the teen years. I would have on my best torn/shredded jeans and be on the way out of the house and Mom would look me over and ask in a critical tone, "Is that what you're wearing?" Yes. "Outside of this house?" Yes. "In public?" Yes. "For people to see?" Yes. I knew the drill, but still I would bite. Why, Mom? Do you not LIKE my outfit? "No, it's fine," she said . . . "It's fine," she SAID . . . She MEANT: "If you go out of this house dressed that way and people see you they will naturally assume you're on welfare and just out of prison and blame me personally for it, because you KNOW they will . . . It's always the MOTHER'S FAULT . . . well, let me tell you that I will just DIE of embarrassment and I don't need to tell you how many slow deaths that kind of agony feels like." I would happily bound out the door and into my day. Yet somehow, mysteriously in all mom's cleaning the next day, I'd find my best torn/shredded jeans staring back at me when I lifted the garbage can lid to drop in a new sack of trash. It was always a mystery and we could never figure out exactly how my jeans got there.

After high school I went through a period of indecision

and searching. I was greatly lacking direction or motivation. I was also in dire need of a reality check. I was certain
that I would be making tons of money soon with my dark
and adolescent poetry, that I was on the verge of being
discovered for my great talents and brilliance and that I
would never have to resort to the likes of the desperate
masses who did things like working real jobs. So, I would
ponder and reflect and be a great thinker. So, with no job
and no plan, I stayed adrift on my listless journey of finding my voice and finding myself for awhile. It was an aim-
less period. It was a grace period. Of about three days.

"All right! I've had it." Mom yelled at me as she slapped
my feet right off the coffee table, threw my Twinkie in the
trash and turned off MTV. (It was all in one continuous
fluid motion like a great karate movie or a scene right out
of *Billy Jack*. Mom was MAD.) "These are your choices," she
informed me as she dropped a stack of employment applications, a community college catalog and an admissions
application in my lap. Wow, this was scary. Mom had been
busy. She had done her homework, the legwork and she
even had thrown (right straight at me HARD) a PACK of
pens. (Black ink, for applications.) She paced and I sat up
straight and listened; horrified by this new, aggressive
side of her I'd never seen. She laid down the law. She was
the marshall and I was the outlaw captured in this God-
forsaken town and she had me. "I will not (It's how she
spoke when I was in really big trouble and she was yelling
so loudly all her lung capacity was used up in about five
to seven words) have you sitting on your lazy BUTT! All
day! Every day! Like you have been! Doing NOTHING
ALL DAY! And if you! Are going to! Sit around here!
Waiting to get published! You can just leave!" At one point
I was waiting for her head to start spinning. I was sure she
was breathing fire. "You can get a job! Like a responsible
person! Or you can go to school . . . FULL TIME! But you're

going to do SOMETHING. ALL DAY! DO you understand ME?"

Okay, that's what she SAID. What she MEANT was "Sweetheart I love you. I want you to do better for yourself than I did. I don't want you to have to struggle and swallow your pride and have to work two or three jobs just to make it. You have been given a gift in this world. You're talented, smart, funny. Please don't throw all of that away. Please don't disregard opportunities you have that I didn't have. Just in case the world's not as quick to notice your greatness as I am, I want you to be able to pay your bills in the meantime and to get that piece of paper. I will love you with or without a college degree but the world has different standards and you need that paper to have choices. It will be like a key that opens many doors. I didn't get the key or the choices and ended up with whatever doors were left open. Doors that I'd have never chosen on my own, had I been given another choice." (So . . . I have two associate degrees and twelve hours left on my bachelors.)

"Did you take your vitamins? What are you having for lunch? Is it low fat? Low cholesterol?" she asked me on the phone. And I rolled my eyes. "Yes, Mom! How many years have I been two to you?" She sighed. We were both disgusted. "Well, I can't make you eat right, Donna. And you're a big girl and if you don't care about your health, it's none of my business," she SAID.

She MEANT, "No matter how old you get, you'll always be my baby. And I will always love you, so much that if you became unhealthy and something happened to you, it would just kill me. I wouldn't have you to talk to or be friends with or remind about vitamins and truly, it would break my heart."

"Hi, Mom. How was your day, today?" I ask her as I kiss her on the cheek.

"Fine," she says, "We didn't really do anything."

"Well, that's my favorite day!" I offer, trying to cheer her up (and maybe me). And after a few quiet moments of handholding, I ask her, "Are you eating well? They must be treating you well . . . You look wonderful! So pretty." I SAID. I MEANT: "How did this happen to you? You're so frail. And so tired. And I miss you so much everyday. One day you'll be gone and I don't know what I'm going to do without you. Seeing you this way completely breaks my heart. Will you ever know how much I love you?"

I crawl into the bed with her and snuggle up. I hold her small, fragile body close. And I brush away her tears as she cries. And then I brush away my tears as I cry. And I tell her in soft, whispering, reassuring tones, "Shhhhh . . . no more tears. There's nothing to cry about." But she cries and she says, "You're my littlest angel. I love you so much." And I say, "And, I'm here now so there's no need to cry! Everything's okay . . ." And she settles into my embrace and says she's tired. I kiss her on the forehead as she drifts off into her dreams. And we both say exactly what we mean. She says, "You're my angel. I love you . . ." and I say, "You're mine and I love you, too."

Donna Lee

Take My Hand

We are together, my child and I. Mother and child, yes, but sisters really, against whatever denies us all that we are.

Alice Walker

We strolled through the aisles of the Venture Store in downtown St. Mary's, her little hand tucked in mine. The weather had turned cold abruptly as a southerly forced its way across New South Wales, Australia. It was time for winter clothes, warm pajamas and woolly underwear. She was barely seven years old but was catching up with me overnight, it seemed. I still towered over her . . . *but not for long,* I thought.

In the bottom of my bag was a detailed shopping list, and we only had one day to get it all done. School was starting tomorrow.

Scarcely had we entered the store when she needed to go potty. I groaned but made the detour, thinking, *What's with these kids, anyway?* Playing the patient mother, I stood outside the cubicle, then turned watchdog to be sure she washed her hands thoroughly before we continued our excursion. It was promising to be a long day.

First we tried on sweats and then footed pajamas, followed by cotton knit jerseys and corduroys. She begged for new boots and a warm jacket with a hood. We took turns hauling our packages around the store ... *me* more than *she* ... slipping sweaters over her head and trying on shoes.

At seven years old, she was beginning to exercise her own tastes in clothing. I was careful to put several of her selections back on the shelf, opting for quality over fashion. It was amusing to watch her as I observed from the "mommy chair" just outside the dressing rooms—but she tired quickly. What had started out as a fun fall shopping spree became a chore by late afternoon, and she fought going one step further.

"Mummy, let's sit *down* somewhere, my legs are *tired*," she complained.

We found a kiosk near the front of the store, dropped our bags into a heap, and ordered hot chocolate for two. She was fading fast, so we did not linger. I emptied my change on the table, buttoned up her sweater, and we headed for the parking lot.

It was a mother-daughter kind of day. I, the mother ... she, the daughter.

We strolled through the glass entrance to the Galleria in the suburbs of St. Louis ... my hand tucked in hers. The leaves were turning and a cold spell had hit town overnight. It was time for winter clothes, warm pajamas, new sweaters and boots.

She was barely twenty-seven years old, but had definitely caught up with me, and I noticed for the first time that she was the taller. Perhaps it was her shoes, I observed.

Somewhere in my bag was a detailed shopping list, and we only had today to get it all done. I was leaving town tomorrow.

Scarcely had we arrived at the Galleria when I had to go potty. She rolled her eyes but smiled and made the detour with me, thinking, *What's with these old people, anyway?* Playing the patient daughter, she waited outside the cubicle, then turned watchdog to be sure I hadn't forgotten to pick up my purse after drying my hands. It was promising to be a long day.

First stop was Dillards . . . second floor . . . sweaters. Each of us grabbed an armload of turtlenecks, cardigans and pullovers. She was careful to put several of my selections back on the shelf, saying that in her opinion, I needed to buy a different style . . . a more fitting size.

"Try this one," she encouraged me. "It makes you look thinner."

Then she plopped down in the "mommy chair" just outside the dressing room. From this position she could monitor my every purchase. Round and round the stores we walked . . . trying on khakis, cotton blouses and the latest in sweater sets. We took turns carrying the shopping bags, *she* more than *me.* But I tired quickly, and what had started out as a fun, fall shopping spree soon became a chore. By late afternoon, I fought going one step further.

"Honey, let's go sit *down* somewhere, my feet are *aching,*" I complained.

So we loaded our bags into the trunk of the car, found a California Pizza near the entrance to the mall and ordered Diet Cokes and dinner for two. I was fading fast, so we did not linger.

She whipped out her credit card to pay for the meal, then helped me collect my purse and sweater from the booth before we strolled back to our car in the parking lot.

It was a mother-daughter kind of day. She the mother, I the daughter.

Charlotte A. Lanham

"Mother, teach me to shop."

Thanksgiving Dinner and Infant Seats

We can not do great things; we can only do small things with great love.

Mother Theresa

I had visited a friend on the Friday before Labor Day and was turning in my visitor's pass at the hospital desk, when I overheard an argument between the receptionist and a distraught man. The receptionist was explaining that his newborn baby couldn't leave the hospital without a car seat.

He looked so dejected as he said, "Where can I get a car seat at this time and where can I get the money to buy one?"

"I'm sorry, sir, but this is now the state law. No one can take a baby out of the hospital without an infant car seat."

My hackles were rising. Were they going to ask this man (or the taxpayer) to cover an additional four days in the hospital for lack of an infant seat? But when the receptionist said, "Your wife can go home with you today, but the baby can't leave unless she's in a car seat," I had to intervene. Leaving a newborn baby in an impersonal hospital for four days without her mother because there was no car seat? I knew from my mother how important that early bonding can be for a baby—and the mother.

So, being the daughter of a woman who never hesitated to jump in and help strangers, I said, "Sir, I have an infant car seat in my house that my sister just returned to me. I'd be glad to give it to you, but I live about twenty-five minutes away." Beaming in amazement and relief, the man said, "I'll follow you in my car."

As I debated whether I had done the right thing or been foolish in inviting a stranger to my home, the flashback happened. I remembered being in my parents' apartment in New York City for Thanksgiving dinner. Lots of us were there and it was very festive. Too much food, of course, and laughs and good times—and my mother frequently peering out the window of the eighth-floor apartment.

"What's going on, Julie?" asked my father.

"That man has been sitting on the sidewalk all day. He looks cold and hungry. I'm going to take him a Thanksgiving dinner," said my mother. And the protests arose from the group. He may reject it, he will know where you live, he'll think you're a softie and may bother you later, it's not safe. . . .

Undaunted, my mother packed up a big Thanksgiving dinner, complete with pie wrapped in foil, grabbed some utensils and napkins, a few Thanksgiving candies and a nice heavy wool sweater of my father's that he didn't wear much in their warm New York City apartment and charged out the door.

We all watched out the window. My mother walked right up to him and we could tell that they were talking. The man seemed agreeable, took everything and thanked my mother profusely. As she walked back to the building, we watched the man. He carefully placed the plates and things on the sidewalk, took off his thin jacket, put on the wool sweater and put his jacket back on. Then he opened the food and began to eat. We stopped watching, feeling we were invading his privacy. Later he returned the plate and utensils to the doorman, whom my mother had alerted.

When my mother got back into the apartment, she was obviously moved by the man's plight and his appreciation of her Thanksgiving gift. And so were all of us. The man never bothered her and the gift was exactly the right thing to do. It stayed with me for many years—and popped into my head as I stood at the hospital debating whether to offer this man my infant seat.

When we got to my house, I offered him other never-to-be-used again baby things. He accepted. But there was nothing abject about his receiving the gifts. It was as if he knew people give to people and it's the right way to live. And he accepted my baby equipment as a new father from a longtime mother.

They say what goes around, comes around, and I believe it's true. My mother's good example comes around again and again through me, her daughter who learned by watching her. Silently, I thanked her for the lessons in generosity that she had given me.

Frances Firman Salorio

Letting Go and Holding On

Give to the world the best you have and the best will come back to you.

Madeline Bridges

Recently, I was gathering a few things to take to the dry cleaner. I keep a bag in my closet where I theoretically put my dry-cleaning items after I've worn them, but usually I have to do some gathering. Since my closet door is partially blocked by my dresser, I asked my daughter to slip in there and pick up anything that should go to the cleaner.

A sweater came flying out, then a pair of pants, followed by a skirt and a couple of shirts. Then Alex stuck her head through the door. "I'm not sure about this one," she said. I waited a second, and a tan coat appeared where Alex's face had been.

"Do you need to take this?" she asked, struggling to hold the coat off the ground.

"No," I said. "I'll hang it back up."

"You should take it to the Goodwill since you never wear it. There are people who need coats when it's so cold."

She's right. I've never worn this coat. It's not me.

"Don't you want to take it? It has something on the pocket."

"No, it's fine. I'll take care of it."

This coat was my mother's. Whatever is on the pocket was probably hers, too. It's about the only thing of hers that I ended up with. When she died pretty much everything went to charity, but I managed to grab this coat and have kept it through more moves than I can count. It always winds up at the back of my closet.

The funny thing is, I can't remember her ever wearing this coat. This, like so many details, has faded from my memory. Where there was color and texture is now only an outline, a rough sketch, a stick figure scribbled on the back of a napkin.

I would probably not recognize her handwriting if I saw it today, except for the way she always wrote the word "and" at an angle, as though she wanted to keep it out of the way of the other, more important words.

"Your mom sounds like she's from Texas or something," my friends used to say when they met her. I never really noticed her Southern drawl; it was normal to me. Now I can't even remember her voice. I remember her hands, only because in pictures they look just like mine.

In the later photographs, the ones from her thirties, her hands look slightly arthritic, also just like mine, a detail I don't remember. I remember her tiny watch and her gold shoes and the half-glasses she bought at a drugstore. I remember her green bathrobe and her mashed potatoes and her goofy sense of humor.

It seems so strange that someone who was such a part of my day-to-day life is just not here anymore. She hasn't been here for a long time, so I should be used to it. But every once in a while, I actually think I see her on the street, on the train, at the grocery. At first, it's not apparent to me who I think it is. I just think, I haven't seen her in a long time. Occasionally, I think I should call her up and tell her something or just find out what she's been up to. Then I remember.

When my daughters were babies, I lamented the fact that they never had a chance to know my mom. She would have been a wonderful grandmother—her mother certainly was. She would have enjoyed these years with fun, energetic children, minus the burden of day-to-day parenthood. She seemed to get along best with kids, to lose her insecurity and inhibition and just have fun. She'd love going to their sporting events and sewing Girl Scout badges on their vests and having a good laugh over a game of Monopoly at the kitchen table.

The truth is, though, that my daughters do know her. They know her because I go to their sporting events and sew their badges and play Monopoly with them. I cut sandwiches diagonally and fold towels in this bizarre way that I can't even describe, because she did. I put notes and comics in my kids' lunches and take them to McDonald's every Monday for dinner. I support their nutty ideas and let them cook dinner even though it means lots of extra cleanup for me, because that's what she did with me. They know her because they know me.

Alex is right. Someone probably needs that coat, but I don't. Next time we take things to the Goodwill, the coat will go. It's not the only thing I've managed to hold on to.

Lisa West

7

LOSS AND HEALING

*F*ear knocked at the door. Faith answered.
No one was there.

Old Saying

Mama-Cat

Do not follow where the path may lead. Go, instead, where there is no path and leave a trail.

Ralph Waldo Emerson

When I was nearly four years old I was just a mere bit of a girl. Curly hair framed my happy little freckled face, and my lively blue eyes looked at everything in curious anticipation of delights yet to be. One beautiful September day, my mother stretched out on the sofa and called to me. She asked me to bring her a cool, wet cloth for her forehead. She said she had a headache. I was happy to do such a grown-up thing and felt very important as I brought her the cloth. With that done, I skipped outside to play in my yard.

I never saw her again. My mother died of polio three days later—just one week before I turned four years old. The loss was total, irreversible and devastating. And I could not change it. No matter how I cried. No matter how good I promised to be. No matter how many threats I issued. No matter how desperately I wanted her back. My mother was gone—never to return to me. Never again to hug me close, or brush my hair, or tuck me in bed, or sing softly to me as I drifted off to sleep in perfect peace. Nor would she ever again gaze at me with love. And tragically, all too soon after she died, she began to fade from my memory. It was difficult to remember what her face looked like—or remember the tender gaze that always transmitted how much she loved me.

I was tormented by the idea that perhaps my mother left me because I was bad. I couldn't remember what I had done, but I must have done something to cause her to leave. That burden weighed heavily on my heart. There was no peace for me. Only dreadful longing and unutterable guilt.

Soon after her death, while trees were still dressed in scarlet and gold—before the leaves had floated to the ground and left limbs bare, I overheard the mailman speak to a neighbor of mine. He called out as he passed her home, "Those are sure cute kittens." Although I had been withdrawn and listless, the idea of seeing kittens drew me to the neighbor's home. I avoided being seen by anyone as I entered the backyard. There in a wooden tool shed was a box that held a beautiful white cat who had recently given birth to kittens. She was tucked away in the corner of the neat, dry shed. It was a cozy place. The mother cat snuggled close to her babies. It reminded me of the times I had snuggled close to my own mother. The grief that had engulfed my heart began to ease a little at the sight of the mother cat. I wanted my mother, but I could not have her anymore. After a few minutes, my four-year-old mind came up with a simple plan. I would become a kitten. And this beautiful mother cat would be my second mama. And since she was a mother herself, I reasoned, I could talk to her about my own mother. I knew she would understand. The eyes of the mama cat seemed to transmit the sweetest love to her kittens, and it reminded me of the special loving look my own mother used to gaze at me with. For the first time since my mother died, I smiled.

Each day I would visit Mama-cat. She liked being gently stroked by my little hands. Her fur was silky and soft and somehow comforting to me. Mama-cat purred loudly and talked to her babies in soft meows. She began to include me in her circle of love, too. She would gaze at me and purr loudly whenever I was near. I knew what she was saying—a four-year-old just knows these things—she was saying, "I love you, my babies," and I knew she included me in that, too.

I talked to her about my mother and how much I missed her. Mama-cat always seemed to understand. I could not speak to anyone else about the confusing jumbled-up pain that was in my heart, but I could talk to Mama-cat. She always listened patiently, and she seemed to be very wise.

My heart began to heal during the days that followed as Mama-cat showed me how much she loved all of us. I was absolutely certain that when I was with my Mama-cat I was a kitten. I believed if someone were to glance into the tool shed he or she would not see a child—they would see me as a kitten, so strong was my imagination as a four-year-old.

As time passed, and the kittens grew bigger, they no longer listened to the mother cat as well as they should have. They would ignore her worried meows to behave and stay close. They would race in and out of the tool shed and even climb way up a tree. I could always tell when Mama-cat was worried. My own mother used to get the same worried look when I would climb too high on my swing set after being told not to. She would rush over, lift me down and chide me for not listening to her. Then she would kiss me, smile and extract a promise that I would be more careful, though the following day I would be back up on the top of the swing set again.

In watching how much Mama-cat loved her misbehaving kittens, I came to understand the profound truth that my mother didn't leave me because I was bad, nor had she stopped loving me when I disobeyed her. Knowing that eased the ache in my heart.

For one very special season, I took refuge in the innocent land of make-believe. Within my young mind, I was one of the kittens this mother cat loved. That Mama-cat loved me was certain. That she eased a profound loss was also true. And her tender acceptance of me helped me fix the memory of my mother in my mind forever. When Mama-cat snuggled against me and comforted me, it was always a reminder of when I had snuggled in my mother's arms. Mama-cat was always glad to see me, just as my real mother had been. She would gaze at me with love —as my real mother had done.

No one else looked at me that way anymore. No one else was glad to see me. No one else worried about me, yet Mama-cat did, I was sure of it—just as my real mother had done. Mama-cat helped me keep the sweetest memories of my real mother from fading.

Many years later I became a mother. When my son was an infant I would hold him in my arms and gaze at him with tenderness. As he grew older, each year brought more delight, and my heart would fill with love. And sometimes, my heart would wander back to the tender memory of my own mother's love—and to a Mama-cat that helped a lonely, motherless little waif of a girl come to terms with loss. In my mind, even now, I can still see the face of my own mother and her tender loving gaze. And I can still see the sweet loving acceptance in the eyes of Mama-cat.

Lynn Seely

Reprinted by permission of Donna Barstow.

All My Mothers

Nothing we learn in this world is ever wasted.

Eleanor Roosevelt

Jennie to kindergarten, Kelly to college. The refrain repeats in my mind this year as my oldest sister and I send our children into wider orbit. The partings feel familiar. Being set out to swim in larger ponds came early in our family.

I was two when my mother died, and like any smart young animal I collected substitutes right away. On Mother's Day I send more cards than most. "To the one who has been like a mother to me," says one. "To my friend's mother," says another. Tante Minnie, Susanna, Ginny, Toni, Palma, Tetta, Woodie, Helen. My list goes on and on. Some of these women have been lost through time and circumstance, but each has etched my life with indelible strokes. Instead of just one mother, I have had many, which saddles you with a heady combination of freedom and sadness. On one hand, you're always that bewildered seven-year-old, neatly printing "deceased" on school registration forms. On the other hand, you're a parent unfettered by "Mother-always-did-it-this-way" rules, whether it's discipline, decorating or dishwashing soap you're after.

My oldest sister taught me to sew, and as a child I'd sit behind a chair in my grandmother's house, needle and thread in hand, inhabiting the same secret hiding place my mother favored when she hemmed as a girl. But I never picked up her vibes there. Today I use a whipstitch learned at the knee of Mrs. Parker, my seventh-grade home economics teacher.

That same year, I saw Lucinda Mirk's mother set chocolate-chip cookies to cool on brown paper bags, and that's still my method thirty years later, my cookie recipe cadged from a friend. I learned to write thank-you notes and answer wedding invitations in a book by Amy Vannderbilt (green-cover, circa 1952); it was a great find for fifty cents at a yard sale, I went to one summer.

My father was an eager and energetic parent, and he shepherded my two sisters and me through the snares of childhood with a bustling enthusiasm and confidence that belied our collective sorrow. We rarely talked of my mother's death, and then only in surface ways. Each of us adopted an attitude reflecting the truth as we saw it: We had a happy life together. We were young when she died. We didn't remember her.

Neighborhood moms escorted us to Girl Scout mother-daughter dinners. A string of housekeepers cooked our meals. And when coming-of-age came about, Dad steered us toward the nearest female and departed with embarrassment and grace. "I don't know whether to buy them garter belts or baseball bats," he'd cry out jokingly to friends, raising his arms toward the sky.

My best luck came as a teenager. I met Ginny, the sophisticated widow across the street. Her apartment had moody lighting and was decorated totally in purple, her favorite color. She curled up on an undulating black fur lounge chair in her living room to read *Cosmopolitan,* and I hung around her place after school, while my dad was at work, and struck the same poses. Lots of times I'd stay for supper: broiled chicken breasts and corn in butter sauce boiled in a bag. These dinners seemed as slim and sleek as Ginny herself, a heady menu for a girl more accustomed to Dinty Moore and powdered milk.

From Ginny I inherited not my nose or curly hair, but a no-fail parallel-parking technique and an abiding enthusiasm for miniature golf, bold jewelry and betting at the track. At Halloween, it's Ginny's custom to send five dollars to each of her grandchildren, and my Jennie is always on her list.

Our earliest infant recollections never leave us. They are emotional bonds, passed to us without words. These gifts from my mother are not lost. I care for my daughter instinctively, knowing that as I squeeze the bath sponge over her narrow shoulders and I brush her hair in long strokes, I am echoing love from many mothers, including my own. "Hang in there," I cry at the soccer field, echoing my friend Helen's sage advice. "Let it out," I murmur when my child cries, rocking her in my arms as Tante Minnie did for me so many years ago.

A mother died in our town last year; her son goes to my child's school. I don't know him, but I searched for his face among class photographs as if looking for myself—hoping he will find loving arms and a neighborhood mom cooling chocolate-chip cookies on brown paper bags, knowing the world is full of angels.

Mary Seehafer Sears
Family Circle

The Ring

Gratitude is the fairest blossom which springs from the soul.

Henry Ward Beecher

When the one-year anniversary of my mother's passing came around, I found myself in the kitchen preparing some of her favorite dishes. I hadn't planned this, but there I was one hot August afternoon, making her famous soup from the turkey I had roasted the day before.

As I poured myself into cooking, some of the deep sadness I was experiencing at this one-year mark moved through me. I loved my mom's turkey soup, how she cooked the egg noodles right in the broth, and how they soaked it up and tasted almost like dumplings. I remembered the time she made some especially for me. It was summer then, too, and I had a terrible head cold. She arrived unexpectedly one afternoon at my work place with a huge jar of her turkey noodle soup. I thought about the bread she used to bake and about how much butter she would slather on it, and how we loved to dip it into the broth. I began to feel a little more buoyant amidst the pain of losing her.

While the noodles boiled in the broth in my kitchen, I realized that I was reconnecting with my mother through food. I laughed a bit at myself when I reflected on all the dishes I had cooked that week. Without knowing it, I had created a beautiful ritual to honor my mother and to comfort myself at this vulnerable time. I suddenly felt my mother at hand and was filled with her presence. I was so uplifted and excited that I began talking to her, imagining she were there.

"What else should we make?" I asked of us both, wanting to keep the ritual from ending.

"Irish potato pancakes," was the reply.

I hesitated. The thought of these brought up another loss. The last time I made potato pancakes was two and a half years ago. I had taken off my engagement ring to make the dough, and never found it again. Since then, I resisted using that recipe even though I really liked those pancakes. It's sort of silly, but whenever I considered making them, I felt resentful of their participation in my loss, as if they were partly to blame.

My mom should know better than to suggest these, I thought. (I don't even remember her ever making them.) She knew how upset I was about losing my ring. I had always called her whenever I lost something, even when I was away at college, even from across the country, even when I traveled abroad. She had a knack for helping me find my way to lost things, except for this time.

But despite these hesitations, I found myself caught up in the joy and celebration of the moment, and I reached for the cookbook without another thought of the ring. My mom did love Irish things, and these were delicious. I opened the large coffee-table cookbook and turned to the pancake recipe. At once, something at the bottom of the page caught my eye . . . it sparkled! I gasped in utter amazement! There, pressed into the pages of this book, was my diamond ring!

Chills ran up and down my body as my mind raced to ponder how this was at all possible. Hadn't I used the book for other recipes in the course of almost three years? Wouldn't the ring have slipped out during the packing and unpacking of two household moves? Hadn't I checked the book for the ring when I had lost it?

My mind was subdued as my heart overflowed with the magic of gratitude and wonder. I slipped my ring onto my trembling hand, and a smile filled my soul as I whispered, "Thanks Mom."

That day, I made potato pancakes in the shape of hearts.

Kelly Salasin

Hold Your Head up High

Facing it—always facing it—that's the way to get through. Face it!

Joseph Conrad

I was fifteen months old, a happy carefree kid . . . until the day I fell It was a bad fall. I landed on a glass rabbit which cut my eye badly enough to blind it. Trying to save the eye, the doctors stitched the eyeball together where it was cut, leaving a big ugly scar in the middle of my eye. The attempt failed, but my mama, in all of her wisdom, found a doctor who knew that if the eye were removed entirely, my face would grow up badly distorted, so my scarred, sightless, cloudy and gray eye lived on with me. And as I grew, this sightless eye in so many ways controlled me.

I walked with my face looking at the floor so people would not see the ugly me. Sometimes people, even strangers, asked me embarrassing questions or made hurtful remarks. When the kids played games, I was always the "monster." I grew up imagining that everyone looked at me with disdain, as if my appearance were my fault. I always felt like I was a freak.

Yet Mama would say to me, at every turn, "Hold your head up high and face the world." It became a litany that I relied on. She had started when I was young. She would hold me in her arms and stroke my hair and say, "If you hold your head up high, it will be okay, and people will see your beautiful soul." She continued this message whenever I wanted to hide.

Those words have meant different things to me over the years. As a little child, I thought Mama meant, "Be careful or you will fall down or bump into something because you are not looking." As an adolescent, even though I tended to look down to hide my shame, I found that sometimes when I held my head up high and let people know me, they liked me. My mama's words helped me begin to realize that by letting people look at my face, I let them recognize the intelligence and beauty behind both eyes even if they couldn't see it on the surface.

In high school I was successful both academically and socially. I was even elected class president, but on the inside I still felt like a freak. All I really wanted was to look like everyone else. When things got really bad, I would cry to my mama and she would look at me with loving eyes and say, "Hold your head up high and face the world. Let them see the beauty that is inside."

When I met the man who became my partner for life, we looked each other straight in the eye, and he told me I was beautiful inside and out. He meant it. My mama's love and encouragement were the spark that gave me the confidence to overcome my own doubt. I had faced adversity, encountered my problems head on, and learned not only to appreciate myself but to have deep compassion for others.

"Hold your head up high," has been heard many times in my home. Each of my children has felt its invitation. The gift my mama gave me lives on in another generation.

Vickie Leach

The Lost Heart

*She never outgrows the burden of love, and to
the end she carries the weight of hope for those
she bore.*

Florida Scott-Maxwell

Maura was my middle daughter. Ahead of her was
Sharon, always in the lead and always in command of the
trio. Behind her was Sheila, determined from the beginning to always have my attention. They were all one year
apart and very different. Maura was the quiet one, lured
ahead or behind by the moment. In between, she read and
created. Our special bonding started when Maura was
eight years old and diagnosed with lymphosarcoma. We
were in London and she was hospitalized for six weeks for
surgery and radiation treatments and given a 5 percent
chance of survival.

"Mommy, am I going to die?" she asked. I answered the
only way I could: "I hope not."

"Mommy, is it true I can't have babies when I grow up?"

"Yes," I answered gently, "but the radiation will save
your life, and that is more important."

It did, and Maura and I grew up together, learned to fight the disease together, always looked for tomorrow, and shared the pain of each day. We learned to squeeze hands for all the needles and bone-marrow tests, and tried to pretend it didn't matter when she lost all her hair, even the second time when she was a senior in high school and didn't get to the senior prom.

The cancer finally left her body when she was eighteen and never returned. We shared the joy of life after cancer when she soared like an eagle into the academic world, excelling in everything she touched, challenging even her graduate school professors with her ideas and ambitions. Maura had learned early on how precious life is and she fought to the end to hang on to every morsel of it.

Cancer stepped into the background of our lives. I remember the day when she told me, "Mom, I can drive myself to my annual check-ups in Boston. You don't need to come anymore."

Eight years later it was discovered that the last chemotherapy drug used to cure her cancer had, over time, damaged her heart. Her life was in jeopardy, and as her only hope, she was accepted at Brigham & Women's in Boston as a heart transplant candidate. Now in graduate school at Princeton, she fell in love with a chap from Australia who devotedly cared for her as her heart weakened. They married sooner than planned, in my living room, sitting down. They honeymooned in my same-floor bedroom with candles lit as their romantic get-away.

Three months later, the new heart still hadn't come. Cardiac arrest put her in intensive care on life support, as I prepared my students for their big ballet performance. I rushed to the hospital instead of the theater. Maura was first on the national list for the needed heart. Three days passed. We stood at her bed joining hands, my daughter Sheila, and Maura's husband, as the life-sustaining machine was turned off. Sharon, the eldest, the leader, very pregnant, stood near and held tightly to her husband. Maura's father stood alone.

Maura died the day taxes were due. We got an extension. On Easter Saturday we buried her in the woods of Wildwood Cemetery. Sharon's water broke. Maura's dried bridal bouquet was placed on her coffin, and as soon as she was lowered, Sharon and her husband raced to Brigham & Women's in Boston to welcome a new life.

As Sharon entered the lobby of the hospital where Maura had died a few days earlier, she passed a familiar couple. "Hi," the man said. "Remember me?" The man had been a patient on Maura's floor, also waiting for a heart transplant. "Tell Maura I got my new heart," he told Sharon as they passed. He was checking out as Sharon checked in. He couldn't know that Maura was not as lucky as he.

On Easter Sunday, I was back in Boston at the same hospital that had been my daughter's last hope. As I held my grandson in my arms, the emotional pendulum was swaying much too fast. As I stood there in the weak light of that April afternoon, the heart transplant team social worker walked through the door: She had come to welcome our new heart, and to grieve with us for our heart lost.

Therese Brady Donohue

Blessings

Luck is a matter of preparation meeting opportunity.

Oprah Winfrey

The sharp smell of smoke woke me out of a deep sleep. Opening my eyes I saw pulsating flames engulfing the bedroom. Seized by panic, my heart took up the beat of an African drum, strong and loud. A whispery voice from deep within me could barely be heard above its booming beat. Instinctively, I followed the voice's advice, *Heat rises, stay low to the ground. Call 911 after you're out of the house. Get people out first. Leave things behind.* Impaired by thick smoke and searing heat, I clung to my husband and baby and dashed out the front door.

Then I woke up.

It had all been a dream. A nightmare to add to my growing list of waking ordeals. In the past six months I had quit my job and become a first-time mom, and my husband Alan had suddenly been laid off from work. Sleepless and stressed, I desperately needed relief from life's tribulations, not invasive nightmares. Looking for the positive, I used the dream's prompting to install new batteries in my home's smoke detector.

My mom's visit to meet her new grandson had been a high point in that stressful time. She flew up from California and took over kitchen duty. Dressed in her green-flowered muumuu, she performed kitchen magic. The aroma of comfort foods lulled me back to treasured childhood memories. Tucked into Mom's suitcase, beside her cold cream and bottles of vitamins, was the baptismal gown my four siblings and I had worn. After all these years, the white silk kimono, covered with tiny embroidered bows, was still purity itself. The long pleated under gown and the lace-edged bonnet were immaculate. At my mother's urging we called the local church and set a date for Zander's baptism.

Days later, the once familiar smell of spicy frankincense wafted through a heavy wood door, as we stepped into the church. The organ's deep chords vibrated through our bodies. This baptism was an offering to my mother. Dressed in the family heirloom, Zander cooed quietly while blessings and fluttering hands passed over his head. Mom stood in proud attendance. Alan and I held Zander's head as he was immersed in the ancient ritual, irreverently known as "the dunking." Not partial to cold water, Zander let out an ear-damaging scream. Taking him from our arms, Mom rocked Zander with a gentle swing and sway of her hips. Tilting her head toward his ear she whispered, "You'll be just fine, sweet stuff."

Mom beamed as she held her grandson for photos. He was cute, he had good strong lungs, and he wouldn't go to hell for lack of a proper baptism. What more could a grandma ask for?

None of us knew that would be the last time we'd all be together as a family. Mom headed back down to California feeling slightly tired. Weeks of rest left her weaker, not stronger, and within a month she was dead. Cancer had spread undetected throughout her body and no amount of modern medicine or old-fashioned prayer could keep her on this Earth.

Dizzy with grief, I mourned the loss of my mom. Depression tried to lure me into its quicksand. I struggled to remain semi-sane. My husband was going through his own grief, and my child's safety and well-being were dependent on my keeping a finger hold on sanity.

Christmas loomed ahead. Yet the joy of the season eluded me. My belief in miracles was at an all-time low. I forced myself through the motions. I missed my mother.

The morning after my fire dream, Zander and I spent the day in the attic wrapping presents and listening to different versions of "Jingle Bells" and "Silent Night." Remnants of the dream stubbornly clung to my psyche. Mentally, I relived our fire escape and planned out better routes. Unaware of his mother's preoccupation with disaster, Zander giggled the day away, decorating himself with leftover bits of paper and ribbon. A small space heater kept us warm while snow clouds formed outside. By day's end, I had accomplished a lifetime goal as I finished wrapping gifts before Christmas Eve.

That night the first snowflakes of the year covered the ground. It looked as if we were going to have a rare white Christmas in Seattle. I eagerly anticipated seeing Zander's reaction to this cool white stuff. Dawn seemed too far away.

In the dark hours between night and morning, our smoke detector started beeping. "Damn it," I fumed. "Why is it waking me up with its blasted beeping?"

Floating into consciousness, I opened my eyes to a room filled with smoke. My mind raced back to the night before and my nightmare about a house fire. Was I now having serial fire dreams?

My eyes stung, and my nose was clogged with

blackness; this was the real thing. Alan and I raced around our house searching for the fire's source. He checked the basement, and I raced to get Zander. Pausing outside his bedroom, I checked the attic stairs. Slamming the door against the hissing fire, I grabbed Zander out of his crib and raced out the front door with Alan. Glancing back over our shoulders, we saw the kitchen, right next to our son's room, explode into flames. Words slowly stumbled out of my mouth, "If the alarm had gone off a few minutes later . . ."

A flashback of the fire nightmare played out in my mind. Could it have been a warning? A message from my mother? The thought sent shivers up my arms and a glow of warmth to my heart. Without a doubt the dream had prepared me for our house fire. With what little emotions I had left, I gave heartfelt thanks for the miracle of our survival and for the dream I had originally scorned. I longed to hear my mom's comforting voice but had to be content with her ethereal presence. Internally, I could hear her whisper soothing words. The tone of voice and cadence were just as I remembered.

In the light of day, we returned to assess the house's damage. As we stepped through the doorway, the smell of smoke overwhelmed us. Devastation was everywhere. With leaden legs, we surveyed the remains of our worldly possessions. Tears streamed down my cheeks as I found my smoke-damaged wedding dress, destroyed family recipes, fire-scented letters and piles of melted toys. Ghostly images of picture frames and figurines were silhouetted against a backdrop of black, smoke-streaked walls.

As Alan and I gingerly climbed the fire-damaged steps to the attic, little drifts of snow fell through the few remaining rafters. This had been my refuge, the place I'd stored all my childhood treasures after my mom's sudden death. It was also the heart of the fire, caused by a cheap extension cord, they told us. Picking through charred remains, I found little to salvage. Books, files and those beloved stuffed animals I saved for my children, were all destroyed. What more could I lose?

Alan found the fire-scorched box that held the family baptismal gown my mother had brought up for Zander's christening. Before tossing it into the trash pile, I felt compelled to peek inside, one last reminder of my mother. Opening the blackened lid, my fingers picked up flakes of burned cardboard. But inside, the tissue paper was miraculously unsinged. Lifting my family's heirloom gown, a stillness embraced me, just as it used to when my mom would whisper, "Don't worry, sweet stuff, you'll be just fine." My breathing slowed as I brushed off my hands and gently traced the gown's tiny, embroidered bows. And I knew my mom was right. I would be fine.

Colleen Foye Bollen

The Prom That Almost Wasn't

*If you paint in your mind a picture of bright
and happy expectations, you put yourself into a
condition conducive to your goal.*

Norman Vincent Peale

My daughter Beth's bright blue eyes sparkled as they
caught mine in the mirror at the beauty salon.

"She looks beautiful," said our hairstylist Elaine, who
had just put the finishing touches on Beth's updo style.
Beth's smile of pleasure spoke volumes. This remarkably
lucky young woman felt like the belle of the ball, which is
a fitting way to feel on prom night. But just six short
months ago, as doctors fought to save my sixteen-year-old
daughter's life, I would have never dreamed she would
recover enough to attend her junior prom.

At approximately 10:30 P.M. on November 10, 1999, Beth,
a passenger in a tiny Dodge Neon, was heading to a friend's
house to watch a video in celebration of a day off from
school. The driver lost control of the car as he sped through
some curves. He buried the right front fender in a tree at the
edge of the road less than a quarter mile from our home.

At midnight we received the knock at the door every parent dreads. A deputy sheriff stood on the doorstep. After he ascertained that Beth was our daughter, he told us she had been involved in an accident. As the blood drained from my body and my knees suddenly became too weak to support me, I asked, "How bad is it?"

"It's her legs," he said, "They're bad. They're very bad."

Beth was rushed to the University of Tennessee Medical Center for surgery. The prognosis was grim. She suffered a broken right hand, leg and hip and a fractured left leg and foot. X-rays showed six major breaks and dozens of tiny fissures and cracks in the pelvic region.

Her initial chance for survival was questionable. The orthopedic surgeon, thinking he was just patching her up so we could say our final good-byes, inserted steel rods above and below the knee in her right leg and three four-inch screws in her hip. An external fixator, a series of metal rods protruding from her hips, kept her crushed pelvic bones in place.

I was not allowed to see Beth after the accident until regular trauma intensive care unit visiting hours at ten o'clock the next morning, nearly a dozen hours after the accident. Beth spent five critical days in ICU fighting for her life. A collapsed left lung and internal injuries and bleeding caused grave concern. She eventually received six units of blood before she began to stabilize.

Ten short days later, the insurance company deemed her ready to be released. She remained bedridden for nearly two months and was put on a collection of drugs including a blood thinner, Coumadin, to help keep blood clots from forming in her legs, which might lead to heart attack or stroke. Coumadin helps prevent these clots, when taken at the right level. However, too much Coumadin can result in serious internal bleeding.

As her classmates were preparing for Christmas break,

Beth was enduring daily blood draws. As they were ringing in the New Year, Beth was weaning herself off pain pills. And as they were pouring over catalogues and magazines full of prom dresses, Beth was retraining her muscles from the waist down.

By the end of January, the rods were removed from Beth's hips and she could begin the journey to walking once again. Jo Scott, our home health physical therapist, gave Beth a list of daily exercises. From the beginning, Beth was determined to succeed. She surpassed Jo's expectations and went from walker to crutches in just a few days. Two weeks later she tossed the crutches and wobbled about on her own.

By May first, Beth was almost back to normal, and she wanted to go to the prom. I was concerned that the evening would be too much for her to handle, but she insisted. As I watched Beth whirl and twirl in prom dress after prom dress, I reveled in a moment I may once have taken for granted.

The accident has changed Beth's perspective and appreciation for life. She is grateful for the little things like being able to take a shower or hold her baby sister. She never fails to wear a seatbelt and chides her friends when they forget to snap their own. Although her gait is different now and she limps when she is tired, Beth's recovery is nothing short of astounding.

This year's prom theme was, appropriately enough, "What Dreams May Come." Thanks to a miracle and her own determination, Beth still has many dreams to fulfill.

As she walked out the door with her date on prom night, I smiled as I told her I loved her. More important than any prom dream, my dream for her recovery had come true.

Kate Clabough

The Cosmic Click

Man never made any material as resilient as the human spirit.

Bern Williams

On the other side of the world is my shadow. I have never seen her; there is no sunshine bright enough to bring her into focus. But once a year I know, for sure, that we are connected. Today is my daughter's birthday—Rose is five! An exuberant, swirling, twirling, graceful, beautiful girl. This is the fifth time I have planned her birthday party, bought presents, kissed her goodnight for the last time at a certain age. And today, as on birthdays past, my heart has gone to my shadow—the woman who left an infant near a police station in Dongguan, China.

As Rose rips the wrapping paper off her roller skates, she is radiant with happiness. My eyes meet my husband's, and we smile over her head, silently telling each other that all is well; our little girl is A-okay. I love sharing this with him and, later, with my parents and friends who will come to pay homage to a cherished child. But I am also missing something. What I want more than anything, on *this* day, is to be able to walk down some narrow street in China, knock on a door, and hug this other woman who is connected to Rose. I know nothing about her—no name, no address, no medical info. What made her give up her baby? We haven't a clue—just the general knowledge of life in China (poverty? unmarried? pressure to have a son?). As Rose grows up she will fantasize about this woman, and I hope we will be able to share our images with each other. Mine are of a beautiful young woman who, sobbing, kisses her beautiful infant a thousand times—and then a thousand times more, before saying good-bye.

Right now I am sitting in my office, while Rose shares Dunkin Donut holes with her kindergarten classmates. Before I pick up Rose and frost the cake, I want to take these two hours to sit with my shadow, knee-to-knee. I want to fill my backpack with photos, sling my video bag over my shoulder, and magically be transported to that little house in China. I would show her the pictures of Rose learning to get up on the couch using our dog as a step stool, Rose riding on her daddy's shoulders, Rose eating corn on the cob, Rose caught just as her plastic bat smacks a baseball. I would use the video screen on my camcorder to let her hear Rose singing the alphabet song and Twinkle, Twinkle. The movie of Rose meeting her little brother, just brought home from Vietnam. The scenes of all her past birthday parties. We won't need to talk, my shadow and I, the images will be enough. I want to let her know, by seeing her lost child, that Rose's life is filled with joy, and that I am a good mother to her.

When we traveled in China, everyone gave us the thumbs-up sign, smiled, pointed to our baby and gestured "good luck." We had taken a baby whose fate was "very, very bad" and given her the chance to be lucky, lucky, lucky. On this yearly anniversary, I think of Rose's shadow mother, and want her to know exactly what occurred when I was handed her underfed, shining-eyed miracle. I think of it as a cosmic, mind-boggling, wondrous "click," as Rose's fate switched from a Chinese trajectory, heading in a direction I cannot even imagine, to join mine in lockstep, glued together for life; new mother and child.

Rachel Fink

A Legacy of Love

*A woman is like a tea bag. You never know
how strong she is until she gets into hot water.*

Eleanor Roosevelt

From time to time, an experience of astonishing grace
can instantaneously transform our relationship to self,
others and the universe in a way that leaves us renewed.
The story of my mother's death and our mutual rebirth
was that kind of luminous event.

My mother's answer to the perennial question of why
bad things happen to good people was deeply affected by
her losing many of her family in the Holocaust. Her faith
was shattered by Hitler. To her, the world was a Godless
place where nice guys finished last. After my father fell ill
with leukemia and committed suicide when medical treatments had rendered his life unbearable, my mother
became a hermit. She saw only family for the last thirteen
years of her life.

When my mother's health failed and she became
bedridden, I wondered how she felt about death. After all,
my entire professional life consisted of working with

people in passages like my mother's. But with her, I felt stymied. It was a case of the shoemaker's children having no shoes.

I wanted my mother to taste the healing, the peace of mind and forgiveness that I had witnessed in hundreds of other people. In retrospect, this was my need, not hers. Perhaps it was really a need of forgiveness before her death. But our track record for intimate conversation was poor, and discussion of our mutual feelings about life and death was no exception. We had no shared vocabulary for feelings. So for the most part, our conversations centered on politics, family and sports.

Sitting in my mother's bedroom, watching television and making small talk, I continued to search for some way to make a deeper spiritual connection. One evening my former husband crawled into bed next to her, held her in his arms and lovingly recounted inspiring near-death experiences we had heard. She pushed these away with good humor, commenting that we could believe in such things if it made us feel better, but they didn't speak to her in the least.

A few weeks before she died, Spirit provided an experience that spoke to her. Mom, an avid baseball fan, was a Bostonian, and the Red Sox were naturally her team. Like most of Boston, she had followed the saga of Wade Boggs, a third baseman, with great interest. Boggs's mistress had spilled to the newspaper some nasty gossip he had told her about his teammates, and he was publicly humiliated.

The media had a field day with his indiscretions. Even though I'm not a baseball fan, my attention was caught one day by a newspaper article that queried why Boggs was doing so well in the stressful situation. The answer was nothing short of astonishing. Boggs's mother had recently died, and he reported that she had come back to him as a full three-dimensional apparition! She assured him that we learn from our mistakes and that he should take responsibility for what he'd done and go on. At the same time, she had appeared to Boggs's sister, who was confined to a wheelchair with multiple sclerosis so advanced that even her vocal cords were paralyzed. She asked her daughter to give the eulogy at her funeral, and her daughter recovered sufficiently to do so!

Filled with the most delicious excitement, I phoned my mother and read her the article. For once she was speechless. Just a few weeks later, I was with her when she went into respiratory distress. I called an ambulance, and we rode through the snow to the hospital for the last time.

In the ER, a very kind nurse, whom she knew well from previous stays, told Mom that she was close to death and asked if she was at peace with that. Barely conscious up to this point, Mother was fairly resurrected with her own version of the good news. "Am I at peace with death?" she crowed. "Have you heard about Wade Boggs's mother?"

As she lay dying, Mom pondered the perennial questions in a new way. Never once did she question that her soul would live on—apparently the apparition of Mrs. Boggs convinced her of that. Instead, she pondered about whether my father, her brother and her parents would be there on the other side to greet her. The hope of reunion gave her tremendous peace.

The morning of her death, she was taken down to the hospital basement, where the radiology department was located. She was bleeding internally, and they wanted to diagnose the source of the bleeding. When she had not reappeared after several hours, the family dispatched me to look for her. I found her alone, on a stretcher, in the hospital corridor. She was waiting her turn for X-ray.

Although I'm not usually an assertive person, I lambasted the young doctor in charge and demanded that they let my mother go back to her room, where the family was waiting to say good-bye. He commented dryly that first they needed a diagnosis for her bleeding. Mom retorted, "*You* mean I've been waiting here all day for a diagnosis? Why didn't you just ask me? I'm dying—that's your diagnosis." He couldn't argue with her logic, and, surprisingly, let her go.

I rode up in the elevator next to her stretcher. Holding hands on that brief ascent, we accomplished the work of a lifetime—the exchange of forgiveness and the realization of a deep mutual love.

Joan Borysenko

A Message for the Bride

"The way you're fussing over this wedding!" my mother said with a cluck-cluck of her tongue. "You'd think it was the royal wedding of Princess Diana!"

I bristled. "I want things to be perfect for Cathy," I said. "She's our most romantic daughter, and she's been quietly dreaming of her wedding day all her life."

"Well, you can't get things perfect," Mom grumbled. "That's Murphy's Law."

"Maybe so, but we can try," I said, and continued going over and over the list of pre-wedding details.

It would be the first wedding of our three children, and Cathy, at age twenty-seven, was entitled to a "perfect day," if there was such a thing.

And maybe it was a little bit for my own sake. Our 1959 wedding had been marred by a wrinkled train behind my gown, noticed only when it was too late to iron it correctly. I'll never forget walking down the aisle feeling like some kind of last-minute, pathetic and wrinkled bride.

Therefore this one—Cathy and Brad's big day—must have no glitches. We met each night to plan every small detail. My husband ordered the finest of prime rib dinners at a really elegant catering hall. We certainly weren't wealthy people, but this event became a priority; it had to be "perfect." There would be no wrinkled dress in this wedding!

One problem was that Cathy missed her dearest childhood friend. Deirdre had died eight years before, a cancer victim at age nineteen. But life had to go on, and Cathy accepted that she couldn't have Deirdre there as a treasured bridesmaid.

The wedding day arrived at last. We had it all under control—except that cloudy skies opened up for a blustering April rainstorm like no other in history! How could we possibly get those girls to the church in even a semi-dry state?

As the limo service drivers protected the bridal party with black umbrellas, we wrapped the bride in a large sheet of clear plastic and kept her gown from getting soaked.

Patting myself on the back during the nuptial Mass for averting the rain, I heard the priest say, "Well, we wouldn't have had this rainstorm if the mother of the bride had remembered to place a rosary on a tree last night."

I turned purple with mortification. I was horrified. First of all, I'd never HEARD of such a custom; and second, if I had, I would have festooned all the trees in Connecticut if it would have helped my Cathy's wedding.

Even though everyone knew the priest had made the remark in a joking way, I felt like a failure. Déjà vu: It was the wrinkled train all over again. Murphy's Law, after all.

After the ceremony, we gathered in the rear of the church for an indoor receiving line. I rushed over to my bride/daughter, my once-tiny, curly haired toddler, to straighten her flowery headpiece.

And that's when I did the thing I'd been planning since Cathy's friend passed away years before.

"Honey, you look absolutely radiant today," I whispered so that only she could hear.

"Oh, Mom!" Tears flooded Cathy's eyes and she grasped

my arm in a tight grip. "How did you know? How'd you know to say that?"

My eyes also filled with tears. "I knew, honey. Deirdre told me, years ago, the last time I saw her."

Deirdre and Cathy, very best friends, had this secret, ironclad plan: Each of them would say to the other on her wedding day: "You look radiant." They planned it since third grade . . . and it was vital to them both.

As Deirdre lay dying in the hospital, she told me of their vow—and asked, "Mrs. H., will you say the radiant thing to Cathy for me? In case I'm not there on her wedding day?"

I nodded yes, my heart splintering. Here was a precious life disappearing before my eyes—a sweet and sassy and beautiful young lady who'd leave a gaping hole in all of our lives . . . and most especially in Cathy's.

"You do look radiant," I repeated now to my daughter. "And if Deirdre were here, she'd say it, just the way you girls planned."

"Oh, Mom . . ." My little bride had to dab her eyes with a tissue. "Just your saying that . . . I know it seems crazy but . . . I think Deirdre IS here. She is."

"Yes." We clasped hands and shared a moment. "Yes, hon, she is here right now."

Wedding guests were pushing to get at us, to kiss and congratulate. Our quiet little mother-daughter moment was over; tears rolled quietly down my face.

So, Mrs. Mother of the Bride, you did do something correctly, I told myself. And I felt a soaring sense of joy, thankful that we'd given our daughter a perfect day after all.

Thanks for saying that radiant thing for me, Mrs. H., a voice seemed to be whispering in my ear. I know it was Deirdre, with her impish little grin.

A "perfect wedding," indeed.

Eileen Hehl

Lunch Dates

If you give your life as a wholehearted response to love, then love will wholeheartedly respond to you.

Marianne Williamson

Mother was delighted when I became a nurse. A long time ago, she had dreams of becoming a nurse, too, but that was before marriage and children. We enjoyed spending precious time together on our "lunch dates" after I was married and had two children of my own. The time we had together meant more than simply sharing a meal. Being together was a cherished gift—a gift we gave to each other—a gift we enjoyed as time allowed. The word "time" is short and simple—and often taken for granted. We shared our hearts and souls during our uninterrupted moments in time.

My life was hectic and occasionally chaotic. There never seemed to be enough time to juggle everything that had to be done, let alone what I wanted to do. Keeping all of the balls in the air at the same time was an almost impossible task. Still somehow, Mother and I always managed to make the time to have our special "lunch dates."

One afternoon in early April, the two of us drove to the mall for a morning of shopping before we "did lunch." After walking for only a few minutes, Mother pointed toward a display of brilliantly colored spring dresses. "Let's stop in here," she said with a childlike voice full of excitement. This was an unusual day because Mother didn't indulge in the luxury of spending money on herself very often.

We walked over to the finery, and she eagerly shuffled through the hangers. After scrutinizing each dress, she finally pulled one out and held it up with an inquisitive glance.

"Look at this beautiful blue one," Mother exclaimed. "Do we have enough time for me to try this on, dear?"

Without a moment's hesitation I said, "Certainly. After you have it on come out and model it for me." Mother was of a generous size, and it was wonderful to see her rare excitement over a new dress. She appeared from behind the fitting room curtains, and slowly sauntered toward the full-length mirror, turning around and around, to view every angle. She looked at me with the wide-eyed enthusiasm of a schoolgirl.

"Where could I wear this if I did buy it?" she inquired.

I was thinking ahead to our son's college graduation in the spring. We both agreed this would be the perfect opportunity for her to wear the new dress.

As we walked out of the store Mother tried to disguise her discomfort. I noticed she was walking more slowly than on previous outings, and she was breathing harder with each step. She stopped frequently to window shop and discuss the displays, but I knew she was trying to disguise her need to catch her breath. When I mentioned it she dismissed the subject with her usual, "I'm just fine, dear . . . not used to walking in these darned sandals."

We seemed to be closer than ever. We shared feelings and thoughts about everything and everyone in our lives. I saw her in a different light. We surpassed mother and daughter. We were now close friends—two adult women, connecting.

Two weeks later, on a Sunday afternoon, my father telephoned, hysterically mumbling something about paramedics. He instructed me to meet him at the emergency room as quickly as I could. I drove to the hospital with trembling hands and a racing heart. I gripped the steering wheel for support. This was the hospital where I worked, and my car seemed to pilot itself.

The emergency room nurse was waiting for me at the door. She escorted me into an office where my father sat, shaking and sobbing. He stood up as I walked over to him. We hugged. His tear-filled eyes disclosed the dreadful truth.

He managed to choke out a few words. "She never knew what happened. Her heart just stopped. I did all I could for her but . . ." Then he fell into my arms, and we both cried. It seemed like a nightmare—so unreal. The soft-spoken nurse gave us a few details about Mother's condition and assured us that death had come quickly. Then she left the three of us alone for our final farewells, telling us to take as long as we needed.

Mother was lying so peacefully on the stretcher, covered almost entirely by a white sheet, except for her pale face and shoulders. Although I had seen many patients die, this was different. This was my one and only mother, and my first experience with losing a loved one. Dad and I held on to each other as we cried.

That shopping trip suddenly seemed ages ago. Thank God I had the chance to get to know and appreciate my mother while she was still alive. Not everyone has this miraculous opportunity.

The funeral director requested that we bring Mother's burial clothing with us the next day when we finalized the arrangements. When Dad and I stepped into her closet, the first piece of clothing we saw was her new blue dress, with the tags still dangling from the sleeve. I choked back the tears as I remembered her recent question, "Where could I wear this if I bought it?"

I held up the dress and said, "I know Mother would want to wear this one." Dad looked up with tears streaming down his cheeks and nodded in agreement.

Mother looked beautiful at the viewing in her blue dress.

Laura Lagana
Previously appeared in Touched by Angels of Mercy

Angel Escort

Faith is the daring of the soul to go farther than it can see.

William Newton Clark

I peaked anxiously into the living room where my grand-mother was dozing in a morphine-induced euphoria, appar-ently free from pain, and lulled by the soothing scratchiness of carols on the radio. It had been three weeks since the Hospice Foundation released her to my care. At the age of ninety-two, she developed cancer of the gallbladder. The oncologist gave her less than a month to live, and dis-charged her to my home in Fishkill, New York, to die.

She sat in the overstuffed recliner, that appeared more like a cloud with my son's pale blue blanket draped across the broad arms of the chair. Her skin was so white it was blue, disappearing into the color of the soft, woolen folds.

"How has she been?" I asked, strangling with concern.

My husband continued to stir his bubbling tomato sauce, tasting puddles of it from the wooden spoon, and shaking spices into the pot accordingly.

"She's fine. Terry has been driving me nuts, though. I

know it's tough for you to deal with that son of ours right now, but . . ."

I slumped into a kitchen chair, amid the damp, crumpled bags and rolling oranges.

"Were you able to get the 'good' kind of Parmesan?"

"Yes. The man at the deli counter grated it fresh," I assured him as I walked into the living room.

Gingerly pulling my son's wooden rocking chair close to Mum, I stroked the coolness of her gnarled and freckled hand. The lights of the Christmas tree refracted through the thin whiteness of her hair, lending an unearthly glow. She appeared as if she belonged atop the tree instead of beside it. Mum opened her eyes with the slow deliberate-ness of an ancient sea turtle. Her eyes were clouded from cataracts, watery with wisdom.

"You're home, dear. I was getting worried. Are the roads bad?"

"No, Mum. It's that big, fat 'cartoon' snow that doesn't stick to the roads," I explained licking salty tears from my upper lip.

"Christmas Eve snow. Remember how you used to think it was magic?"

"I still do . . ."

She reached up and touched the droplets in my hair, lightly brushing the bangs from my eyes. Looking past my head, Mum strained with her fingers outstretched.

"I see a blue light behind you, and little gold bells in your hair . . ." Her voice weakly trailed off, and then her face widened with a look of realization.

I listened, almost as an intruder. She was on the other end of a conversation that I could not hear.

"I will always love you, dear. Nothing can ever change that. And I will always be with you, even forever. Promise me, you won't be afraid . . ."

"I promise, Mum," and I kissed the inside of her wrist as I replaced her hand in her lap.

But I was afraid. I didn't know how I would get through the rest of my life without the strength of this tiny woman. Mum, as I always called her, had raised me from infancy, whenever my mother's frequent and episodic manic-depression interrupted her maternal tasks.

My grandmother was an oasis of sanity and calm, and she faced all of life's adversities with quiet dignity. I could no longer pretend to be brave for her, or anyone else. I stopped praying for a miracle to save her, and asked God to show me a way to get through the loneliness I would know when she was gone.

"Who's having shrimp?" was my husband's signal that the traditional Christmas Eve feast was about to begin, whether I was ready for it or not. He came out of the kitchen, unfolding my grandmother's walker, and motioned for me to get our son.

The first angel arrived Christmas afternoon.

I was watching my son play obliviously with his new toys, when Mum began to shriek. When I reached her, she was huddled in a corner of the bed, her eyes glowing like a cat hit with light.

"Elissa, you have to save me! I'm dying!"

She clawed my forearms and pleaded for me to deny the sudden reality, all the while staring at the blank bedroom wall as if a ghost stood before it.

I held her quivering shoulders—that had become a human hanger for her nightgown—firmly to my chest until I felt her relax against me.

Slowly, her countenance softened and her eyes shone with the familiar recognition of an old friend. She smiled and resigned herself to me as I placed her limp frame onto her mountain of pillows.

Days suffused to nights without my noticing, as Mum

slipped into a purgatory world, and the hospice nurse informed me that my grandmother was "actively dying."

I was understandably alarmed when she began speaking to deceased relatives and friends as if they were standing behind me. In the week or more that passed, though, I accepted it as naturally as I did drawing water up a 50-cc syringe to drop onto her cracking tongue. One by one they came, all of her lost loved ones. I especially remember the smile on her face when her brother, my great-uncle, joined the angel visitors. I could almost see the brightly colored medals shining on his chest as Mum's eyes welcomed him home from the war.

"How 'bout this little girl here, Bill? Isn't your niece taking good care of me?" and I sensed the end was near from the warm pride in her voice that was present whenever her younger son was near. I caught myself praying for God to just let her go to him. Even the experienced hospice nurse could not explain why my grandmother was hanging on.

Twelve mornings had passed since Christmas, and I looked at my church calendar that notated the Epiphany.

"You have to eat something," my husband reproached as he removed my untouched plate of eggs.

"I don't know how much longer I can go on like this! I can hardly tell the real-life callers from the unearthly ones! I'll end up like my mother if I don't get some rest."

"It won't be long, now, honey," Steve reassured me with a shoulder squeeze. "I didn't want to upset you, but I heard Mum talking to your father before you woke up. I knew it was him when she mentioned the 'flashlight.'"

My father was the official family escort who owned every kind of flashlight on the market. Mum and I had buried him with his favorite, a high-tech contraption that appeared as if it belonged on top of an ambulance. We joked that he would come for us with it, one day.

"Of course, who else would she go with?" and I walked down the hallway to the bedroom, steadying myself on the paneled walls. I offered my farewell, at last, cradling Mum's stiffening hands to my cheek, and assuring her that it was time to leave me.

I never saw the angel escort. Nor was I aware of the exact moment of Mum's passing. But, as I looked out the window at the circling snow, I felt the cool, connective threads of unending love, and the strength to go on without her.

Elissa Hadley Conklin

The Club

You never will finish being a daughter.

Gail Godwin

The doctor cuts the umbilical cord at birth, but I believe it remains an invisible connection throughout the lives of both mother and child. In utero, the cord that joined my mother and me flowed with blood, rich in food and oxygen. After birth, my mother provided me with emotional and spiritual sustenance. When my mother died and our connection was severed by her removal from the physical world, I floundered. I felt displaced and disoriented. There are still times, years later, when I feel deprived and bewildered without that invisible cord in place to nurture and nourish me.

I recall the day my mother joined the club. I was eleven and had come home from school for lunch. That day, as with many days that preceded it, I had been followed home by two girls who teased and taunted me every step of the way. I was crying by the time I reached my door and I needed my mother. I rushed blindly into the kitchen and fell into her arms, sobbing and trying desperately to tell her how hurt I was. I saw my father and wondered why he was home in the middle of the day. I then looked up into my mother's face and saw it streaked with tears and contorted with her own misery. I thought, *Wow, she is really upset about the teasing, too!*

My father broke the silence and announced, "Your grandmother died this morning." Only after I joined the club years later did I begin to comprehend the wrench she was feeling that day at lunch. The cord to her mother had been cut, and she was struggling to breathe on her own for the first time.

I have heard that time heals all wounds. I do not believe this. The person who has lost a limb never stops missing the arm or leg that is gone, but somehow time permits that person to cope eventually with the loss. The cloud of grief that isolates, suffocates and blinds us will lift.

I was a mother of two when my mother died. There have been three babies born since, and sometimes the pain of not being able to share the smallest and most insignificant moments that I know she would understand paralyzes me briefly, and I feel angry and cheated.

My mother is physically gone, but she still sustains me. A glance at an old photograph, the sight of her handwriting on a recipe card or the remembrance of a moment long ago can evoke a memory so powerful and vivid, I swear sometimes I can hear her calling my name. Her obvious presence in my five children continues to inspire and motivate me even when I am tired, lonely and scared. One's meticulous attention to detail, another's smile and another's unflagging optimism resurrect her when I need her the most.

My mother has not left me, even though the cord has finally been cut, and I have joined the club I never knew existed.

Susan B. Townsend

Mother's Goblets

*Hope is a thing with feathers
that perches in the soul,
And sings the tune without words
And never stops at all.*

Emily Dickinson

I can't remember the last time I saw my mother. Actually, I don't remember her at all. She died shortly before I turned three. The stories I've heard about her are other people's memories, not mine. Life cheated me out of hearing her voice and feeling her touch. She remained out of focus, a shadowy figure, until the day I found her glasses. Suddenly, thirty-three years after her death, she was real as if she reached out to help me when I needed her most.

Don't get me wrong. My life was good. My wayward father wisely left me with his in-laws who gave me pretty much everything—especially a home filled with love. Growing up, I was vaguely aware of several mysterious boxes that had something to do with my elusive mother. Since I was too young for the contents to mean anything to me, my aunt faithfully guarded her sister's belongings for over twenty years.

Eventually, I got married and moved into my own house. My aunt, feeling her tour of duty was over, gave me the boxes. Like treasure hunters, we eagerly opened each carton. A teacup collection. Fine china. Tarnished silver. Exquisite crystal. The most beautiful glasses I'd ever seen—clear and delicate and etched with roses. We hand-washed and arranged them in the china cabinet. They came out only on holidays or special occasions along with the china and silver. I proudly used them until the day the water goblets broke.

I can't remember how it happened. An accident, I'm sure. No one's fault really. Two water goblets simply broke. Carefully picking up the pieces, I set them way back inside the china cabinet with a promise that one day I'd have them repaired. From then on, no one could touch my mother's glasses. Forbidden. I couldn't risk losing any more.

Some time later, at an antique show, I found a man who repaired crystal. I took the broken pieces to him hoping he'd make them whole again. To my bitter disappointment, he couldn't repair them without destroying the rose etchings.

"Are you sure there's nothing you can do?" I asked with the slightest hope.

"Let me show them to my wife," he offered, noting my distress. "Maybe she'll have an idea."

He carried the pieces to a woman seated on the other side of the booth and asked her if they had any similar glasses back in their shop. She only laughed, "Where in the world would I get expensive glasses like these? They're Heisey Roses!"

"What are Heisey Roses?" I wanted to know, my curiosity aroused.

Pulling out a magnifying glass, the man pointed out a tiny diamond with an "H" inside it, engraved on the stem of each glass. "These glasses are worth about forty dollars each. They were made by the Heisey Company of Ohio. I really am sorry that I can't fix them."

If he was sorry, I was sorrier. "Do you think I could buy two water goblets to replace these?"

"Chances are a million to one you'll ever find these glasses anywhere."

Feeling bad, but determined to find replacements, my search began. Antique shops. Antique shows. Yard sales. Garage sales. Rummage sales. Flea markets. Michigan. Ohio. Florida. Massachusetts. California. Pennsylvania. Anywhere. Everywhere. Years went by and still no glasses, but something inside me wouldn't give up.

As time passed, I developed severe back pain that only grew worse. The diagnosis? Scoliosis, curvature of the spine. The solution? Surgery. Possibly two surgeries and no guarantee that things would improve. With two small children depending on me, it wasn't an easy decision to make. I prayed for a sign—something to let me know whether I was on the right track. No sign came.

My doctor scheduled surgery for early January. Mid-December, he changed his mind. Instead, he wanted me to consult with a doctor in Minnesota—one of the finest spinal surgeons in the country. It was winter, and Minnesota seemed so far away, but my husband insisted we go. More discouraged than ever, I continued to pray for that sign, but still none came.

The Minnesota doctor described a relatively new surgical procedure that would accomplish everything I needed in one grueling twelve-hour session. The good part? I wouldn't need a second operation just when I started recovering from the first one. The bad part? The surgery had to be done in Minnesota, a very long way from home.

I made no commitments that morning. No final decisions. I needed time to think. Besides, I still hadn't gotten that sign I'd been waiting for.

We left Minnesota right after the consultation. It was a long drive, and we were anxious to get home before any bad weather hit. Out of habit, we watched for antique shops and malls along the way. If we could find one right off the highway, it would be a nice way to stretch our legs. We passed up a few shops: one was closed, the other out of the way, and one we just couldn't find. We hit the jackpot at an exit in Tomah, Wisconsin. Not only was there an antique mall, but a cheese shop, a gas station and a pay phone so we could call the kids. What more could we ask for? Only that darn sign I hadn't stopped praying for.

We filled the gas tank, made our call and bought some cheese. Our last stop was the antique mall. Once inside, the number of dealers selling hundreds and hundreds of items overwhelmed us. As we passed the first couple of booths, something caught my eye. I held my breath as I peered closer into the locked display case. My mother's glasses! Not just water goblets, but salad dishes, cordial glasses, an ashtray and more! A Heisey Rose dream!

I couldn't take my eyes off them. Refusing to move from the spot, I sent my husband to find someone who could unlock the cabinet. Once the glass case was opened, I picked up one goblet at a time studying every inch, making sure there were no mars or chips. The glasses were perfect and the forty-dollar price tag just didn't matter. After all these years, I'd finally found my mother's glasses!

As the saleslady wrapped the goblets, my thoughts ran back to the man who repaired crystal. He had told me so long ago that my chances of finding these glasses were a million to one. *A million to one!* So how did I end up here? What brought me to this place? I suddenly realized that I hadn't just found my mother's goblets, but the sign I'd been so desperately praying for. My mother came through loud and clear. Words couldn't have been more to the point. Now, there were no more doubts. I had to return to Minnesota for the twelve-hour surgery we discussed with the doctor just hours earlier! And I learned something else. My mother has always been with me. I just never knew it, until the day I found her goblets.

Debra Pawlak

8

TIMELESS WISDOM

Life is not an easy thing to embrace. It is like trying to hug an elephant.

Diane Wakoski

"Is It Fun Being a Mommy?"

*If you think you're too small to have an impact,
try going to bed with a mosquito.*

Anita Roddick

I didn't know Rachel was paying close attention to me one ordinary evening. I did know that nothing slipped past my bright, inquisitive second-grade daughter. Like all mothers, I bragged about my child's brilliance, but once again I was caught off-guard by her insight into adult behavior.

From the time Rachel arrived home from school that particular Tuesday afternoon until after our family dinner, she observed me prepare a snack for her and her little brother, help her with her homework, cook dinner, wash dishes, and sweep and mop the floor. Then I prepared to begin the daily laundry routine. When her dad walked in the door from his day's work, she observed him leisurely reading the evening newspaper, working on a crossword puzzle, stretching out in the recliner, watching television, eating dinner and retreating to the backyard to play catch with her brother.

"Ummm," Rachel wondered what was wrong with this picture. In her mind, the score wasn't quite even. She decided this issue demanded immediate resolution.

As I checked a load of clothes in the dryer, Rachel approached me with a puzzled look.

"Mom, is it hard being a mommy?"

"No, dear," I moaned as I trotted to the bedroom with a load of hot sheets and towels to fold. "I love being a mommy."

"You do?" she asked in amazement.

"Yes, I do, sweetheart," I moaned again, as I gathered up a pile of grimy play clothes to start yet another washer load.

"Why do you ask?"

"Well, to me, it looks like mommies get all the hard work and daddies get all the fun."

"This is what stay-at-home moms do. It's part of my work. You didn't see Dad working hard all day at his office. Now it's time for him to relax and have fun with his family."

"Oh, okay," Rachel conceded. "So, when is it your turn to have fun?"

Good question. I wondered if I had a good answer. Before I replied, my son called for Rachel to come outside and play ball. As I folded and stacked towels, it occurred to me that as Rachel observed me that evening, she didn't see a contented homemaker, happy to stay home and care for her family by maintaining an orderly home. What my daughter watched was a madwoman frantically rushing about the kitchen throwing hamburger meat into the microwave. She witnessed an impatient woman who thought the story in the second-grade reader would never end. She saw a weary woman who seemed to prefer scrubbing sticky pots and pans to playing baseball in the backyard.

This wasn't the picture of motherhood my daughter needed to model. She deserved better. (I deserved better, too!) She needed not a picture of perfection, but one of joy and contentment in a mother doing the same old household chores again, and again and again.

In her daddy, Rachel noticed a man who took time out for himself and his family. It was my turn to try that approach to life as well. I decided immediately that the laundry could wait to be folded. I joined my half-pint ball team by the swing set. My relaxed, new and improved outlook on life paid immediate results. My family watched in amazement as my home-run baseball cleared the backyard fence.

DeAnna Sanders

"I'll start Christmas dinner just as soon as I finish the Thanksgiving dishes!"

Reprinted by permission of Dave Carpenter.

Résumé of the Heart

My daughter waited while I stitched the final threads, anchoring a button to the shirt she was about to put on. As her nimble fingers tucked the last button through its hole, I reached up and untangled the golden strands of her ponytail. I wrapped my arms around her in a hug. Then she disappeared through the doorway and onto the waiting school bus.

I knew in that moment that my accomplishments of the past years would never be listed in the *Who's Who* of life. I loved being a mother. Still, I often witnessed the puzzled faces as unknowing souls asked, "What do you do all day?" Most people could not understand my choices; after all, there's nothing heroic about hugs—unless you're on the receiving end.

Despite an extensive education and diverse opportunities, my résumé couldn't tout prestigious positions or high salaries. Instead, it was marked by the tiniest increments of time when I'd lent a helping hand, opened a storybook or shared in the discovery of a moment. I'd spent endless hours taxiing between practices, applauding little accomplishments and discerning temporary hurts from great big wounds of the heart.

Mine was the kiss that melted the pain of a scraped knee. Mine was the heart that swelled while witnessing each new triumph. Mine was the smile that bravely encouraged independence, while silently wrestling with the ache of letting go.

There is no place on a résumé for the wisdom of life experiences, compassion or nurturing relationships. The logic of my choices over the years would be appreciated by only a few, and never in the *Who's Who* of life.

But as my front door opened again later that afternoon and growing arms embraced me, I knew I had been blessed with a résumé of the heart. The real *Who* in life had already given me just enough prestige and salary to be the *Who* I was meant to be.

Kathleen Swartz McQuaig

Girls

How do you tell your mother that you feel you're getting . . . old? If I'm old . . . then what is she?

Gail Parent

How old do you have to be before you stop calling yourself "one of the girls?"

Frances Weaver, cruise-ship lecturer, humorist and senior citizen, recalls telling her granddaughter that she was getting ready for a party that afternoon because the "girls" were coming to play bridge. Her granddaughter replied, "Oh, you mean the girls with grandmother faces?" And that became the name of her first book.

Even though both my daughters have children of their own, I haven't any grandchildren. They are simply "my girls' children."

If I live to be a hundred and my daughters live to be seventy-five and seventy-eight, I will probably still call them "the girls." Somehow they've remained in a Peter Pan limbo all these years, and I imagine them floating through space, with Tinkerbell in tow, singing, "I won't grow up, I won't grow up," while I nod my head in vigorous agreement. The fact that they might not be "girls" anymore was brought to my attention recently when Javier Moreno from the Spanish tourist board called to discuss our upcoming trip to Spain.

"Do you think your daughters might enjoy horseback riding on the beach along the Costa del Sol? We have some fine Andalusian stallions there!"

I was hesitant. "I'll have to ask the girls. Offhand, I don't know if that's something they would like."

At the next opportunity I called my older daughter Linda. "Would you and Leslie like to spend a day riding horseback on the beach in Spain?"

Linda was horrified. "I'd rather run with the bulls!"

"Don't be ridiculous! There's nothing frightening about it. I was just thinking it would make such glamorous picture for the magazine . . . the two of you on black stallions at sunset, your hair floating behind you as you gallop through the waves."

"Ma! I have short hair now. My hair hasn't floated behind me since I was sixteen years old."

"We could get you a fall," I said hopefully.

"You want a picture of me with a fall? Well, think about me falling off the horse, my foot catching in the stirrup and me dragging behind the silly animal. How does that strike you?"

I was apologetic. "I just thought you girls. . . ."

"Ma, we're not girls anymore! Leslie's forty-five years old and I'm—ah—slightly older than she is. We are no longer girls."

"Oh," I whimpered. "Then what does that make me?"

"You're the mother of two middle-aged. . . ."

I put my hands over my ears to shut out the dreaded sounds. "I refuse to listen to that. When you're around me, you will always be the 'girls' and that's that! So . . . do you girls want to go to Spain or not?"

Linda was thoughtful, "Well, when you put it that way . . ." She gave a girlish giggle.

"That's my girl," I said happily.

Phyllis W. Zeno

The Little Jungle

Children are the anchors that hold a mother to life.

Sophocles

"Look, Mommy. Look!"

There is such gleeful excitement in the little-girl voice that it cuts through even the preoccupation of traffic, and deadlines, and meetings looming and being *late.*

"What is it, sweetie? I don't see anything."

"Over there, see?"

A glance in the rearview mirror reveals a tiny hand waving enthusiastically toward the left, but I see nothing over there except the concrete embankment of a culvert, overgrown with weeds. I feel a brief flash of annoyance at the unsightly mess; I pay enough taxes that you'd think the city could at least keep the weeds cut back.

"I'm sorry, honey, I must have missed it. It's hard for me to see all the things you see when I'm driving, because I must pay attention to the other cars. What was it, a bunny or a squirrel?" We are stopped at the traffic light. *Won't it ever change?*

"No, no, Mommy, look! It's a little jungle!"

Jungles and rain forests have been the topic at kinder-garten this week, so suddenly it makes sense. I glance at the overgrown patch again.

"Oh, yes, baby, it does sort of look like a little jungle. Very nice."

The light changes finally, *but why are all these people driving so slowly today? It's late; don't they know that?*

Several blocks later, the small voice chimes again. "What kind of animals do you think might live in that jungle, Mommy? Snakes, I bet. Do you think it would be big enough for maybe a little baby fox to live there? It would be nice for a fox. And chipmunks, because I saw one. Did you see the chipmunk in the little jungle, Mommy? Did you?"

"Sorry, baby. I didn't see the chipmunk. I was busy driving." I'm distracted, brusque, *late.*

"Oh."

The disappointment and hurt cuts through everything else, realigns the priorities back into their proper order. In my mind's eye, I look again at that patch of green by the culvert, and really see it this time, see it as she saw it from the first. Several young saplings bend and sway with the breeze, the clustered leaves of sumac recalling palm fronds. Honeysuckle twines around them, sweet-smelling flowers peeking out like small golden stars in a firmament of deep green. The grass is lush from all the recent rain, and morning dew sparkles like diamonds on the leaves of dock and thistle and milkweed. It *is* a jungle in miniature; perfect in its tiny wildness, stubbornly carving a place for itself amid the concrete and asphalt, a small niche in which all manner of creatures might find refuge.

"I don't think it was big enough for a fox, sweetie, but I'll bet a bunny lives there. And maybe a toad, and yes, maybe even a snake. A snake could sun himself on the concrete during the day; he'd like that. And lots of bugs, and butterflies. It was a very nice little jungle." Another look in the rearview shows the delighted smile that is worth far more than being on time.

"Yeah, a monarch butterfly! Like the one we hatched at school!"

For the rest of the ride, we talk about the little jungle and the creatures that might live there. We pass other small jungles, and it becomes a game to point them out. All too soon we are at school, and it's time for me to go. One last hug and kiss, then she scampers away toward her friends. I watch her go for a moment, and then as I turn to leave, she stops and runs back.

"Mommy, will we see the little jungle on the way home again?"

I smile and steal another quick hug. "Yes, we'll see it on the way home. And tomorrow, too. We can check on it every day as we go to school. It can be our very own little jungle."

A giggle: "Kylie's Jungle!"

"Yep, Kylie's Jungle. Now go on, and be good today!"

"Okay, Mommy! Bye!"

Back in the car, the commute continues as I think about a tiny jungle tucked into a culvert that I could not, would not see. When was it that I started to see the weeds instead? When did my life narrow to deadlines and traffic, commutes and commitments, black and white, cut and dried? When did I begin to see realities instead of possibilities?

The drive takes longer than usual, but that's okay. I'm looking for jungles and finding myself. When I finally arrive, late, someone asks if the traffic was bad. I just smile.

"Oh, you know how it is; it's a jungle out there."

And I swear I can smell the scent of honeysuckle drifting through the open window.

Donna Thiel-Kline

I Love My Body . . . Now

Too much of a good thing can be wonderful.

Mae West

It has been about five years since I've worn a swimsuit. I've been overweight since elementary school, and I've had a poor body image ever since I can remember. I've spent much of my life feeling bad about my body, avoiding mirrors, leaving dressing rooms in tears, and mentally beating myself up over what I look like. I was so ashamed of and embarrassed by my body that I hated to let even my husband see it. I would try to hide myself if he came into the room while I was showering or getting dressed.

When I found out I was pregnant, I was certain that having a baby would be the end of any chance I might have had of eventually being happy with my body. I cringed every time someone mentioned my growing belly. I knew it was all part of the childbearing deal, and that everyone else knew that. But for someone who has spent most of her life feeling embarrassed and self-conscious about her girth, suddenly having strangers and friends commenting on it can be pretty painful.

We had moved and I needed a full-length mirror for the new place to help me when getting ready in the mornings, but my husband kept finding little excuses not to buy one. So when I did catch a full view of myself at nine months pregnant, I was shocked and dismayed. And he admitted that this was why he had been avoiding buying the mirror—not because of what he thought of my appearance, but because of what he knew I would think.

My baby girl was born in July of 2000. She is, without question, the most amazing thing that has ever or will ever happen to me. I am simply astounded when I look at her and realize that she is what I felt moving inside of me all those months. Here is a beautiful, wonderful little person. She is perfect. I love her perfect little hands, little round eyes, little legs, little feet, little pinchable bottom and little mind that I can see developing along with her body. Every day I can see how she is changing and growing as a separate human being, yet I still feel as if she is somehow a part of me. I love her and love being her mother with every fiber of my being.

And here's what I've come to realize. This wonderful little person grew inside of my body. My body provided the ingredients that became her. It then sheltered her, protected her and provided every single thing her body used to develop and become her. It wasn't something my mind did. For the first weeks, my mind wasn't even aware of the process my body was carrying out. I didn't will her into being, and it had nothing to do with my intelligence, determination or perseverance. It was my body that did everything. Then, when her body was ready to leave the protection of mine, mine did just what it was supposed to do. Without any instructions or experience, it went into action and delivered life into the world.

Yet the process wasn't over there. Once my baby was born, my body continued to provide for her. It immediately began producing exactly the kind of food she needed as a newborn. I didn't study medicine or take the right pill or eat a certain food to cause it to do this. It simply did. And three days later, when she was ready for a new and different food, my body provided it. For six months after, my body continued to provide all the nutrients and antibodies she needed, complete and perfect for her, and in just the right amount. In short, my precious daughter's very existence is a function of my body.

My body just gave me the greatest gift I've ever received. How could I possibly dislike it now? I look at my stretch marks and I see a visual reminder of what has happened, a reminder I'll be able to carry with me my whole life. I don't look in the mirror and see fat anymore; I see an amazing and wonderful life grower. I'll never look anything remotely like a super model. My society and culture will never declare me a beautiful woman, and men will never turn and watch me go by or whistle as I pass. There will always be people who will look at my body and consider it average, unattractive, even ugly. Frankly, I don't care. Those people don't know or understand what makes a person, or a person's body, beautiful and wonderful. This is my body. And I love it . . . now.

Regina Phillips

"I should warn you now, we Wagner women have *always* had pear-shaped bodies."

Thank Heaven for My Mother-in-Law

*Whatever you do, put romance and enthusi-
asm into the life of your children.*

Margaret Ramsey MacDonald

When I met my husband, Benn, it was from across a room at a youth group reunion at a hall with five hundred people. He was in town, vacationing for a week, from Florida. The reunion was in Michigan where I had lived my entire life. We connected, the way it happens sometimes, and spent the entire week together before he had to return home. As I got to know him, I was intrigued by the love this man had for his mother, who had passed away. She was a large influence in his life, and he missed her terribly. So when he returned to Florida I decided to pray to his mother. I said, "If you believe that your son and I belong together, make it happen. I put it in your hands."

I never told anyone about this prayer; it was my secret. I received a call from Benn asking me to come for a visit. Two weeks later, I went for a long weekend. Benn picked me up at the airport and took me directly to a nightclub that had live entertainment. He asked me to dance a slow, romantic dance; of course, I accepted. As he held me close, he whispered in my ear, "You're the one."

I replied, "And how do you know?"

"My mother just told me," he whispered. The rest is history.

Judy Perry

The Unwrapped Gift

A mother doesn't walk, but runs, to smooth the human pathway she knows her child must tread.

Jeanne Hill

"Mom," came the frantic call from my teenage daughter's bedroom, "Come here quick!"

I opened one eye, still tired from the last-minute details of Christmas Eve, and was on my feet just as Jennifer cried out again. Waves of dizziness struck me, almost knocking me back into bed. *What was going on?*

I managed to make it to my daughter and saw her sitting up, pale-faced and holding her stomach. She looked like I felt.

"What's the matter, Jennifer?" I asked.

"Mom, I've got the stomach flu, and it's Christmas!"

"Well, if it's any consolation, I don't feel so great myself." And, with that, I ran to the bathroom. I lay on the cold tile and thought, *Oh, God, why today of all days? Not today, Lord, not today.*

By now, my husband, hearing all the commotion, was up preparing breakfast. He assumed our noisy hoopla was the excitement of Christmas morning. Popping his head into the bathroom he said, "Bacon and eggs are on when you're ready." A closer look and he discovered his *faux pas* and slipped quietly back out of the room.

Our other two children went to church with him while Jennifer and I moaned encouragement to each other across the hall. After an hour of this, I thought, *This is silly . . . we certainly can't catch anything from each other, so why not bunk together?*

Jennifer came and got in our king-size bed with me. We spent the day talking, sucking ice chips and sleeping. When we were awake, we talked about boys, life at her new high school and friends she had made when she had changed schools midyear.

I told her how hard it was to be a working mother and still stay on top of all the family activities. I confessed that I had missed sharing with her lately, and we made a pact to spend more time together. We told each other secrets, giggled and laughed at our predicament. We became closer that day than we had been in a long time.

Many years have passed, and my daughter is grown with a husband and two children of her own. Yet not a Christmas goes by that one of us doesn't say, "Remember the Christmas when . . . ?" We both laugh, knowing we received a gift that year better than any we found under the tree.

Sallie Rodman

Sunflower Success

Success is not the key to happiness.
Happiness is the key to success.
If you love what you are doing, you will be
successful.

Albert Schweitzer

My mother was the expert gardener. She patiently tried to pass her skills on to me but to no avail. Her pumpkins were larger than the family dog. Mine usually grew to the size of the gerbil. She told me potatoes were easy to grow. I planted a potato from the kitchen and received healthy-looking foliage. When I dug them up, I couldn't decide if they were potatoes or moon rocks. One potato had seven other potatoes growing on it. They could have put it in the next *Star Wars* movie. My mother quietly thanked me for my potatoes, and they disappeared into the back of the refrigerator. The next season, I decided to try some carrots. The carrots couldn't decide if they wanted to be single, twins or triplets. I can imagine my mother standing at the window wondering how her daughter managed to grow mutant vegetables next to her award-winning ones. My carrots went the same way as the potatoes. My cucumber and melon vines never produced anything. They just grew and grew and became a hazard for tripping over. I guess I could have cut them and given them to the neighborhood children to jump rope with.

With an increasing array of evidence, my mother gently informed me that maybe vegetables weren't my thing and suggested I try flowers. We went to the local nursery to pick out summer annuals. She said I might want to try flowers that said "hardy" on the tag. I picked out sunflower seeds. My mother assured me they were hard to kill, and we went home to plant. My neighbors' sunflowers were peeking over the fence. I know they had seen my vegetables and looked almost sadly down at the seed package of their cousins. The package said they would sprout in eight to ten days. Mine took almost a month. Then they grew, and grew and grew. They surpassed me in height, then they grew taller than the flowers from over the fence. My mother took a picture to put in the family album of "plant successes." It was my first picture. I was looking back at this album shortly after my mother passed away. Under my beaming face next to my flowers, I noticed a caption. It read, "The last ones to bloom are always the most beautiful."

Kristal M. Parker

Reprinted by permission of Kathy Shaskan.

A Mother Listens

They are so small and fragile, you are afraid you will
  not hear—
you lay awake and . . . listen

They are little and just in the next room, suddenly it
  is very quiet—
you go to the doorway and . . listen

They are bigger and have so much to tell you about
  their day—
you are busy and very tired but you make the time
  and . . . listen

They are a little bigger and so secretive, they do not
  say much anymore—
you must find different ways to . . . listen

They are teenagers and talk a strange new language—
you try hard to hear without commenting and
  just . . . listen

They are growing up, all at once they know it all—
   it's best to let them think so and . . . listen

They are becoming adults, they want to talk and ask
   your advice—
there might be things you do not want to hear, but
   you . . . listen

They grow up and go away—
   you hate the silence, the phone rings, you can't
   wait to . . . listen

They come to visit with their kids, all demanding
   your ears at once—
someone shouts "be quiet!", no it's all right, it's so
   wonderful to . . . listen

They get older, you get old, they speak loud as if you
   are deaf—
it's okay, you nod your head and . . . listen

You pass on, and when they pray, they do not ask for
   God—
they need to talk to you, God is gracious, and once
   again He lets you . . . listen

Carolee Hudgins

If I Could Be a Mother Again

*Life is a great big canvas; throw all the paint on
it you can.*

Danny Kaye

If I could be a mother all over again, I know one thing
I would never change . . . how much I loved each of you. I
wanted to be a mother from the time I was a little girl. I
played with dolls long after the other girls had given them
up. So being a mother and holding and rocking and nursing and caring for you was the joy of my life. But I look
back on it now, and I think I probably treated you like my
dolls. I picked you up if you cried. I held you when your
ears ached. As long as you were in pain, I wanted to be
there with you. But keeping you happy, safe, healthy,
polite and studious seemed to be the range of my mothering. Happy could be lots of things: sleigh riding, picnics,
swimming, parties for you and your friends, learning to
bake or sew, or even learning to skate or ride a bike. Those
were things that I was familiar with and knew how to help
you learn.

But today looking back on how rich I might have made

your lives if I had known then the things I have learned now—oh, how exciting it would be.

I would begin with sight. Not having your eyes tested for glasses: that I knew about and did—but learning to really see things. To see the way the sky changes color with just a little gust of wind. To see the leaves twist in the wind and shimmer with light, then plunge into the shadows. I'd like to teach your eyes to take in the shades of green and blue that rush across the waves or the sky, to see shapes and forms, not as objects but masses of color that change as you turn away from them; to see the world as an exciting masterpiece; to see a flower as a perfect vision. When the motto used to be "Stop and smell the roses," I didn't realize just what was being said. Yes, that is what I would do if I could start all over again with each of you. I'd stop and smell the roses with you and look at their colors and enjoy the fact that they exist.

I wouldn't stop with nature, I would help you learn about seeing people: to see the planes and curves of an eye, an ear or a cheekbone; to see how we are alike and yet vary in many ways; to see how people live different lives, but carry similar values; to see compassion and bravery and dedication. The world would seem to have more color, more variety, more beauty were I to teach you about it today.

Hearing, I'd teach you about really hearing. I know that I miss lots of words that I used to hear. I'm eighty-three and can't hear much anymore. I know that my taste in music has not changed with the times, and I never wanted to hear your music! But also I now listen to the sound of the surf, or a train whistle in the night, or a loon over the lake in the early morning. Those are sounds that I appreciate today, and I wonder if I ever told you about the beauty of those sounds. Yes, I would have a new approach to teaching you about listening and hearing, not just to human words or to be quiet when adults are speaking, but to the sounds that are always around us. The city sounds of rumbling buses and taxi doors slamming, of street vendors hawking their wares or sirens telling us of an emergency, or the country sounds that are quieter and more peaceful, but often frightening alone at night. Yes, I think I would teach you about the beauty that enters through our ears.

And also I'd teach you to hear people's feelings and hopes and dreams, the truth behind their words. I'd help you to hear pain and need, and I'd help you know how to respond. I'd help you to hear the whole world, in all its complexity.

"If onlys" aren't much good though. I'm not a mother again, and my two daughters are both mothers and my four granddaughters are on their way to becoming mothers! No more babies to hold, children to teach. I miss that from time to time, but I notice that even though I don't have those children to teach, I have never stopped teaching myself.

Julie Firman

More Chicken Soup?

Many of the stories you have read in this book were submitted by readers like you who had read earlier *Chicken Soup for the Soul* books. We publish at least five or six *Chicken Soup for the Soul* books every year. We invite you to contribute a story to one of these future volumes.

Stories may be up to 1,200 words and must uplift or inspire. You may submit an original piece, something you have read or your favorite quotation on your refrigerator door.

To obtain a copy of our submission guidelines and a listing of upcoming *Chicken Soup* books, please write, fax or check our Web site.

Please send your submissions to:

Chicken Soup for the Soul
P.O. Box 30880, Santa Barbara, CA 93130
fax: 805-563-2945
Web site: *www.chickensoup.com*

Just send a copy of your stories and other pieces to the above address.

We will be sure that both you and the author are credited for your submission.

For information about speaking engagements, other books, audiotapes, workshops and training programs, please contact any of our authors directly.

Supporting Others

The authors of this book are deeply appreciative of the opportunity to share a portion of the proceeds with two organizations whose mission over many years has been to help individuals and our world. Both organizations continue their commitment to mothers and daughters through workshops, trainings and groups.

The Synthesis Center

The Synthesis Center, in Amherst, Massachusetts, is a grassroots nonprofit organization whose goals are to have a positive impact on real people and to support the conscious evolution of individuals, groups, society and the planet. The center was the original home for the mother/daughter workshops that have now become national events. The center now offers ongoing mothering groups and workshops, a mothering newsletter, *MotherWoman Journal* and training for leaders of mothering groups.

The Synthesis Center also offers professional training in psychosynthesis, a holistic psychology, as well as counseling, workshops, online coaching services, a correspondence course on "Making Meaning with the Mandala" and a book service that publishes, distributes and sells *Daughters and Mothers: Healing the Relationship,* the Firmans' first book. The book service also carries *Chicken Soup for the Mother and Daughter Soul,* available online.

The Synthesis Center can be reached at:

www.synthesiscenter.org

or

274 N. Pleasant St. Amherst, MA 01002

Omega Institute for Holistic Studies

Founded in 1977, Omega is recognized worldwide for its broad-based curriculum, distinguished faculty and unique community spirit. What began as a bold experiment in life-long learning is now one of the largest and most trusted holistic education providers in the world. In 2001, Omega Institute welcomed more than 20,000 guests to its Rhinebeck, New York, campus, international travel programs and conferences held in cities nationwide.

In a world of division, Omega's mission is integration—integration of each person's body, mind and spirit, and integration of the people of the world. To this end, Omega creates an environment where guests can learn about themselves and each other, and discover new, more healthful, and meaningful ways of being in the world so they can grow into their most enlightened and generous potential.

The Crossings, an Omega center, celebrates its opening in 2003. The Crossings is a progressive learning center and meeting place located in the Texas Hill Country just outside of Austin. Situated on more than 200 acres in the Balcones Canyonlands Preserve, The Crossings provides a peaceful place for individuals to renew and grow.

Mothers and Daughters: Working Toward Well-Being, a weekend workshop with Julie and Dorothy Firman, has been offered at Omega each summer for more than twenty years and also in the opening season of The Crossings.

For further information call 800-944-1001 or visit *www.eomega.org* or *www.thecrossingsaustin.com.*

Who Is Jack Canfield?

Jack Canfield is one of America's leading experts in the development of human potential and personal effectiveness. He is both a dynamic, entertaining speaker and a highly sought-after trainer. Jack has a wonderful ability to inform and inspire audiences toward increased levels of self-esteem and peak performance.

He is the author and narrator of several bestselling audio- and videocassette programs, including *Self-Esteem and Peak Performance, How to Build Maximum Confidence, Self-Esteem in the Classroom* and *Chicken Soup for the Soul—Live.* He is regularly seen on television shows such as *Good Morning America, 20/20* and *NBC Nightly News.* Jack has co-authored numerous books, including the *Chicken Soup for the Soul* series, *Dare to Win, The Aladdin Factor, 100 Ways to Build Self-Concept in the Classroom, Heart at Work* and *The Power of Focus.*

Jack is a regularly featured speaker for professional associations, school districts, government agencies, churches, hospitals, sales organizations and corporations. His clients have included the American Dental Association, the American Management Association, AT&T, Campbell's Soup, Clairol, Domino's Pizza, GE, ITT, Hartford Insurance, Johnson & Johnson, the Million Dollar Roundtable, NCR, New England Telephone, Re/Max, Scott Paper, TRW and Virgin Records.

Jack conducts an annual eight-day Training of Trainers program in the areas of self-esteem and peak performance. It attracts educators, counselors, parenting trainers, corporate trainers, professional speakers, ministers and others interested in developing their speaking and seminar-leading skills.

For further information about Jack's books, tapes and training programs, or to schedule him for a presentation, please contact:

Self-Esteem Seminars
P.O. Box 30880
Santa Barbara, CA 93130
phone: 805-563-2935 • fax: 805-563-2945
Web site: *www.chickensoup.com*

Who Is Mark Victor Hansen?

Mark Victor Hansen is a professional speaker who in the last twenty years has made over 4,000 presentations to more than 2 million people in thirty-two countries. His presentations cover sales excellence and strategies; personal empowerment and development; and how to triple your income and double your time off.

Mark has spent a lifetime dedicated to his mission of making a profound and positive difference in people's lives. Throughout his career, he has inspired hundreds of thousands of people to create a more powerful and purposeful future for themselves while stimulating the sale of billions of dollars worth of goods and services.

Mark is a prolific writer and has authored *Future Diary, How to Achieve Total Prosperity* and *The Miracle of Tithing.* He is coauthor of the *Chicken Soup for the Soul* series, *Dare to Win* and *The Aladdin Factor* (all with Jack Canfield), and *The Master Motivator* (with Joe Batten).

Mark has also produced a complete library of personal-empowerment audio- and videocassette programs that have enabled his listeners to recognize and use their innate abilities in their business and personal lives. His message has made him a popular television and radio personality, with appearances on ABC, NBC, CBS, HBO, PBS and CNN. He has also appeared on the cover of numerous magazines, including *Success, Entrepreneur* and *Changes.*

Mark is a big man with a heart and spirit to match—an inspiration to all who seek to better themselves.

For further information about Mark, write:

MVH & Associates
P.O. Box 7665
Newport Beach, CA 92658
phone: 714-759-9304 or 800-433-2314
fax: 714-722-6912
Web site: *www.chickensoup.com*

Who Is Dorothy Firman?

Dr. Dorothy Firman is a psychotherapist, life coach, author, consultant, speaker and trainer. She has worked in the field of mother and daughter relationships for more than twenty years, offering workshops, seminars and keynote presentations with her mother Julie. Their book, *Daughters and Mothers, Healing the Relationship,* now in its fifth printing, is designed as an active workbook for women wanting to become more whole in relationship and in themselves.

Dorothy is a founding member of the Association for the Advancement of Psychosynthesis, a spiritual psychology that she first encountered in her early years as a student and colleague of Jack Canfield. For twenty-five years, Dorothy has been a trainer of helping professionals in the field of psychosynthesis, offering people the opportunity to deepen their experience of aliveness, presence and the ability to serve. Her training is run through The Synthesis Center, a nonprofit educational organization co-founded by Jack Canfield in 1976. The Center is dedicated to making therapy and therapeutic groups available to all in need. It specializes in the teaching of psychosynthesis, cancer support work and mothers' groups.

Dorothy has been a psychotherapist in Amherst, Massachusetts, for more than twenty-five years. Her work focuses on helping to create meaning, purpose and values in life, while addressing issues of trauma and personal need. She has specialized in work with people with cancer, has worked in the inner city with teenage mothers, done consulting work for groups throughout the United States and presented her psychosynthesis work in Europe, the United States and Canada.

Dorothy has three incredible children, and one wonderful granddaughter. She has been married to her best friend for twenty-six years. Dorothy's work includes online coaching and distance-training programs. She is available for speaking engagements and workshops.

For more information, contact Dorothy Firman:

The Synthesis Center
274 North Pleasant St.
Amherst, MA 01002
413-256-0772
SynthesisC@aol.com
www.synthesiscenter.org/ or *soupforMDsoul@aol.com*
www.motherdaughterrelations.com/

Who Is Julie Firman?

Julie Firman is the mother of two daughters—her coauthors—and one son. She has eight grandchildren and one great grandchild. She has been married, happily, for more than sixty years. Julie has been a school teacher and school administrator. In her fifties, she returned to college to get a master's degree, and she became an active psychotherapist, group leader, trainer and speaker. She and her daughter, Dorothy, are the authors of *Daughters and Mothers, Healing the Relationship*. They lead workshops on the mother/daughter relationship at numerous conferences and centers around the country, including Esalen, Big Sur, California; The Synthesis Center, Amherst, Massachusetts; The Wellness Program, Columbus, Indiana; the Common Boundary Conference, Washington, D.C.; Armstrong State College, Savannah, Georgia; Women at the Crossroads, Salem, Massachusetts; Chestnut Hill Healthcare, Philadelphia, Pennsylvania; and The Family Therapy Networker Conference, Washington, D.C. They have given mother/daughter workshops every year for over twenty years at the Omega Institute for Holistic Studies in Rhinebeck, New York, and hope to continue to do so for many more years.

At eighty-three, Julie thinks about giving it up but continues each year because she has so much fun. She reminds herself that it is not the number of years that govern what you do but how you feel and what your goals are. Learning, teaching and growing are her goals still.

She can be reached at:

28 Woodlot Road
Amherst, MA 01002
JulieFirm@aol.com

Who Is Frances Firman Salorio?

Frances Firman Salorio is a solution-focused marriage and family therapist. Her work in family systems over the years has involved individuals, couples and families with many differing goals. She began her work career as a teacher many years ago and has continued to do teaching and training in a variety of settings. She founded and ran Ashbrook Center for Brief Therapies with several colleagues and, in addition to psychotherapy, they held groups, seminars, coaching and training sessions and therapist gatherings for mutual support. She worked at the Christian Counseling Center in Norwalk, Connecticut, for a number of years. Through that Center, she worked in the courts doing an experimental alternative-to-sentencing program for first-time offenders; she did therapy and group work with a prison halfway house for mothers and their children; she did goal-oriented coaching groups for small business, and extensive psychotherapy with a wide range of clients.

She says that, as a family systems therapist, she has watched many mother-daughter relationships in the works and has been privileged to help a number of those relationships sort themselves out. She is the mother of two adult children, and she has commented that she thinks her own mother/daughter stories, as either the daughter or the mother, would be different each year because experience accumulates, understanding deepens, hurts fade and judgments soften.

Since moving to Amherst, Massachusetts, she has done private practice psychotherapy, as well as telephone therapy and coaching sessions, workshops and trainings. You can contact her at:

fsalorio@aol.com
or
The Synthesis Center
Mother Daughter Relations
274 North Pleasant St.
Amherst, MA 01002

Contributors

Several of the stories in this book were taken from previously published sources, such as books, magazines and newspapers. These sources are acknowledged in the permissions section. If you would like to contact any of the contributors for information about their writing, or would like to invite them to speak in your community, look for their contact information included in their biography.

The remainder of the stories were submitted by readers of our previous *Chicken Soup for the Soul* books who responded to our requests for stories. We have also included information about them.

Donna Barstow says it is a joy to draw and write cartoons! Her quirky drawings appear in over 200 publications, including *The New Yorker, Los Angeles Times, Reader's Digest, Harvard Business Review, Wall Street Journal* and many calendars and books, including other *Chicken Soup for the Soul* books. Her book about women and cats will be published in 2003. Her favorite topics are relationships, computers and pets. You can see more of her work at *www.reuben.org/dbarstow*.

Mary Alice Dress Baumgardner received her B.A. from Gettysburg College and M.A. from Marywood University. She writes and illustrates children's books and inspirational stories for adults. She may be contacted at: P.O. Box 55, Waynesboro, PA 17268; or via e-mail: *baumgarm@earthlink.net;* or the Web site: *www.marialys.com*.

Julie Bete lives the good life in southern Vermont. She spends her days playing Simon Says, dancing with fairies and breastfeeding the unquenchable nursling. She enjoys gardening, reading, writing, plant spirit medicine, local organic produce and giving birth at home. Her husband and daughter bring laughter to her days.

Elizabeth Bezant works as both a freelance writer and speaker in Perth, Western Australia. Her inspirational, uplifting stories on life have been published worldwide as have her interactive educational ideas. Her goals are to encourage a positive and fun outlook on life. Elizabeth can be contacted through her Web site: *www.writingtoinspire.com*.

Cynthia Blatchford is an aspiring writer with profound hopes of helping others heal through the written word based on her life's experiences. Her interests include reading, crafts and a vast love of movies. She may be reached by e-mail at: *cindy_700@hotmail.com*.

Alice Lundy Blum, a New Mexico native, is a freelance writer, focusing on women's issues and raising social consciousness. She is also working on a book about losing her mother to cancer. Alice lives with her husband, Tom, and black Lab, Cassie, at 15852 Garrett Path, Apple Valley, MN 55124.

Colleen Foye Bollen is a professional writer. Her upcoming book focuses on dreams, dolphins and her spiritual awakening. Colleen conducts workshops about writing, spirituality and creativity. She lives in the Pacific Northwest with her family and numerous smoke detectors. Contact Colleen at Turtle Island Press, P.O. Box 77598, Seattle, WA 98177; email at *heartwork4u@yahoo.com*.

Joan Borysenko, Ph.D., is trained as a medical scientist and licensed clinical psychologist. She is the co-founder and former director of the mind/body clinical programs at the Beth Israel/Deaconess Medical Center and a former instructor in medicine at the Harvard Medical School. Her work encompasses mind/body medicine, women's health and spirituality. Author of many books including the *New York Times* bestseller *Minding the Body, Mending the Mind,* Dr. Borysenko's work bridges medicine, psychology and the world's great spiritual traditions. As president of Mind/Body Health Sciences in Boulder, Colorado, Dr. Borysenko provides lectures, workshops and consultations for healthcare providers, corporations, clergy, civic organizations and the general public. She has been described as "a rare jewel: respected scientist, gifted therapist and unabashed mystic."

Tonna Canfield is a wife, mother, teacher and speaker. She and her husband are church youth leaders. They also teach a Bible study for teenagers in their home. Tonna teaches Sunday school and ladies' Bible study. She is writing a ladies' devotional book. Reach her at 606-329-9408 or at *tonnacanfield@att.net*.

David Carpenter has been a full-time cartoonist since 1981. His work has appeared in a number of publications such as *Harvard Business Review, Barron's, The Wall Street Journal, Reader's Digest, Good Housekeeping, Better Homes and Gardens* and *The Saturday Evening Post*. Dave's cartoons have also appeared in several of the *Chicken Soup for the Soul* books. Dave can be reached at *davecarp@ncn.net*.

Kim Childs is a writer and certified Kripalu yoga teacher who guides all kinds of people worldwide through group classes and private lessons. She also sings, acts and leads workshops on conscious eating, body loving and artful living (based on Julia Cameron's *The Artist's Way*). Please visit her at *www.kimchilds.com*.

Kate Clabough is a freelance writer and historian. She writes regularly for regional newspapers and magazines. Currently, she is working on two local history books and a historical romance. Kate lives with her husband and children near the Great Smokey Mountains in East Tennessee. You can reach her at: *dv121212@earthlink.net*.

Elissa Hadley Conklin is a freelance writer and poet whose work has appeared in *Guideposts, Writer's Journal, Hudson Valley Parent, Mature Life* and *Muscular Dystrophy* magazines. She is married and has two sons. Her book, a biography about Joan Crawford, is to be published. She may be reached via e-mail at: *CONKSPIRIT@aol.com.*

David Cooney's cartoons and illustrations have appeared in numerous *Chicken Soup for the Soul* books as well as magazines including *USA Weekend* and *Good Housekeeping.* David lives with his wife, Marcia, and two children, Sarah and Andrew, in the small Pennsylvania town of Mifflinburg. His Web site is *www.DavidCooney.com* and he can be reached at *david@davidcooney.com.*

Paula D'Arcy is an author, speaker and retreat leader. She has a master's in education in counseling psychology from the University of New Hampshire, 1970. Among her works are *Song for Sarah, Gift of the Red Bird* and *A New Set of Eyes.* Learn more at *www.redbirdfoundation.com/.*

Therese Brady Donohue has lived in Amherst, Massachusetts, for thirty years where her family moved to enable her daughter Maura to be treated at Boston's Jimmy Fund Clinic. Ms. Donohue founded the Amherst Ballet Centre. She has received awards from the Town and Citations from the Massachusetts Senate and House of Representatives. She holds a B.A. from Maryland's College of Notre Dame.

Julia Alene Doyle is an aspiring writer and photographer. A native of Waukegan, Illinois, she lives in Alexandria, Indiana, and is employed by the newspaper industry. Her passage is dedicated to her nieces and nephews who remain a constant source of pride and inspiration. She can be reached at *jules_274@hotmail.com.*

Karen C. Driscoll lives in Connecticut with her husband and their four children, age five and under. She has a master's degree in elementary and special education and is currently a full-time mom. Her writing has been published in anthologies, magazines and online. She can be reached at: *kmhbrdriscoll@hotmail.com.*

M. M. English delivers her sometimes quirky, sometimes irreverent views with honesty and humor in her newspaper column, "It'll Be Fine." She lives with her husband and five children in northern Alberta. For more of her work, including books and cards, please visit *www.echoecho.ca.* Contact her at: *wordsmith@echoecho.ca* or Box 207, Fox Creek, AB, T0H 1P0, Canada.

Rachel Fink teaches developmental biology at Mount Holyoke College. She lives with her husband, two children and shaggy hound dog in a little house by the edge of the woods. She enjoys writing essays about international adoption, motherhood and being a scientist.

Winfield Firman is a successful businessman, Boy Scout leader and bomb disposal officer during WWII, who, as a retiree, is a giving and wise volunteer in many organizations. His writing has appeared in *I Like Being Married.* He is a supportive, loving father, grandfather and husband.

Nancy B. Gibbs is a pastor's wife, mother and grandmother. She is the author of *Celebrate Life . . . Just for Today,* a weekly religion columnist and freelance writer. Her stories have appeared in numerous books and magazines. She has contributed several other stories to the *Chicken Soup for the Soul* series. Her e-mail address is *Daiseydood@aol.com.*

Randy Glasbergen is one of America's most widely and frequently published cartoonists. More than 25,000 of his cartoons have been published by *Funny Times, Woman's World, Cosmopolitan,* America Online and many others. His daily comic panel "The Better Half" is syndicated worldwide by King Features Syndicate. He is also the author of three cartooning instruction books and several cartoon anthologies. To read a new cartoon every day, please visit Randy's Web site at *www.glasbergen.com.*

Anne Goodrich is a Web and graphic designer for an educational agency in Kalamazoo, Michigan, and Webmaster of *www.OhAngel.com,* an angel and inspirational e-card site. She is blessed to have a number of earth angels in her life, especially her daughter Kelly, and her sons Gordon and Carman.

Hallmark Licensing Inc. is an ever-expanding company. Through licensing leadership and joint ventures, Hallmark continues to expand its product formats and distribution avenues. Its headquarters are based in Kansas City. Hallmark is known throughout the world for its greeting cards and other personal expressions of celebration, love and loss. The *Hallmark Hall of Fame* is a well-known and time-honored dramatic television series.

Jonny Hawkins' cartoons have been published in over fifty books and in over 265 publications over the last sixteen years. His most recent book, *The Awesome Book of Heavenly Humor,* can be purchased by contacting him at: *jonny-hawkins2nz@yahoo.com* or by calling him at 269-432-8071. He lives in Sherwood, Michigan, with his wife Carissa and their two boys, Nate and Zach.

Eileen Aquina Hehl, a proud grandmother of four children, has sold more than three hundred short magazine stories. Twenty of her novels were published, fifteen of them for young readers. Her book *Lucky in Love* was nominated for Romance Writers of America's RITA Award, and she's a longtime member of Connecticut RWA. She and her husband Tony live in New Milford, Connecticut.

Judy Henning is a registered nurse and mother of three beautiful daughters, all nurses, and a son, an artist. In addition to her work, Judy loves to hike, canoe, dance, garden and throw pots. She writes for pure pleasure and has been a member of a writing group for ten years. Contact her at: *judy100@sover.net.*

Win Herberg, formerly an English teacher, now enjoys working as a studio potter and operating an art and craft gallery near Centuria, Wisconsin. Children Leif, Brandon and Nissa are the inspiration for some of her writing. Win is currently working on her parents' biography/memoirs. Please reach her at: *winterboo@centurytel.net.*

Donna M. Hoffman is a retired teacher. She cannot remember when reading and writing were not a part of her life. She has a MA in reading/writing education. She has published numerous articles and stories in periodicals for children, women and mature adults. Mrs. Hoffman is currently working on a woman's novel and a fantasy novel for children. Widowed in late 1997, she remarried in June of 2002 and lives happily with her husband and two cats in Westminster, Colorado. Her daughter, son-in-law and grandson, Jared, live nearby.

The Reverend **Melissa Hollerith** graduated with a bachelor of arts from Tulane University in 1984 and received a master's of divinity from Yale University in 1990. She lives in Richmond, Virginia, and works at St. Christopher's School. She and her husband Randy, who is also a priest, have two children: seven-year-old Marshall and four-year-old Eliza.

Carolee Hudgins lives in Chesterfield, Virginia. She spends most of her time with her husband, grown children and her grandchildren. She has always enjoyed writing poetry. The poem in this book was inspired by her mother, Ruth Tellefsen, who died in 1985 after a very long and valiant fight against breast cancer. And she is sure she is still listening.

Barb Huff, after seven years serving children and families at the YMCA of Central Stark County, is now the youth and children's director at Otterbein United Methodist Church in New Philadelphia. Barb is also a writer specializing in children's ministry, fiction and parenting nonfiction.

Annette Marie Hyder's work appears in magazines, books and newspapers throughout the United States and internationally. Being a mother informs and nurtures her writing in countless generative ways. Of her occupations, writing, editing and mothering, her favorite "job" is being a mother, because, she says, "You can't beat the perks!" Contact her at *adhyder@frontiernet.net*.

Kendeyl Johansen is an award-winning author and contributing editor for *iParenting Media* and the national magazines *Pregnancy, Woman's Health & Fitness* and *Baby Years*. Her work has also appeared in *Woman's World* and several literary journals. You may contact her at: *larsken@burgoyne.com*.

Brenda Jordan is a fifty-five-year-old retired high school teacher in Huntsville, Alabama. She now works at EarlyWorks, a children's history museum. She teaches young children about Alabama's early history.

Kathy Jublou is a full-time, stay-at-home mom to two teenage boys. After retiring from the Naval Reserves as a Commander, she became active in civic affairs. She enjoys her daily gym workouts and is a longstanding member of a drawing workshop that uses colored pencils as the primary medium.

Paul Karrer has had five stories published with *Chicken Soup*. He is regularly heard reading his stories on First Person Singular on radio station KUSP 88.9 FM, in Santa Cruz, California. When not writing or annoying his wife, he is a fifth-grade teacher. He may be disturbed at: *pkarrer123@yahoo.com*.

Betty King writes inspirational and humorous articles for a variety of mediums and is highly published on the Internet. She is a Heartwarmer Gem on *heart-warmers4u.com* and writer of the month on *www.2Theheart.com*. She has publishing credits in a number of mediums and is the author of the books *It Takes Two Mountains to Make a Valley* and *But—It Was in the Valleys I Grew* waiting release. You can contact her at *Baking2@charter.net*.

Jean Kinsey, a Franklin, Kentucky native, writes a bimonthly column for *FACES*, a publication of the American Syringomyelia Alliance Project. Jean was stricken with the rare disorder, syringomyelia, in 1983. She is in the process of writing a novel based on the disorder. Jean is also active in her church.

Houstonian **Karen O. Krakower** is editor of a national health magazine, an essayist and humorist. Her writings have appeared in over fifty publications. She spends her free time playing guitar with her son, schmoozing with her daughter, and exhaling with friends and family. And then there's the dog, *Oy*. Another story.

Bella Kudatsky started writing when her senior center needed another workshop participant. Reluctantly, Bella joined. Surprisingly, it became her therapy, and later, her hobby. She is also dismantling her vast collection of worldwide seashells. Bella can be reached at 617-244-0552. She lives in Newton Centre, Massachusetts.

Laura Lagana is a professional speaker, registered nurse, author of *Touched by Angels of Mercy*, coauthor of *Chicken Soup for the Volunteer's Soul* and frequent contributor to the *Chicken Soup for the Soul* series. She may be reached at P.O. Box 7816, Wilmington, DE 19803; via e-mail: *NurseAngel@LauraLagana.com*; or at her Web site: *www.LauraLagana.com*.

Anne Lambert was a navy wife, taking advantage of exotic locations to become a research and travel writer. She's a generic reader, reading anything and everything. She is the author, with her husband, Jeff, of three novels: *Thief by Moonight, Magic's Logic* and *Realms of the Shadows*. She enjoys gourmet cooking and long walks on the desert mesa.

Charlotte A. Lanham is a storyteller, freelance writer and columnist. She has been writing stories and poetry ever since her eighth-grade English teacher wrote the simple word "Astute" across the corner of a term paper. Her collection of memoirs, featured in a weekly column, "Over a Cuppa," reflect a lifetime of humorous and heartwarming tales. In her files are dozens of children's books, songs and poems, written during her years as a teacher in New South Wales, Australia. Now retired, she writes from her home in Duncanville, Texas. Charlotte can be reached by e-mail at *charlotte.lanham@slocglobal.net*.

Vickie Leach is assistant principal at Stamford High School. She and her husband Michael have two grown sons and live in Riverside, Connecticut.

Donna Lee is a freelance writer and video producer from Charleston, South Carolina. She is a regular columnist for a travel Web site. She has worked in educational television as well as in television news and radio broadcasting. She is currently working on a short film adaptation of "Mom SAID/She MEANT."

Eda LeShan was the author of more than thirty books for adults and children, including *When Your Child Drives You Crazy* and *It's Better to Be Over the Hill Than Under It*. She was also a playwright. Her play *The Lobster Reef* premiered in New York City on June 6, 1995. She was a renowned family counselor, and a former columnist for *New York Newsday* and *Woman's Day Magazine*.

Patricia Lorenz, the mother of two daughters and two sons, makes her living as a writer and speaker. With stories in over a dozen *Chicken Soup* books, she is one of the most prolific *Chicken Soup* story writers in America. Patricia is the author of three books, over four hundred articles, has stories in numerous anthologies, is a contributing writer for fourteen *Daily Guideposts* books, and an award-winning regular columnist for two newspapers. To contact Patricia for speaking opportunities, e-mail her at: *patricialorenz@juno.com* or by phone at 800-437-7577.

Karen Majoris-Garrison is an award-winning author, whose stories appear in *Woman's World, Chicken Soup for the Soul* and *God Allows U-Turns*. A wife and mother of two young children, Abigail and Simeon, Karen describes her family life as "heaven on earth." You may reach her at: *innheaven@aol.com*.

Judith Marks-White is a columnist for the *Westport Connecticut News* where her column, "The Light Touch" appears every Wednesday. She freelances for newspapers and magazines throughout the country, lectures on humor writing and is an adjunct professor of English at Norwalk Community College in Connecticut.

Kathleen Swartz McQuaig shares stories from the heart shaped by her deep faith. As a writer, speaker, teacher, wife and mother, she lives to encourage others. After earning her master's degree in education, and living in military communities stateside and abroad, Kathleen and her family settled in Carlisle, Pennsylvania.

Carol Sjostrom Miller lives in New Jersey with her husband, Jack, and daughters Stephanie and Lauren. Her essays, articles and humor pieces—written while her family sleeps—appear in dozens of local and national print publications, as well as online and in inspirational anthologies. E-mail: *miller_carol@usa.net* or *miller.carol@verizon.net*.

Tekla Dennison Miller is the author of two memoirs: *The Warden Wore Pink*, about her corrections career, and *A Bowl of Cherries*, about herself and her sister. She taught in riot-torn South Central Los Angeles and worked with mentally challenged enlisted men in Germany. Ms. Miller lives in Colorado.

Ferna Lary Mills is the author of "The Rainbow: Words of Inspiration, Faith and Hope." She cites writing stories of faith as her greatest love. You may reach her by e-mail at *ferna@rainbowfaith.com* or read more of her stories and poems at her Website at *www.rainbowfaith.com*.

Jacquelyn Mitchard, the mother of three daughters and three sons, is the author of *The Deep End of the Ocean,* Oprah Winfrey's first book club selection, a contributing editor to *Parenting* magazine and author of the new novel *Twelve Times Blessed.*

Christie Kelley Montone is a writer and photographer currently living near Buffalo, New York. She enjoys creating unique family portraits at locations special to her clients. Now a mother to a precious little boy, she hopes to instill in him the same wonderful values she learned from her mom. She can be reached at *nabeam1@aol.com.*

Cassie Moore enjoys being a full-time mom to her son Brady. She likes to read, write poems and short stories, and spend time with her family and friends. She wrote 'The Magic Jar Years' in memory of her mom, Gloria, who continues to be her inspiration from above. Cassie, her husband Scott, and Brady reside in Spanish Fort, Alabama. You can email her at *cbsmoore@att.net.*

Alicia Nordan is a psychotherapist in private practice and counsels adults who struggle with issues of separation, grief and loss. *The Nightgown* is the result of a promise she made to her mother in 1981 to write about the events of one night during her mother's treatment for pancreatic cancer. Alicia lives in Pittsburgh, Pennsylvania, with author Lewis Nordan and their two adopted greyhounds.

Jennifer M. Paquette lives in Toronto with her two children. Her writing, on topics ranging from computer viruses to spiritual step-parenting, has been featured on national radio and appeared in both mainstream and spiritual publications. She is also a published fiction writer. Visit her on the Web at *www.geocities.com/j3fer.*

Mark Parisi's "off the mark" comic panel has been syndicated since 1987 and is distributed by United Media. Mark's humor also graces greeting cards, T-shirts, calendars, magazines (such as *Billboard*), newsletters and books. Lynn is his wife/business partner and their daughter, Jenny, contributes with inspiration, (as do three cats).

Kristal M. Parker attends college in San Diego, California. She enjoys traveling, writing and scuba diving. She is looking forward to a career working with children. This is her first published work.

Debra Pawlak, a freelance writer from Farmington, Michigan, lives with her husband, Michael, and children, Rachel and Jonathon. She is currently writing a book on Farmington history and recently completed a screenplay about Clara Bow. Debra contributes regularly to *The Mediadrome, (www.themediadrome.com)* an online magazine for thinking people. E-mail her at: *mjpawlak@msn.com.*

Melissa Peek is a wife and full-time mother of four. She also owns an online fan club, is a radio advertising rep and copywriter, has been self-employed in construction and real estate speculation, and has appeared in a Snapple commercial. You may e-mail her at: *melhi@a5.com.*

Judy Perry lives in Florida with her soulmate, Benn. She is an advocate for small business owners and represents NFIB, the National Federation for Independent Business. Judy enjoys art, travel, friends and family.

Cindy Phiffer credits her mother Lu Flatt for teaching her how to be a good mother. Cindy, whose sons are past rocking age, manages Durrett Cheese & Gift Gallery in Murfreesboro, Tennessee. She is the author of *The Edible ABC's, My First Book of Prayers* and *My Body, My Choice.*

Regina Phillips holds a bachelor's degree in social work and currently works for a legal information service company. She lives in Columbus, Ohio, with her husband and their daughter. She can be reached by e-mail at *ginamp1976@yahoo.com.*

Stephanie Piro is a cartoonist, designer and mom. She considers her fabulous daughter, Nico, her greatest inspiration. She is one of King Features cartoon team, Six Chix (she's Saturday!) and she also self-syndicates "Fair Game," a daily cartoon panel and designs T-shirts and other items for her company, Strip T's. Contact her at: *piro@worldpath.net* or *www.stephaniepiro.com* or write to: Stephanie Piro, P.O. Box 605, Farmington, NH 03835.

Mindy Pollack-Fusi left a PR career to focus on creative/freelance writing including articles for *The Boston Globe,* an essay column in *The Minuteman,* a prior *Chicken Soup* story in *Unsinkable Soul,* and a hopefully-soon-to-be-published memoir. Reach her at *mindy@tiac.net* in the Boston area.

Marilyn Pribus, a freelance editor and journalist, lives with her husband near Sacramento, California. They have two sons. Her mother, Marian Groet, a musician, weaver and much-loved grandmother, lives in a nearby retirement center. Marilyn's e-mail address is: *mailto:pribus@compuserve.com.*

LeAnn R. Ralph earned a bachelor's and a master's degree from the University of Wisconsin-Whitewater. She is a reporter for two newspapers in Wisconsin and is writing a book of true stories about her childhood on a Wisconsin dairy farm. E-mail her at: *bigpines@ruralroute2.com.*

Rebecca Reid is a photographer and psychotherapist living in Amherst, Massachusetts. She has two grown children, Sarah Reid and Anna Nguyen, both of whom weathered adolescence and came out fine, and one grandson who is eight years old. Rebecca and Sarah both live in a co-housing community in Amherst.

Pam Robbins has worked as a journalist and freelance writer and editor in western Massachusetts for more than thirty years. The author of *Laughing Matters: Selected Columns by Humorist Pam Robbins,* she is working on a book about her mother. She can be reached at 413-569-0976.

Sallie Rodman is a freelance writer residing in Los Alamitos, California, with her husband, a dog and a cat. She has a certificate in professional writing from California State University, Long Beach. Her work has appeared in *Chocolate for a Woman's Courage, Byline, The Mystery Review* and *Good Dog!* She enjoys writing about the synchronicity of life in everyday events. E-mail her at *srodman@ix.net-com.com.*

Kelly Salasin is a "recovering" teacher and long-time overachiever. In refocusing her life around "being" rather than "doing," she is uncovering the path of her dreams. Kelly lives with her husband, Casey Deane, and their sons, Lloyd and Aidan, (all three a dream-come-true), in the Green Mountains of Vermont. She can be reached at: *kel@sover.net.*

DeAnna Sanders is a freelance writer and mother of two, Rachel and Johnny III. She lives in Duncan, Oklahoma, with her husband, Johnny. DeAnna is the author of two books, *Quest Challenges* and *Quest Reflections,* written for *Woman's Missionary Union.* She contributes regularly to the teenage missions magazine, *Accent.* Contact her at: *Sanders@texhoma.net.*

Sandra Schnell is an unabashedly proud mother of a teenage son and daughter and a loving wife to her husband of twenty-plus years. A graduate of Keene State College in New Hampshire, she worked as an administrator at Bowie State University in Maryland. After relocating to Japan, she taught English classes at Hitachi, Casio and Toshiba, and then worked as a teacher at an American elementary school. She recently moved to Hawaii with her family and is pondering her future exploits. Reach her at *Senseimom@juno.com.*

Anne Schraff is the author of more than 150 books including fiction, biography, science and history. She enjoys hiking in the wilderness. She especially enjoys writing fiction for teenage reluctant readers and feels blessed to introduce a kid to the wonderful world of books.

Anne Tews Schwab is a writer, household engineer, doctor, psychiatrist, chef, maid, and all-around handy person. In other words, Anne is a full-time wife and mother of three children. Anne graduated from Wellesley College, and received her master's degree from the University of Minnesota. She currently resides in Grant, Minnesota.

Mary Seehafer Sears grew up in Northbrook, Illinois, and graduated with honors from The American University in Washington, D.C. She is a former magazine editor, and has authored more than a dozen books on gardening and interior design. She lives with her husband and daughter in New Jersey.

Lynn Seely is a book author and freelance writer with a unique heartwarming style. She is published in *Chicken Soup for the Soul, Cup of Comfort* and *Listening to the Animals.* Seely's completing a book about her hero cat Aggie, seen on TV's *Miracle Pets.* E-mail her at: *cataggie@usa.net* or write: P.O. Box 2545, Martinsburg, WV 25402.

Kathy Shaskan ditched a successful career as a marketing communications executive to pursue her interest in humor writing. (This fact alone, she says, was enough to cause hysterical laughter among her friends.) Since then, her witty sayings have appeared on t-shirts ("A little gray hair is a small price to pay for this much widom"), mugs ("I maintain a balanced diet . . . I carry a cookie in each pocket") and cartoons. She has also written two humorous children's books for Penguin/Putnam that will be published in the near future. Kathy can be reached at *Motherbeee@aol.com.*

Vahan Shrivanian drew cartoons for Air Force newspapers and taught fighter-pilot gunnery in WW II. *Post* war, his first sale was to the *Saturday Evening Post.* He has been selling to the *Post* and hundreds of other magazines ever since. Vahan was named Best American Cartoonist six times.

Deborah Shouse lives and writes in Prairie Village, Kansas. She is a speaker, writer and creativity catalyst. Her writing has appeared in *Reader's Digest, Newsweek, Woman's Day, Family Circle* and *MS.* Visit her Web site at *www. thecreativityconnection.com.*

Deborah Dee Simmons is a freelance writer whose work, including greeting cards, a newspaper column, anthologies and award-winning poetry, has appeared in numerous online and print publications. Deborah has completed a children's book series and is now working on compilations of her humorous and inspirational stories. Reach her at: *jdsimmons@chartermi.net.*

Cie Simurro, like her mother's mother's mother, who was the healing woman of her village, has been a healer and writer all her adult life. She does private healings and training in Shamanic practice, joyous empowerment, and Earth stewardship. Cie writes a monthly column for an East Coast magazine and is working on two books.

David Sipress graduated from Williams College and attended the master's program in Soviet studies at Harvard University for two years before leaving to pursue a career as a cartoonist. His cartoons appear regularly in *The New Yorker,* the *Boston Phoenix* and the *Spectator of London,* among many others. David was the winner of the Association of Alternative Newsweeklies 2000 editorial award for his cartoons in the Boston Phoenix. David is also the author of eight books of cartoons, and lives in Brooklyn, New York, with his wife, Ginny Shubert, a public interest lawyer.

Susan Spence is happily married, works as a veterinary technician and writes whenever possible. She also does rottweiler rescue for southern states.

Linda Sultan is the winner of two national poetry awards for humor. Her work has appeared in *The Baltimore Sun, Light, Welcome Home* and a variety of other magazines and newspapers. Her book of humorous verse, *Family Life & Other Strife,* is available through the Internet at *www.amazon.com.* Please reach her at: *lsultan@juno.com.*

Annmarie Tait is the youngest of five children born to an Irish family. She lives in Conshocken, Pennsylvania, with her husband Joe and their little dog Sammy. A published essayist and poet, Annmarie is an accomplished vocalist who takes pride in singing the folk songs of her Irish and American heritage.

Donna Thiel-Kline is the publisher/editor of *Demensions,* a bimonthly Webzine of speculative fiction (*www.demensionszine.com*). She lives in Pennsylvania with her husband, Matthew Cook, two cats, a cockatiel and, of course, her tutor in life's little lessons: her daughter, Kylie. Contact Donna at: *editor@demensionszine.com*.

Susan B. Townsend is a writer and stay-at-home mother to five children ranging in age from three to seventeen. She and her husband, Tom, live on a 300-acre farm in southeastern Virginia with a multitude of pets. Susan is at work on her first novel. She can be reached at *monitor@visi.net* or by calling 804-834-2245.

Elizabeth Sharp Vinson is a full-time mom and homemaker. She has three teenage children and has always enjoyed journaling and writing stories based on her family's life experiences. Elizabeth enjoys quilting and music and she volunteers at her children's school and her church. She can be reached at *JSEVinson@prodigy.net*.

Lisa West lives with her two daughters in Tigard, Oregon. In addition to freelance writing, she is on the editorial staff of *The Einkwell* (*www.einkwell.com*), a weekly e-zine, where she also writes a column. She enjoys sports, reading and hanging out with her daughters. Contact Lisa at: *thateditor@einkwell.com*.

Polly Anne Wise was born in Baltimore, Maryland, to Paul and Betty White in June of 1964. She currently resides in Westminster, Maryland. Polly Wise is the mother of two: Jeffrey Scott and Samantha Nicole. She now works as general manager of a convenience store chain, Jiffy Mart. She also is a cheerleading coach and her team has been National Champions for the last three years.

Phyllis W. Zeno is the editor-in-chief of *AAA Going Places*, a magazine she founded in 1982, which goes to 2.1 million AAA members in Florida, Georgia and Tennessee. She travels extensively with her two grown daughters, Linda Aber and Leslie Metzler. Please reach her at: *Phylliszeno@aol.com*.

Also Available